When *the* Church Was *a* Family

When *the* Church Was *a* Family

Recapturing Jesus' Vision
for Authentic
Christian Community

JOSEPH H. HELLERMAN

ACADEMIC

NASHVILLE, TENNESSEE

ISBN: 978-0-8054-4779-8

Published by B&H Publishing Group
Nashville, Tennessee

Dewey Decimal Classification: 262
Subject Heading: CHURCH FELLOWSHIP\FELLOWSHIP—BIBLICAL
TEACHING\
FELLOWSHIP—RELIGIOUS ASPECTS—CHRISTIANITY

Printed in the United States of America
2 3 4 5 6 7 8 9 10 11 12 • 17 16 15 14 13 12 11 10 09
VP

CONTENTS

INTRODUCTION

S piritual formation occurs primarily in the context of community. People who remain connected with their brothers and sisters in the local church almost invariably grow in self-understanding, and they mature in their ability to relate in healthy ways to God and to their fellow human beings. This is especially the case for those courageous Christians who stick it out through the often messy process of interpersonal discord and conflict resolution. Long-term interpersonal relationships are the crucible of genuine progress in the Christian life. People who stay also grow.

People who leave do not grow. We all know people who are consumed with spiritual wanderlust. But we never get to know them very well because they cannot seem to stay put. They move along from church to church, ever searching for a congregation that will better satisfy their felt needs. Like trees repeatedly transplanted from soil to soil, these spiritual nomads fail to put down roots and seldom experience lasting and fruitful growth in their Christian lives.

Then there are those who leave to avoid working through uncomfortable or painful relations with others in the church family. Running away does provide immediate relief from the awkwardness of a hurtful relationship. It is the easy way out in the short term, and there are legitimate reasons to leave a local church. But people who leave to escape the hard work of conflict resolution are often destined to repeat the cycle of relational dysfunction with another person in another church somewhere else in town.

It is a simple but profound biblical reality that we both grow and thrive together or we do not grow much at all. None of this is terribly novel. We all know it to be the case. So why do we so often sabotage our most intimate relationships, seek help from others only after the damage is irreversible, and continue to try to find our way through life as isolated individuals, convinced somehow that God will remain with us to lead us and bless us wherever we go? Why do we continue foolishly to operate as if our own immediate happiness is of greater value than the redemptive relationships God has placed us in? Why are we seemingly unable to stay in relationships, stay in a community, and grow in the interpersonal contexts that God has provided for our temporal and eternal well-being?

I count myself blessed to serve on the pastoral team of a vibrant Christian church. We consistently emphasize the inviolable maxim that spiritual formation occurs primarily in the context of community, and we have in place an extensive support and accountability network designed to help our people grow in their abilities to relate to others in a healthy way both at home and in the church.

Our fellowship is average in size: some four hundred persons of all ages attend on a given Sunday. But not a month goes by in which the pastor-elders are not summoned to intervene in some kind of interpersonal crisis among the members of our church family.

Sadly, much of our intervention has little lasting effect upon the health of the relationships involved. In spite of the counsel and support provided by our leadership team and others in the congregation, people in crisis frequently insist on going it alone—following their individualistic, often self-destructive pathways. Roberta's pilgrimage is but one example of such behavior.

Roberta's Story

Roberta (not her real name) is a bright woman in her forties with a highly charged emotional attachment to Jesus. Roberta loves to sing in church, and her passion for worship infuses those around her with a desire to know God more deeply. Unfortunately, Roberta's family background has set her on an apparently irreversible course to relational confusion and heartache. After a failed marriage, Roberta lived with a sister for more than a decade, spending hours each week involved in various charitable causes. The sister's death brought to the surface a host of family and financial crises.

Roberta's grief process was highly intensified due to years of dysfunctional family relationships. She was dangerously despondent. It was clear to us that Roberta needed outside help in order to gain a proper perspective on herself and the world around her. Roberta's current money problems were only the latest in a history of such fiscal fiascoes, suddenly intensified by a squabble with her surviving siblings over their sister's estate.

Roberta is loved and highly appreciated by our church family. Our leaders sincerely desired to do something tangible to help Roberta get on her feet again, both emotionally and economically. We offered to meet the most pressing financial needs immediately. But we knew that our assistance would benefit Roberta only if accompanied by several nonnegotiable conditions.

We informed Roberta that the money would be hers if she met three conditions. (1) She would see our staff therapist (initially at the church's expense) on a weekly basis in order to find short-term support and guidance in dealing with the loss of her sister. (2) She would meet with a financial adviser who is a member of our congregation (again, *pro bono*) to come up with a game plan to dig herself out of debt. (3) She would agree to attend church regularly and partner with others in the church family in some area of ministry.

What we asked of Roberta was really quite straightforward: relational accountability. We challenged Roberta to quit trying to find her way through life as an isolated individual and, instead, to take advantage of the guidance, community, and accountability offered by her brothers and sisters in the family of God. Only in this way would Roberta begin to grow up to become the healthy person God had designed her to be.

Roberta declined our offer and rejected our advice. Like many people in our churches, she chose to chart her own course and to bear her pain alone rather than to integrate herself into the body of Christ through the vehicle of strong relational accountability. We no longer see Roberta at Oceanside Christian Fellowship anymore.

American Individualism and a Church in Crisis

A story like Roberta's impacts more than just the individual involved; it takes its toll on a whole church family. On more than one occasion I spent a great deal of time with Roberta on the phone as the above crisis unfolded. We also dedicated an hour or so of our elder board's precious meeting time in our efforts to carefully craft the three conditions (see above) for the financial assistance that she requested.

We have free assistance available through professional counselors and financial planners who are graciously willing to donate their time. And we have a church body ready to receive and encourage anyone willing to embrace our oversight and our guidelines. But Roberta benefited from none of these resources since she foolishly chose to sort out her problems on her own, apart from input from her brothers and sisters in Christ. And we are all the worse for it.

It is tempting to dismiss relational crises like Roberta's as personal expressions of individual sin and selfishness. But the increasing tendency of persons in our churches to make wrong-headed life decisions, and to make them in isolation from the broader church family, demands a more nuanced explanation. Personal sin and selfishness have been around since Adam. Why the marked increase in relational breakdown in our society and in our churches today?

I suggest that it is the unique orientation of Western culture—especially contemporary American society—that best explains our propensity to abandon, rather than work through, the awkward and painful relationships we so often find ourselves in. Social scientists have a label for the pervasive cultural orientation of modern American society that makes it so difficult for us to stay connected and grow together in community with one another. They call it *radical individualism*. What this amounts to is simple enough. We in America have been socialized to believe that our own dreams, goals, and personal fulfillment ought to take precedence over the well-being of any group—our church or our family, for example—to which we belong. The immediate needs of the individual are more important than the long-term health of the group. So we leave and withdraw, rather than stay and grow up, when the going gets rough in the church or in the home.

The influence that our radically individualistic worldview exerts on American evangelical Christians goes a long way to explain the struggles we face to keep relationships together. The incessant failure of marriage after marriage, along with the repeated unwillingness of persons to stay in the local church in order to grow through relational conflict, are only in part due to individual sin and selfishness. Broader cultural values are in play.

Our culture has powerfully socialized us to believe that personal happiness and fulfillment should take precedence over the connections we have with others in both our families and our churches. So we run from the painful but redemptive relationships God has placed us in. The tune of radical individualism has been playing in our ears at full volume for decades. We are dancing to the music with gusto. And it is costing us dearly.

A Different Approach to Interpersonal Relationships

By contrast, nearly all other societies throughout history have been (and continue to be) collectivist in their view of the world. Most persons who have lived on planet earth have simply assumed that the good of the individual should take a back seat to the good of the group, whether that group is a family, a village, or a religious community. People who have been socialized to embrace this "group comes first" mentality are convinced that such an arrangement is in their best interest even at the individual level. So they stay the course when the going gets tough.

For those of us who are new to cultural analysis, perhaps an illustration will help. Nowhere are the differences between the individualist and the collectivist or strong-group approach to society more obvious than in the area of decision making. Two young women, fellow students at a Christian university, found themselves comparing the marriage strategies of their respective cultures. One was an American, the other a student from Iran. The discussion was hardly academic since the Iranian student was looking ahead to an upcoming summer wedding when she would marry a man whom her parents had picked out for her many years before.

The young Iranian bride barely knows her future husband. The American girl is astounded. "How can you let your parents marry you to a man you do not even know?" the American asked. She then proceeded to extol Western marriage strategies and the freedom she had to choose her own spouse. The young Iranian woman was equally amazed. "How can *you* act independently of your parents and contract a marriage which may not contribute to the long-term well-being of your extended family?" she replied.

The cultural distinctives are clear, and so are the different priorities. In choosing a spouse, we in America place the highest value upon our own personal fulfillment and happiness. Marriage is the place, first and foremost, to meet the relational needs of the individuals involved. This can only occur if we have the freedom to choose a mate.

The Iranian woman, like others around the world from traditional societies, had been raised to believe quite the opposite, namely, that the honor and health of the group—in this case her family—should take priority over her own freedom and over her personal satisfaction in a marriage relationship. Accordingly, she was quite content to sacrifice her freedom to choose a mate for the good of her extended family.

Ironically, the Iranian bride will likely end up just as happily married as her American counterpart. One jokester explained it this way: in traditional societies a man's parents choose his wife, and he does not know who she is until after the marriage; and even though the custom in America is completely different, the end result is often exactly the same!

Various approaches to decision making helpfully reveal the radical differences between the mind-set of traditional societies and the "American way," and not just in the area of courtship. Americans clearly relish the freedoms we have to make decisions in all the key areas of our lives. We are generally free to decide *what* we are going to do with our lives (vocation), *who* we are going to do life with (marriage), and *where* we are going to do it (place of residence).

People in traditional, strong-group cultures typically make none of these decisions in isolation. They are made within the context of the family or village community, and the well-being of that family or village takes center stage as the final arbiter in the decision-making process.

I am hardly naive enough to suggest that modern Americans ought to return to the extended family systems of generations ago. We hold on tenaciously to our hard-won personal freedoms. But we must recognize that we have paid a tremendous emotional and spiritual price to be released from the cultural shackles reflected in the strong-group values of our ancestors.

The Robertas in our American evangelical churches are not making foolish and destructive decisions due solely to individual stubbornness and sin. The issue is much broader than this. It has to do with the way in which we have been culturally programmed to view the world around us.

Our uniquely individualistic approach toward life and relationships, so characteristic of American society, subtly yet certainly sets us up for failure in our efforts to stay and grow in the context of the often difficult but redemptive relationships that God has provided for us. Radical individualism has affected our whole way of viewing the Christian faith, and it has profoundly compromised the solidarity of our relational commitments to one another.

Recapturing the Relational Power of Early Christianity

The cultural outlook of the ancient world generated a markedly different approach to interpersonal relationships. The world in which Jesus and His followers lived was a distinctly strong-group culture in which the health of the group—not the needs of the individual—received first priority. And the most important group for persons in the ancient world was the family. It is hardly accidental that the New Testament writers chose the concept of family as the central social metaphor to describe the kind of interpersonal relationships that were to characterize those early Christian communities. There is, in fact, no better way to come to grips with the spiritual and relational poverty of American individualism than to compare our way of doing things with the strong-group, surrogate family relations of early Christianity. This is the central focus of this book.

The New Testament picture of the church as a family flies in the face of our individualistic cultural orientation. God's intention is not to become the feel-good Father of a myriad of isolated individuals who appropriate the Christian faith as yet another avenue toward personal enlightenment. Nor is the biblical Jesus to be conceived of as some sort of spiritual mentor whom we can happily take from church to church, or from marriage to marriage, fully assured that our personal Savior will somehow bless and redeem our destructive relational choices every step of the way.

You may be surprised to discover that the expression "personal Savior" occurs nowhere in the pages of Scripture. We will encounter other surprises in our discussion, some of which will encourage us to reconsider traditional and long-held ways of viewing the Christian faith. It is my intention to demonstrate that our radical overemphasis on a personal relationship with God is an American—not a biblical—theological construction. What we find in the Bible, rather, is a God who seems at least as concerned with His group (me in relationship with my brothers and sisters in Christ) as He is with the individual (me in relationship with God).

Consider Paul's perspective. In his letters, Paul refers to Jesus as "*our* Lord"— that is, as the Lord of God's group—53 times. Only once, in contrast, does the expression "*my* Lord" appear in Paul's writings (Phil 3:8). This speaks volumes about the priorities of the great apostle. Paul's overarching concern in his ministry went far beyond the personal spiritual pilgrimages of his individual converts. Paul's driving passion was to establish spiritually vibrant, relationally healthy *communities* of believers in strategic urban settings throughout the Roman Empire.

Until we get this straight, the Robertas of American Christianity, along with their churches, will repeatedly suffer the debilitating effects of the culture of radical individualism, as it continues to sabotage our most precious interpersonal relationships. We must embrace the fact that our value system has been shaped by a worldview that is diametrically opposed to the outlook of the early Christians and to the teachings of Scripture. As church-going Americans, we have been socialized to believe that our individual fulfillment and our personal relationship with God are more important than any connection we might have with our fellow human beings, whether in the home or in the church. We have, in a most subtle and insidious way, been conformed to this world.

There is great hope, however, for profound transformation. God's vision for community, as reflected in the lives of the early Christians, offers a powerful antidote to the relational ills that so often characterize the lives of modern evangelicals. We need to exercise a degree of cultural sophistication in order to distance ourselves from our own perspective and to embrace the very different values of the early Christian church. Comparing the New Testament church with contemporary Christianity necessarily involves a significant conceptual leap both culturally and theologically.

Therefore, some of what follows will be challenging reading, but a cross-cultural excursion of this sort is absolutely indispensable. Before we can return to the twenty-first century to address the practical people issues of everyday life in evangelical America, we must gain a new understanding of the very different strong-group values of the early Christians. Only then will we be properly equipped to recapture Jesus' vision for authentic Christian community.

Is This Book for You?

It is probably too late to ask that question. You have already bought or borrowed a copy from someone. But it might help to know that I have designed the book for two primary groups of church leaders and leaders-in-training.

Traditional Church Leaders

Many of us serve as church leaders in a traditional congregational environment, or perhaps we are in seminary being trained for such a role. Our churches own buildings, craft budgets, employ paid staff, and regard the Sunday service as our primary community gathering. If this description of church sounds familiar to you, then consider yourself a key part of my target audience, whether you are a paid pastor or a volunteer church leader.

A good portion of those who serve the institutional church sorely recognize the need for renewal and reform in the way we do ministry. Our programs are tired, our services have often become repetitive and nonengaging, and—most notably—we increasingly struggle to keep our people connected with one another in ongoing networks of mutual support and accountability.

We tried for a season to play the consumer game by appealing to our people's felt needs through programs such as "Three Keys to a Healthy Marriage" and "How to Find Success at Work." You have surely heard the sermons, and you may very well have preached them yourself. The spiritual bankruptcy of consumer Christianity has become quite clear in retrospect. Indeed, it has completely backfired where the cultivation of community is concerned. The "let us meet your needs" approach to marketing the church, which became so popular among baby boomers in the 1980s and 1990s, has only served further to socialize our people to "prefer a variety of church experiences, rather than getting the most out of all that a single church has to offer."[1] This hardly encourages lasting Christian community, so we continue to long for genuine renewal.

I trust that those of you who are attempting to revitalize an existing congregation's values and structures will find in this book a promising vision for church as God intended it. But I must caution you in advance to prepare yourself for an acute paradigm shift. A return to the community orientation of early Christianity requires much more than a slight course correction in our weekly programming or the addition of another line item to the church budget.

Contextualizing New Testament social values in our congregations requires us to significantly revise the way that we conceive of church. And there will inevitably be a cost to pay as leaders. For as is generally the case during seasons of renewal, those of us who have the most invested in "church as it is" will inevitably be called upon to sacrifice more than others in order to liberate our people to experience "church as it was" during the New Testament era.

Emerging Church Visionaries

My second target audience consists of another group of church leaders who are passionate about renewal among the people of God. I have in mind here the creative, disparate collection of pioneers who are giving guidance to a movement known as the emerging church.

This phenomenon involves believers from a variety of denominational and theological traditions, and each emerging church is unique in one way or another. But one thing these communities share in common is the conviction that the kind of change God desires is so systemic in nature that it cannot occur within the context of traditional church structures and practices. So our emerging brothers and sisters have left the institutional church to try their hand at church renewal outside the system.

Eddie Gibbs and Ryan Bolger have recently produced a highly informative overview of emerging church thinking and practice. The authors surveyed dozens of young (and not so young) leaders, and they summarized the values of the movement in terms of three "core practices" that they found common to each emerging church.[2] One of the three core practices Gibbs and Bolger identify relates directly to the theme of the book you are reading. That value is "living as community." Authentic community constitutes a bedrock priority for emerging Christianity.

Brad Cecil, a leader associated with the emerging church Axxess in Arlington, Texas, distinguishes sharply between the consumer strategies that character-

---

[1] G. Barna, *The Second Coming of the Church* (Waco: Word, 1998), 18–19.
[2] E. Gibbs and R. Bolger, *Emerging Churches* (Grand Rapids: Baker, 2005), 43–44.

ize certain expressions of institutional Christianity and the relational agenda that
drives his own church vision:

> We are not interested in short-term relationships or meeting a person's needs or
> functioning as a spiritual vendor for people. Rather, we want to be a community
> of people committed to sharing life together.

The shift in priorities directly impacts the way in which Cecil and his peers mea-
sure progress and growth in the church:

> We don't desire growth for growth's sake but rather a community that grows
> slowly through natural introductions. We don't measure our success by numeric
> growth. We have decided to measure by other means, such as, How long do
> relationships last? Are members of the community at peace with one another?
> Are relationships reconciled?[3]

One encounters similar sentiments throughout the literature produced by
emerging church thinkers. The cultivation of lasting community is at the very
heart of emerging Christianity's renewal project.

In fact, Gibbs and Bolger reflect rather extensively on a specific expression of
Christian community, one that has captured the imagination of numerous emerging church leaders: the idea that the church is a family. The authors devote a whole
section of their chapter about community in the emerging church to the theme "A
Family, Not an Institution." They insightfully observe,

> Emerging churches pursue the "new family" practices as modeled by Jesus and
> his followers, and their embodied way of life operates similarly to the life of an
> extended family. . . . If a church begins to look like a family, then all its institu-
> tional practices will undergo change. Church as family is primarily about rela-
> tionships. It is not about meetings, events, or structures. Such rubric questions
> do not make sense when discussing relational issues.[4]

I applaud the longings for authentic community that characterize the values
of emerging Christianity. And I have no problem with our emerging brothers and
sisters seeking to actualize Jesus' vision for community beyond the boundaries
of the institutional church. If you consider yourself part of the emerging church,
I trust you will encounter in the pages of this book a kindred spirit who shares
your desire to recapture the relational values and practices of the ancient Christian
church.

---

[3] Cited by Gibbs and Bolger, *Emerging Churches,* 99.
[4] Gibbs and Bolger, *Emerging Churches,* 97.

But I suspect that you will also be challenged by what you are about to read. Renewal movements have historically tended to emphasize church practice and the various expressions of the Christian life, while giving less attention to careful theological reflection and lessons learned from church history. This scenario is playing itself out all over again among certain expressions of emerging Christianity.

For all the preoccupation in the emerging church with culture and cultural studies, it remains the case that certain aspects of postmodernism—religious pluralism, tolerance, and moral relativism—have the potential to hijack this wonderfully promising expression of renewal in Western Christianity. Apparently even those of us who attempt to be most sensitive to current trends and thinking are not immune to the seductive influences of the dominant culture.

For example, one uncovers a number of highly problematic observations among the otherwise insightful and illuminating musing of the emerging church participants cited in the Gibbs and Bolger survey. One group in the UK invited a Buddhist to instruct their church about Buddhist approaches to prayer: "We didn't talk to him about the differences between our faiths. We didn't try to convert him. He was welcomed and fully included and was really pleased to have been invited."[5] Other expressions of emerging Christianity engage in the questionable practice of dispensing entirely with all forms of recognized leadership.

To their credit, emerging Christians exhibit an ongoing fascination with the ancient Christian church. And so they should. For the early Christians enjoyed all the relational integrity for which the emerging church so desperately longs. Ancient Christianity owed much of its social capital, however, to an intentionally structured approach to leadership and to distinct social boundaries between genuine believers and those who claimed to be brothers but were not behaving like Christians.

Unbelievers were not simply assimilated into the early church with their pagan religious beliefs and practices intact. Paul intended for the unbeliever who was welcomed into the midst of a house church in Corinth to have a rather different experience than the Buddhist guest at the emerging church in the UK. Paul longed for him to be "convicted by all . . . judged by all. The secrets of his heart will be revealed, and as a result he will fall down on his face and worship God, proclaiming, 'God is really among you'" (1 Cor 14:24–25).

To be sure, the early Christians were socially inclusive—and remarkably so. But they sacrificed their very lives to maintain the ideological exclusivity of their loyalty to Jesus. None of these characteristics of early Christianity sits particu-

---

[5] Ibid., 133.

larly well with emerging Christians whose socialization into postmodern culture has rendered them irretrievably jaded and suspicious about matters such as truth claims, recognized leadership, and community boundaries.

We are reminded once again that we must take care to complement the passionate practice of the Christian faith with ongoing historical and theological reflection. Fortunately, the more insightful practitioners of emerging Christianity readily acknowledge as much. They desire to retain all of the best that the early Christians had to offer.

Wise leaders recognize that the false dichotomy we often erect between belief and behavior will ultimately undermine the long-term viability of any expression of the Christian faith—emergent or otherwise. D. Kimball observed that "everything we do in church is a reflection of what we theologically believe, whether we are consciously aware of it or not." Kimball is determined to help his people "consider how theology impacts what they do and practice."[6]

To the Kimballs of the emerging church I offer this book as my attempt to provide a fledgling movement with some biblical and historical moorings where Christian community is concerned. We have all the resources necessary in the New Testament and in other early Christian literature to erect a robust theology of community on the bedrock of early Christian convictions and social practice. The result will be the kind of community that will satisfy the relational longings of both traditional church leaders and our emerging brothers and sisters. It is to that project that we now turn.

---

[6] D. Kimball, prepublication manuscript cited by R. S. Anderson, *An Emergent Theology for Emerging Churches* (Downers Grove: InterVarsity, 2006), 72.

Chapter One

THE GROUP COMES FIRST

*At these [temple] sacrifices prayers for the welfare of the community must take
precedence over those for ourselves; for we are born for fellowship, and he
who sets its claims above his private interests is specially acceptable to God.*
(Josephus, *Contra Apion* 2.197)

*T*he movie *Titanic* went down in history as one of the costliest and most
lucrative films ever produced. The epic production also won eleven
Oscars. Moviegoers sat utterly spellbound by the $200 million worth
of special effects and attention to detail. Among the technological marvels that
garnered the film the award for Best Visual Effects was a near-perfect 1/20 scale
replica of the *Titanic*. But visual fireworks alone did not propel *Titanic* to the
center stage of the 1998 Academy Awards. Only a simple but powerful love story
could do that, and the love story from the movie *Titanic* colorfully illustrates what
happens when our Western individualistic relational priorities collide with the values of more traditional societies.

The interaction between *Titanic*'s main characters, Jack and Rose, epitomizes
Western romance at its best. Jack is a scrappy but charming street kid who is on
the great ship only because he won a boarding pass in a poker game. Rose belongs
to the upper echelon of British society. She is engaged to be married to a man from
her own social stratum with whom she is traveling in first-class accommodations.
The story line makes it perfectly clear that Rose has no affection for her fiancé. In
fact, the fellow is portrayed as an arrogant, obnoxious individual.

In a memorable scene Rose's mother reminds her daughter that the arranged
marriage is in the best interest of her family. It seems that Rose's father died after

squandering away his fortune, so for Rose's mother and her family the impending marriage represents the only hope of maintaining their wealth and preserving their social status. Rose has been set up with a man for whom she has absolutely no affection in order to guarantee an honorable future for her extended family.

But then one evening Rose meets Jack on the deck of the ship, and the encounter ignites the flame of a romantic fling that serves as the main story line for the rest of the movie. Rose is caught in a quandary. She loves Jack, but she is engaged to a highly unappealing man whom she is obligated to marry for the sake of her family. Whom will Rose choose?

Jack, of course. If Rose had chosen otherwise, the movie simply would not have worked for the tens of millions of American viewers who followed the tragic tale. We are quite unmoved by the potential social dilemma confronting Rose's extended family. Rather, our sympathies lie with the heroine's own personal satisfaction. As I watched *Titanic*, I could almost hear the thoughts running through the heads of the viewers in the theater: *Forget your family's fortune, Rose! Ignore your mother's wishes! Dump the rich jerk! Follow your heart! Go after Jack!*

What I want us to see here is that *Titanic*'s love story would not be nearly as well received in cultures like those of the New Testament world. If *Titanic* were shown in first-century Palestine with Aramaic subtitles, the audience would be utterly appalled to discover that Rose would even consider sacrificing the good of her extended family for her own relational satisfaction. They would find Rose's fling with Jack both risky and foolish. First-century Jews would expect Rose to marry the rich fellow and endure a life of emotional dissatisfaction, if such an arrangement could somehow preserve the honor and social-status of Rose's extended family.

The Group Comes First

The markedly different reactions to a love story like the one portrayed in *Titanic* illustrate the most important difference between modern American culture and the social world of New Testament antiquity. We are individualists. Our personal goals and individual satisfaction take first priority when we make critical life decisions. But the peoples of the ancient world exhibit what cultural anthropologists call a collectivist view of reality. Another way of saying this is to refer to the biblical world as a strong-group society. I will use the expressions "collectivist" and "strong-group" interchangeably throughout this book.

What this means is that for people in the world of the New Testament, the welfare of the groups to which they belonged took priority over their own individual happiness and relational satisfaction. This explains why someone viewing *Titanic* in first-century Palestine would expect Rose to go ahead and marry her wealthy fiancé. The social status of her family would take precedence over Rose's individual relational satisfaction. This chapter is dedicated to helping us grasp this crucial difference between the ancient collectivist mind-set and our own Western individualistic (weak-group) worldview.

John F. Kennedy captivated the audience at his 1961 presidential inauguration when he said, "Ask not what your country can do for you—ask what you can do for your country."[1] This memorable quote continues to inspire a half-century later. But few of us in America actually buy into the strong-group values reflected in Kennedy's lofty challenge—not in our personal lives anyway. Think for a moment about how you relate to the various institutions or groups that make up much of your daily life—your employer, your school, and especially your church. Most of us do not ask what *we* can do for these institutions. Rather, we want to know what *they* can do for us.

I view my employer as a source of income to meet my family's material needs, and since I am fortunate enough to enjoy what I do, my job is a source of personal satisfaction. Although I am grateful for my job as a professor, I don't spend a lot of time thinking about my loyalty to Biola University. And what about my students? I suspect that they view the university in similarly utilitarian terms, as a place to get the education they need to qualify them to reach their individual vocational goals. And church? Well, the purpose of church, of course, is to help me continue to grow in my personal relationship with Jesus Christ.

Or so I have been trained by my culture to believe. It is precisely because you and I have been socialized from childhood to view the world from an individualistic perspective that the attitudes outlined above feel so normal and natural to us. We establish our individual goals in life, and then we utilize the various groups and institutions in society to facilitate the realization of these personal goals and objectives. This is simply the way life works—in modern America at least.

To people in the New Testament world, President Kennedy's exhortation— "ask what you can do for your country"— would have served as more than an inspiring challenge. It would have represented an accurate description of daily life. People in the ancient world automatically assumed that the groups to which they belonged took priority over their lives as individuals. This was true whether the group in view was their nation, family, synagogue, or church.

---

[1] D. Lott, *The Presidents Speak: The Inaugural Addresses of the American Presidents, from Washington to Clinton* (New York: Henry Holt and Co., 1994), 315.

Below is a helpful description of strong-group thinking that will serve us well throughout our discussion. What you are about to read accurately reflects the strong-group perspective of the ancient world. It also characterizes the attitudes of people in a number of traditional, non-Western cultures around the world even today. And, as we will soon discover, the quotation properly reflects the value orientation that God desires of His children as we consider our relationships with others in His family, the church. Take a moment to reflect carefully on this description of the collectivist mind-set, paying particular attention to the expressions in italics:

> [In a strong-group society] the person perceives himself or herself to be a
> *member of a group* and *responsible to the group* for his or her actions, destiny,
> career, development, and life in general. Correspondingly he/she perceives other
> persons primarily in terms of the groups to which they belong. The individual
> person is *embedded in the group* and is free to do what he or she feels right and
> necessary only if in accord with group norms and only if the action is in the
> group's best interest. *The group has priority over the individual member,* and it
> may use objects in the environment, other groups of people in the society, and
> the members of the group itself to facilitate *group oriented goals and objectives.*[2]

A person who perceives himself primarily in terms of the group to which he belongs—family, religious sect, ethnic group, or village community—behaves in a strong-group way; that is, he will gladly put the goals of his group ahead of his own personal desires.

The strategy of Rose's mother in the movie *Titanic*—to marry her daughter into a wealthy family in order to preserve the social status of her own extended family—perfectly illustrates this kind of thinking. This "group comes first" social value must serve as the first focal point for our look at collectivist thinking. It represents the clearest and most immediately accessible window through which to gain some perspective on strong-group convictions and behavior, and to gain a new appreciation for the relational solidarity that characterized the New Testament church. We turn now to consider several examples of strong-group behavior, from ancient Mediterranean society and from collectivist peoples around the world today.

Josephus at the Gates of Jerusalem

It was AD 70. The sun was setting over the city of David as another day drew to a close. Josephus tried to wrap his tunic a little tighter around himself—even

---

[2] B. Malina, *Christian Origins and Cultural Anthropology* (Atlanta: John Knox, 1986), 19 (italics added).

in early July those Palestinian nights can be rather chilly. It was only a couple of years ago, Josephus wistfully recalled, that he had been an esteemed Jewish priest, highly respected both by the people at large and especially by his fellow elite citizens in Jerusalem.

How things had changed! It all began with a hopeless peasant revolt that soon escalated into war with Rome. Along the way Josephus had seen his fortunes decline one after another. Initially, he was recruited to serve as the general over Jewish resistance troops in Galilee. That lasted only until Rome marshaled its legions and came storming in from the north, destroying village after village, including Josephus's stronghold, the town of Jotapata.

Only fools fight with Rome, Josephus ruefully reflected, and now, as he looked back, he felt lucky that he had survived at all. Most of his fellow soldiers in Galilee were brutally massacred. Josephus was put in chains and sent southward with the Roman military machine to set up camp outside Jerusalem.

It had now been nearly three months since Titus and his legions (with Josephus and other prisoners in tow) arrived at the gates of Jerusalem—plenty of time for the Romans to erect their siege engines around the walls of the Holy City. As Josephus bundled himself up against the cool night air, he knew that it was only a matter of time. The enraged legions never failed to take a city.

That evening—like every other evening for the past three months—Josephus pleaded with his besieged Jewish brothers to come to their senses and willingly open the city gates to the Romans in order to avoid a battle they stood no chance of winning:

> I know that I have a mother, a wife, a not ignoble family, and an ancient and
> illustrious house involved in these perils; and maybe you think that it is on their
> account that my advice is offered. Slay them, take my blood as the price of your
> own salvation! I too am prepared to die, if my death will lead to your learning
> wisdom.[3]

The story does not end on a happy note. The Jewish zealots rejected his pleas, and Josephus soon saw his beloved city destroyed and thousands of his fellow Jews slaughtered by the Roman army. But the strong-group nature of Josephus's response to the impending calamity should not be missed. "Take my blood," he exclaims, "as the price of your own salvation."

Josephus, in true collectivist fashion, was willing to die if that was what it took for the Jewish rebels to "wise up" and surrender to Rome. He was ready to sacrifice his life for the welfare of his group—the Jewish nation. Another first-century

---

[3] Josephus, *Jewish War* 5.419. All classical sources cited from Loeb Classical Library.

Jewish writer expressed comparable convictions when he exclaimed, "I could wish that I myself were cursed and cut off from the Messiah for the benefit of my brothers, my countrymen by physical descent" (Rom 9:3).

Take another look at the quote from Josephus at the heading of the chapter:

> At these [temple] sacrifices prayers for the welfare of the community must take precedence over those for ourselves; for we are born for fellowship, and he who sets its claims above his private interests is specially acceptable to God.[4]

For this first-century Jewish historian, a person who sets the welfare of the community "above his private interests"—that is, a person with a strong-group worldview—"is specially acceptable to God." It is crystal clear where Josephus's priorities were; they were with the group. Josephus, writing around AD 100, claimed to have lived out this "group first" ethic when he pleaded with his fellow Jews to surrender during the Roman siege of Jerusalem about three decades earlier.

The Group Comes First in Collectivist Societies Around the World Today

Similar sentiments can be found in contemporary societies that continue to hold on to more traditional collectivist values. Among Asians and Latinos the "group comes first" principle still determines the way in which individuals make decisions in various places around the world today.

The Korean Crises and the Sacrifice of Song Tae Seung

Back in early 1998, the nation of South Korea experienced a great deal of economic turmoil. Stock prices plummeted, and the nation drew dangerously close to defaulting on $20 billion of foreign debt. Financial institutions in particular suffered severely, and many persons lost their jobs. Among those who remained employed, as of January 1998, was a fellow named Song Tae Seung. Song was head of research at Dongsuh Securities Co. Ltd., a top securities house, until his company suddenly collapsed.

Put yourself in Song's place. About 1,500 workers at 81 branches face the grim prospect of being out on the street if no third party steps in to buy Dongsuh within the next four weeks. Our typical American individualist would be scrambling around looking for another job: "I'm not about to go down with this sinking ship!" We can just picture him burning up the last four weeks of his time on

---

[4] Josephus, *Contra Apion* 2.197.

the clock at work by feverishly writing and sending off résumés to one potential employer after another.

Not Song Tae Seung. While our American individualist scrambles to secure himself a vocational lifeboat, Song prepared to go down with the ship. Instead of seeking another job, Song spent his last precious 30 days on the job heading up an employee committee that was working to find a buyer for Dongsuh.

But none of this would benefit Song personally, for if he did secure a foreign buyer to take over Dongsuh (a likely scenario due to the economic situation on the home front), he would lose his job. Still, Song and his coworkers remained committed to the company, even at their own expense. "We understand that we may be among those who are fired, but Dongsuh must survive," says Song.[5] The group comes first—even at Song's personal expense.

As a pastor, I come into contact with people from all walks of life who work in almost every conceivable sector of the urban economy. Our congregation includes people employed in construction, education, aerospace technology, computer software design, healthcare, and the arts, to name but a few occupations. I cannot think of a single person, however, who would put his company first, before his own personal goals and desires. Most of the people in my church would have a hard time understanding Song Tae Seung's willingness to lose his job in order to save his company.

During the Korean crisis, similar sentiments were in operation at the national level. I recently sent off my annual tax return to the IRS. I pay my share of federal income tax. But I also do all that is within the tax codes to pay as little of my hard-earned money as possible to Uncle Sam. My sense of loyalty to the government does not extend to a willingness to toss more money into the national piggy bank than I absolutely have to. You likely take a similar approach at tax time. Not so in Korea.

During the crisis mentioned above, it began to appear that the South Korean government might default on their foreign debt obligations. The Korean people responded by donating significant portions of their personal resources to meet the national need. As of mid-January 1998, average folks—not particularly wealthy persons—had tossed more than $135 million worth of gold trinkets into the government's coffers as a way to stoke foreign reserves.

As I am writing this chapter, the state of California is facing its most severe fiscal crisis in decades. But I do not anticipate that my fellow Californians will be sending their SUVs, gold earrings, and Rolex watches to the state treasurer

---

[5] "International/Asia: Is Korea Ready to Explode?" *Newsweek,* January 12, 1998,

in Sacramento any time soon. The Korean people's willingness to sacrifice their personal resources for the good of the nation is a classic example of strong-group values in action. Koreans were more concerned with preserving their nation's honor in the world's eye than in retaining their own individual wealth.

Many aspects of culture in traditional settings around the Pacific Rim continue to reflect the strong-group worldview and the behaviors outlined above. Collectivist convictions, in fact, find themselves deeply imbedded in certain Asian languages. For example, the Japanese word for human person is *ningen*, which literally means "between people." To be human, from the strong-group viewpoint, is to be *together* with others. "Community" is thus built into the very nature of "humanity," as the language serves to reinforce the strongly held conviction that the group comes first.

The Sacrifice of Juan Espiritu

In general the most important group in a person's life is not the company for which he works but his family. Tijuana, the bustling metropolis just across the border from Southern California, has become a mecca for people all over Mexico who come in hopes of a better way of life. Until recently, Tijuana boasted an unemployment rate of less than 1 percent, and opportunities, in comparison to Mexican standards of living, abounded.

In 1988 Juan Jose Espiritu came to Tijuana from Guadalajara with his divorced mother and family. Juan was 13 years old at the time, and he promptly went to work cleaning a stained-glass window studio to help support his mother and his five younger siblings. Ten years later at 23 years of age, Juan earned $480 per month—the salary of many teachers, journalists and bank employees—creating Tiffany style stained-glass windows portraying peacocks and ships. But Juan's success had come at the expense of his own education and (what we would call in America) a normal adolescence, since Juan had dropped out of school and spent most of his waking hours at work during his teenage years.

Juan made none of these sacrifices for the sake of his own individual goals and aspirations. Good collectivist that he is, Juan instead envisioned that his good fortune would give his younger siblings the educational and vocational opportunities that he was denied. He would not allow them to quit school and work as he had. "Perhaps one of them will become a doctor," Espiritu said. "That is my desire."[6] Juan, the individual, lays down his life for the sake of the group. Juan, the sibling, lays down his life for his brothers and sisters in his extended family.

---

[6] *Los Angeles Times*, January 26, 1998.

The above examples have aptly illustrated the quintessential collectivist conviction: the group takes precedence over the individual. Gaining a clear understanding of the "group comes first" principle has prepared us to expand our appreciation of strong-group values in the pages to come.

We turn now to another vital characteristic of strong-group peoples, this one having to do with personal identity and decision making. Just as it is the case among collectivists that the group takes priority over the individual, it is also the case that the individual in a strong-group society finds his identity not primarily in his own personal achievements but in the context of the group to which he belongs. And crucial life decisions are made in the context of that group as well.

Personal Identity in Collectivist Societies

Imagine yourself at an informal church gathering on Super Bowl Sunday. You have turned your church into a mini-stadium to show the big game on a large screen at the front of the auditorium. Halftime rolls around, and you are milling around eating finger food and socializing with others in the crowd. Then you spot a newcomer across the room. You have seen the fellow in church for several weeks, but this is your first opportunity to get personally acquainted. You walk in his direction, intending to make the first move to break the ice. He sees you coming and smiles warmly. Anticipating your intentions, he introduces himself to you first: "Hello, I'm Jonathan, son of William, son of Eric, son of Michael. Who are you?"

A rather odd introduction, wouldn't you agree? When was the last time you heard anyone introduce himself like that? It was probably the last time you read your Bible. Here are a few examples of the way in which biblical characters are typically introduced:

> "Mordecai son of Jair, son of Shimei, son of Kish" (Esth 2:5)
> "Isaiah son of Amoz" (Isa 1:1)
> "Jeremiah, the son of Hilkiah" (Jer 1:1)
> "Bartimaeus (the son of Timaeus)" (Mark 10:46)
> "John the son of Zechariah" (Luke 3:2)

We encounter introductions like these throughout the Scriptures, yet we seldom notice how odd they really are. Only when we paint a picture like the Super Bowl Sunday scenario, above, and proceed to dab a little Bible behavior onto the canvas of our own lives, do we begin to see just how strangely foreign the biblical world really is.

You would not introduce yourself in America today like Jonathan did, and you would be caught totally off-guard if another person introduced himself in this way to you. But these differences in personal introductions are profoundly significant since the manner in which I introduce myself speaks volumes about the way I view myself in relation to others in the world in which I live. In fact, issues of personal identity are at the very heart of the marked differences between strong-group and weak-group thinking about life and human relationships. The way that you and I answer the question, Who am I? tells much about both our view of the world and the degree of commitment we are willing to maintain in our relationships with others.

Decision Making and Identity Formation in American Society

I referred in the introduction to the freedoms we in America exercise in the area of decision making, freedoms to make choices that are quite unique compared to the options available to people in other cultures. We can summarize our most important life-decisions under three headings:

- **Vocation**   What I am going to do with my life?
- **Spouse**   Who I am going to spend my life with?
- **Residence**   Where I am going to live?

As an American individualist, my personal identity is deeply rooted in the decisions I make along these lines, and I alone am ultimately responsible for my choices—choices that determine my very destiny in so many crucial areas of life.

Social scientists use terms like "self-reliance" and "autonomy" to describe this uniquely Western approach to decision making and identity formation. In a practical sense, the process works itself out most significantly in my life as I choose my vocation, my spouse, and my place of residence. The success with which I make these three critical decisions profoundly affects my identity, as perceived both by myself and by others in the world around me. Moreover, it is the first of these three important life-decisions—the vocation question—that is foundational for identity, particularly for American males and increasingly for females.

Go back with me to the Super Bowl Sunday scene above. Assume again that our newcomer takes the initiative with the introductions. A more predictably Western dialogue would run something like this:

Visitor: "Hello, my name is Jonathan. I don't think we've met."
You: "Hi, I'm [your name]. Have you been attending church here long? I've seen you around the last couple weeks."

Visitor:	"Yeah, I've been coming for about a month."
You:	"What's your connection with Oceanside Christian Fellowship? How did you hear about the church?"
Visitor:	"Bill brought me and I liked it, so I've been coming back."

The conversation continues, and before long this small talk leads to the first big identity question. Now you do not just come right out and ask, "Who do you think you are? What makes you special?" But you say precisely the same thing in a more subtle, culturally acceptable way. It goes something like this:

| You: | Jonathan, what do you **do**? |

The dialogue would continue with Jonathan and you going back and forth about your jobs and perhaps the things you like to do with your free time. American men (and increasingly women), define themselves primarily by what they do, by their individual achievements. Our personal identities are rooted in how we answer the vocation question and in what we accomplish in our pursuits in the working world. Think about the last time you were in a group of strangers who were asked to go around and share names and a few tidbits of personal information. Almost invariably—probably without exception in an all men's group—what is shared is what they *do*.

The choice of a spouse and place of residence are similarly defining but in slightly different ways. Lyman Coleman, the facilitator of a training workshop for small-group leaders that I attended, assigned us to groups in order to model the group dynamics theory he was teaching us. Each of us found himself together with total strangers. I was with three other men. To break the ice, Mr. Coleman instructed us to find two or three things in our wallets that we could share with each other to get acquainted with the people in our group. Here is the identity issue, all over again, and you can guess what we pulled out.

I dug out of my billfold my business card and pictures of my two daughters. The other fellows did much the same. After bantering back and forth about work and family, we asked each other where we were from. What were we talking about in this initial get-acquainted dialogue? The areas of decision making outlined above. In a nutshell, we went around the circle asking, "What are you doing with your life? Who are you doing life with? Where are you doing it?" We immediately gravitate to these kinds of questions in settings like this because in America our identities depend on effectively addressing these pressing issues in the courses of our lives.

But how painful and agonizing these decisions are to make! For in Western culture we must ultimately make these weighty decisions—and shoulder the responsibility for their outcome—*alone*. I do not believe that God has designed us to do so, and I hope to convince you of this before you finish reading this book.

Making Big Decisions

Christians long to have God involved in the decision-making process, so we faithfully seek God's will when we arrive at those inevitable forks in the road of life. I served as a pastor to collegians and young professional single adults for more than a decade. This age group wrestles with the defining questions of vocation, relationship, and residence in a most immediate and heart-wrenching way. Much of the pastoral counseling I provided during my years in single adult ministry involved helping people make wise decisions in precisely these three areas.

Attendance down in the singles group? All I had to do was to mail out a flyer publicizing a teaching series on how to find God's will for one's life, and the crowds poured in. Collegians and young singles are well aware that the choices they make in the three areas outlined above will radically affect every area of their lives—for the rest of their lives. But this makes the process all the more painful, and it generates a certain theological dissonance as well because the Bible says almost nothing about making the kinds of decisions that face young adults.

One cannot find a passage detailing a series of criteria for choosing a mate or a text that will help a collegian decide which major to pick. God's Word is relatively silent on these topics. And we should not be surprised. For all its timeless relevance, the Bible remains a collection of strong-group documents written by people who shared a collectivist worldview.

People in biblical times simply did not make major life decisions on their own. An ancient Israelite, for example, typically did not have to determine whom he was going to marry, what he was going to do for a living, or where he was going to reside. All these decisions were made for him by his community, that is, by his family and the broader society to which he belonged.

What Am I Going to Do with My Life?

Consider the vocation dilemma. A person born in first-century rural Galilee would not have had to wrestle with the issue. If your father was a carpenter, you would be a carpenter. Hey, John, you say your dad Zebedee is a fisherman? You had better grab a net. The odds are about a hundred to one that you are going be a fisherman too.

Even today our surnames are often vestiges of our collectivist past. If your name is Smith, you likely had ancestors who worked as blacksmiths or silversmiths. Shoemaker's your last name? Pretty obvious. A cardiologist named Doctor Fuller is something of an oxymoron, for a person will not likely work bivocationally as a medical doctor and as a fuller (bleaching cloth). But once upon a time in the not-too-distant past, Dr. Fuller's ancestors plied the fuller's trade, and children born into the Fuller family had no other option in the vocational arena. The Fuller name is all that remains of that strong-group past. Collectivist societies answer the question about a young person's future vocation simply and categorically: You are going to do what your father and your ancestors have always done.

The lack of choices in strong-group cultures strikes the average American as restrictive, and perhaps downright oppressive. Few of us would want to turn back the clock. I am proud of the hard-working, blue-collar, high school graduate shoe salesman who was my father. But I would not trade my education and my ever-stimulating vocation in local church ministry and university teaching for the working world my father knew. But at this point I want you to appreciate one of the serious liabilities that comes with the freedom we cherish in America to determine our individual vocational destinies.

The choices we possess in our radically individualistic society have come at a tremendous emotional price. We pay dearly in the stress department for our freedom to decide for ourselves, and as a result many of us are now emotionally bankrupt. How much inner turmoil, how much soul searching and self-evaluation, how much pressure do we experience in individualistic America as we make—and take personal responsibility for—these defining and often highly troublesome vocational decisions?

I am 56 years old. It is now estimated that the average person changes jobs seven times during his or her working career, and this makes me a genuine statistic. Over the past three decades I have worked as (1) a musician in a rock band, (2) a production control clerk in the garment industry, (3) a technician in a university music department, (4) a singles' pastor in a local church, (5) a seminary professor, (6) a pastor again, and now (7) a seminary professor again. My training for these professions took me through college, graduate school, theological seminary, and then graduate school again. None of these transitions occurred without great emotional agony and extended reflection on my part.

I sometimes find it almost overwhelming to embrace the sober reality that I—and I alone—am responsible for my own vocational destiny and for the economic well-being of my family. Just ask my wife Joann. She still wonders what I am going to be when I grow up. I tell her that I am not planning on growing up! On a more serious note, this is precisely the problem. Faced with decisions that people were never meant to make in isolation, we self-destruct emotionally and relationally, we never grow up, and we turn to therapy or medication to prop us up against a world that is just too much for us to handle on our own.

With Whom Am I Going to Spend My Life?

What about decisions in the romantic realm? Even more angst and stress here! The choice of a mate is our most significant life decision, and there is no rule book to help us through the process—although people often try unsuccessfully to turn the Bible into a textbook for Courtship 101. During my tenure in single adult ministry I officiated at more than a hundred weddings. Finding a mate always was, and ever will be, the hot topic in singles' ministry. Seventy-five percent of the counseling I did related directly to this issue.

The folks I worked with never ceased to delight in the comic strip *Cathy* and to identify with the protagonist. In a particularly insightful dialogue, we find Cathy out golfing with her boyfriend Irving:

Cathy:	"Here's your ball, Irving! It was over in the weeds!"
Irving:	"AACK! You moved the ball! You're not allowed to move the ball, Cathy!"
Cathy:	"Who cares? We're the only ones out here!"
Irving:	"It's against the rules! You can't break the rules!!"
Cathy:	"You hate rules!"
Irving:	"But this is a SPORT! It's no fun without rules! It's pointless unless everyone plays by the exact same rules!"

As Irving walks away, Cathy follows after, writing in her notebook, "To do after vacation. Get relationships declared a 'sport' and print up rule book for all the men."

Oh for a rule book to navigate safely through the storms of courtship! Unfortunately, there is no such rule book for men or for women. We are left on our own to sort through the sometimes exhilarating, but more often painfully agonizing, challenge of securing a life partner.

People in traditional societies are spared this anxiety. They are paired up with their life partners before they are even old enough to be interested in such things. No courtship games, no risk taking, no rejection. And when people in strong-group cultures do marry, they do not travel very far. A new groom typically stays in his parents' home or in close proximity. A new bride moves in with their husband's extended family, and she regularly returns to spend time with her family of origin during holidays. Nobody, in a sense, ever finally leaves home. People remain connected for life to others in their local extended family networks.

Where Am I Going to Live?

This leads us to a third key area of decision making, the question of residence. In our experience, choosing a place to live does not appear to be as significant as the decisions we make about our vocation and our spouse. After all, details surrounding marriage and work pretty much determine where we are going to set up house. But the results of our highly mobile Western approach to life are equally far reaching in their effects on our emotions and on our view of how we fit into the world around us.

Leaving home is in many ways a uniquely Western challenge. Sociologist R. Bellah has spent much of his life studying American values. He noted, "In a culture that emphasizes the autonomy and self-reliance of the individual, the primary problems of childhood are what some psychoanalysts call separation and individuation—indeed, childhood is chiefly [a time of] preparation for the all-important event of leaving home." But Bellah further observed, "Separation and individuation are issues that must be faced by all human beings, but leaving home in its American sense is not."[7]

This is an important qualification. In traditional Japan the expression "leaving home" was reserved for those entering monastic life, who abandoned all ties of ordinary existence. In other words, people who left home were the exception, the oddballs of traditional Japanese society.

Indeed, the great majority of people in collectivist peasant societies (such as Jesus' first-century Galilee) never leave home. They live in close proximity to parents, siblings, and offspring, working and worshiping with their extended families until death. Such an approach to residence proves emotionally beneficial, for spending one's life with extended family in a single geographical location provides people in traditional cultural settings with a great degree of relational and economic security.

How different things are in America! In contrast to the collectivist orientation, Americans have made leaving home the goal of the whole parenting process. We are each socialized throughout our childhood to become independent of our families of origin—relationally independent, emotionally independent, financially

---

[7] R. N. Bellah, et al. *Habits of the Heart: Individualism and Commitment in American Life* (New York: Harper & Row, 1985), 57.

independent, and geographically independent. The technical phrase adopted by cultural anthropologists to describe the latter idea is "neolocal residence." As an adult, I do not stay in my father's (patrilocal) house. I move out and establish a new (neolocal) place to live. I leave home. It is the American way.

But is it the wisest way? Consider the sense of utter isolation and instability that often results from being separated by hundreds of miles from parents, siblings, and other members of our extended families. Our geographical mobility, like our freedoms to choose a vocation and a life partner, has not come without a price. It is important to acknowledge the fallout that ensues from the freedom we exercise in America to live wherever we choose.

Young mothers in America suffer more than anyone from the acute geographical fragmentation that characterizes our individualistic society. Raising a child is a task for which no new mother can ever be adequately prepared. Collectivist societies recognize this, and young mothers find a great network of support among the more mature women in their extended families.

By contrast, American women with preschool-aged children are often geographically isolated from their own mothers, grandmothers, and sisters. Young moms live at one end of the country, their parents at the other. Even our neighborhoods have become less and less family friendly, as people hole up in their homes and apartments—the descriptive word is "cocooning"—and increasingly find their closest friendships among co-workers on the job. Mothers with little ones are left isolated and alone to sort through the most utterly daunting task imaginable: raising a human being.

The fallout is tragic but not all that surprising. Depression is absolutely rampant among young mothers in suburban America today. As a pastor I am regularly confronted with some crisis in this area, and I only hear the cries of mothers who call upon their church leaders for help. I can only imagine the sense of quiet desperation overwhelming the many young mothers who do not reach out to others when their worlds cave in.

Women fortunate enough to afford the luxury are propped up by weekly visits to their therapists. These young mothers, in turn, do their best to prop up their families, and we all hang on by the skin of our teeth and try emotionally to survive—instead of thrive—from one day to the next. We Americans pay a tremendous price for our cherished freedoms to determine our own vocational, relational, and geographical destinies.

The Cost of Our Freedom in Decision Making:
Individualism and a Therapeutic Culture

We have no accurate statistics on the number of people in therapy in twenty-first century America. But no one can dispute the fact that there has been a tremendous increase in the number of mental health professionals serving the American public since World War II. You might be seeing a therapist yourself. You almost certainly know someone who is. I have seen a therapist in the past. One of my daughters is doing so as I write. We turn to psychologists—and to medication—to assist us in dealing with the stress and emotional upheaval that inevitably come on us in a society that emphasizes self-reliance and individual autonomy at the expense of relational support and accountability.

It might surprise you to learn that our therapeutic culture is a relatively recent phenomenon in world history. As Bellah and others have observed, the origin and popularity of clinical psychology can be directly traced to the increasingly individualistic slant of Western relational values. In other words, the great majority of people on this planet never needed therapy until society began to dump the responsibility for making life's major decisions squarely upon the lonely shoulders of the individual. Our freedoms, as intoxicating and exhilarating as they often are, have pushed us over the edge emotionally. We are reaping the consequences of decisions that were never meant to be made—and lives that were never meant to be lived—in isolation.

Psychotherapy's very methodology reflects our fragmented, isolationist worldview. One of the most fascinating aspects of the field is that the therapeutic relationship itself mirrors the perspective of the society that has birthed and nurtured it. As early as 1976, the authors of an important work entitled *Mental Health in America* astutely observed that

> Psychoanalysis (and psychiatry) is the only form of psychic healing that
> attempts to cure people by *detaching them from society and relationships*. All
> other forms—shamanism, faith healing, prayer—bring the community into the
> healing process, indeed use the interdependence of patient and others as the
> central mechanism in the healing process.[8]

In contrast to traditional forms of healing, modern psychiatry isolates the troubled person from his or her network of real-life relationships and tries to deal with emotional dysfunction in the artificial setting of a professional patient-client relationship. Think about it. We detach hurting people *from* community in order to

---

[8] J. Veroff, R. Kulka, and E. Douvan, *Mental Health in America: Patterns of Help-Seeking from 1957 to 1976* (New York: Basic Books, 1981), 6–7 (italics added).

help them better function *in* community. Perhaps such an approach to healing strikes you, as it does me, as decidedly counterproductive.

To be fair, the above quotation is dated and somewhat one-sided. Therapists who work with family systems do, of course, attempt to treat their clients in the context of real-world relationships. Moreover, the better Christian psychologists, like those associated with the congregation I pastor, partner with the church community in the healing process, for they recognize the necessity of real-life relationships as an indispensable context for genuine relational growth and development. But I cite the above excerpt because I remain convinced that it helps explain the many failures of the therapeutic process, even in the best of settings.

Sadly, the successes of Christian psychology are marginal at best. I readily acknowledge that I have seen significant growth in certain people whom I have referred to skilled therapists. But in a number of instances, the people in our congregation utilize psychotherapy as just another resource to enable them to continue along their own selfish quest for personal autonomy, an autonomy that seeks to escape—rather than courageously to engage—painful, real-life relationships. The result has become rather predictable. In the detached, artificial environment of the therapeutic relationship between client and psychologist, people often "find themselves," only to take their newfound insights *away* from their spouse or church family in order to chart their own, individualistic course for the future.

Hear me well on this one. I do not lay the responsibility for clinical psychology's checkered track record wholly, or even primarily, at the foot of the discipline or its practitioners. Pastors (if we are honest with ourselves) will acknowledge a similarly unimpressive won-lost record in our gallant but often futile attempts to grow our people in the context of relational accountability. Rather, I suggest that therapists, like the rest of us who work in people-helping professions, are outgunned by the thoroughgoing socialization that has seared the consciences of the persons to whom we minister.

Our clients and congregants are American individualists. Convincing them that their ultimate hope for healing lies in engaging *with*—instead of running *from*—significant others is an almost insurmountable task. Pastoral care and psychotherapy are certainly helpful in this regard, but they are clearly not enough. What is required is a wholesale reorientation of our worldview, and a key aspect of that reorientation must involve embracing the strong-group values that characterized the outlook of New Testament Christianity. Only then will we be able to revolutionize the way we relate to one another in our families and in our churches.

Strong-Group Values as a Biblical, Transcultural Reality

One might object at this point that the strong-group outlook is simply one among many perfectly acceptable perspectives a society might adopt to conceive of the relationship between individual persons and various social groups in a particular culture. The Greco-Roman world was a collectivist society in which the group came first. The modern West, in contrast, is a weak-group culture that assigns priority to individual desires and needs. Neither social orientation is intrinsically good or bad. They are simply different. And we must contextualize the gospel—and do church—differently in these different cultural settings.

As reasonable as all this sounds, for the Christian faith a neutral approach to cultural differences proves highly problematic where the distinction between strong-group and weak-group societies is concerned. The reason for this is quite transparent. The collectivist social model is deeply woven into the very fabric of the gospel itself.

The New Testament church was decidedly strong-group in its social orientation, but this was no accident of cultural accommodation. Jesus unequivocally affirmed such an approach to interpersonal relationships when He chose "family" as the defining metaphor to describe His followers. This is a crucial observation and one that I will unpack in a number of ways as our discussion unfolds. For the present, we may simply note that one's family demanded the highest commitment of undivided loyalty, relational solidarity, and personal sacrifice of any social entity in Jesus' strong-group Mediterranean world. And major life decisions were made in the context of the family.

Of course, Jesus was well aware of this when He intentionally adopted "family" as the key relational image for the social organization of the group He was gathering around Himself. So we should not be surprised to discover that for the early Christians the overall health and honor of the church family took priority over their individual needs and desires.

The same should be true of us. After all, Jesus set the ultimate example of this family-first mentality when He gave His life as a ransom for many. As one of our New Testament authors put it, "He laid down His life for us. We should also lay down our lives for our brothers" (1 John 3:16).

Conclusion

The heart of this book is concerned with recapturing the social vision of the early Christian church as a strong-group, surrogate family. We will consider the family behavior of the early church in some detail in later chapters. But I would

encourage you to begin even now to reflect upon the implications of the material
we have covered for your own pilgrimage as a member of God's family. We may
summarize what we have learned so far with a fundamental assertion. Others will
be added later.

> *Principle #1:   In the New Testament world the group took priority over the*
> *individual.*

I further explain and carefully qualify this truth in the pages to come. For the
present it is helpful to conclude our discussion by briefly reconsidering a familiar
biblical narrative with the above principle in mind.

The collectivist mind-set of early Christianity is particularly evident in the
attitudes of church members toward their material goods. In harmony with the
"group comes first" principle that characterized the Mediterranean world, Christians viewed their possessions as belonging to the broader church family rather
than to the individual believer. The sharing of resources we find in the book of
Acts is an expression of this strong-group, family mentality:

> Now the multitude of those who believed were of one heart and soul, and no
> one said that any of his possessions was his own, but instead they held every-
> thing in common. And with great power the apostles were giving testimony to
> the resurrection of the Lord Jesus, and great grace was on all of them. For there
> was not a needy person among them, because all those who owned lands or
> houses sold them, brought the proceeds of the things that were sold, and laid
> them at the apostles' feet. This was then distributed to each person as anyone
> had a need. (Acts 4:32–35)

This is a hard passage to hear for the American individualist. But we ought to
listen carefully to what it has to say, for it is rather sobering to read what follows
in the very next chapter in Luke's narrative: the one unambiguous New Testament
example of divine chastisement resulting in the death of a professing believer. The
chapter divisions in our Bibles were not put there by the human or divine authors;
they were added centuries later. So Acts 4 and Acts 5 must be read together.

In Acts 5:1–11 Ananias and Sapphira claimed to be acting in a strong-group
way as they brought their offering to the apostles. Tragically, they were more concerned to retain their personal resources and still acquire honor and a reputation
for self-sacrifice in the eyes of the church. Their allegedly collectivist behavior
was all smoke and mirrors. God was not pleased, and the couple died on the
spot.

Now I recognize that the duplicity involved in the couple's behavior—not their unwillingness to part with their possessions—is the reason given in the text for God's judgment. Ananias and Sapphira were never obligated to surrender all their belongings to the church. They lied to God the Holy Spirit, and they suffered the consequences.

But the specific connection between the couple's deceit and the issue of strong-group sacrifice—in this case, the sharing of material resources—must not be overlooked. Nor should we miss the fact that the couple's behavior was directly contrasted with the strong-group family ethic that Luke affirmed in the immediately preceding portion of the narrative. The radical discipline Ananias and Sapphira experienced at the hand of God demonstrates that the collectivist "group comes first" conviction constitutes a central principle for New Testament social ethics. To lie about this aspect of discipleship is to undermine the very foundation of the community God is building.

I trust you are beginning to appreciate the value of cross-cultural analysis for interpreting the biblical text. The Christian communities established by Peter, Paul, and others in the Roman Empire were strong-group, surrogate family units in which the good of the group took priority over the desires and aspirations of the individual members. This collectivist worldview resulted in some very specific behaviors and relational expectations that in turn distinguished the Christian church as unique among the various social and religious groups in the Greco-Roman world.

Indeed, the social solidarity that the early Christians enjoyed as a result of living out their strong-group family values ultimately brought a whole pagan empire to its knees. Such was the power of community as God intended it. Such was the power of the church when the church was a family. We now proceed to consider what "family" meant to persons in the world of Jesus and Paul.

Chapter Two

FAMILY IN THE NEW TESTAMENT WORLD

My soul takes pleasure in three things and they are beautiful in the sight of the Lord and of men: agreement between siblings, friendship between neighbors, and a wife and husband who live in harmony.

(Sirach 25:1)

My daughter Rebekah spent her first year in college working part time at a Hallmark gift shop. Rebekah landed her job in late December and went through her on-the-job training in January. She caught on fast and soon grew accustomed to the various responsibilities associated with a small business. Rebekah also adapted rather nicely to the relaxed work pace typical of a Hallmark store during the lull in greeting card sales that follows the Christmas holidays. One day she even took her college textbooks along to occupy herself during the inevitable "down time" behind the cash register.

But then came February 13—the day before Valentine's Day—which, as you might imagine, is the busiest time of the year for Rebekah's employer. The increase in business that day hit my daughter like a hurricane—a male hurricane, that is, since, to put it in Rebekah's words, "There were so many clueless guys in the store that day, Daddy, you wouldn't believe it!" Oh yes I would. I was one of them. And Rebekah's employer made more money off of us in a single day than she makes any other week of the year.

What is it that drives men in droves to the Hallmark shop and encourages women to expect a little special recognition on Valentine's Day? Love, of course!

Romantic love—ignited during the rituals of dating and courtship, cultivated in a lifelong marriage, and celebrated in annual events like Valentine's Day—occupies the top slot in the hierarchy of relational priorities for people in the Western world.

Those of us who live in individualistic societies expect marriage to be our most meaningful, intimate, and satisfying relationship. We hope to find most of our emotional, physical, and material needs met in the context of the marriage bond. Reflect for a moment on your own life. Of all your many interpersonal relationships—with coworkers, siblings, parents, friends—the connection you share with your spouse (or which you envision sharing with a future spouse) is surely the one you rate as most important. It is the one relationship you most want to succeed.

It will likely come as little surprise to you by now to learn that we in the Western world are, once again, somewhat odd in our priorities and convictions. I say "somewhat" odd because romantic love knows no cultural boundaries. A good marriage is a priority in nearly every society. But notice that I said *a* priority, not *the* priority. There are striking differences between the way we do family and the way that strong-group cultures conceive of family relationships.

The quotation at the heading of the chapter serves as an instructive door through which to enter into the strange world of collectivist family sensibilities. The order that our ancient friend Sirach listed these relationships reflects the priorities of the world in which he lived:

> My soul takes pleasure in three things and they are beautiful in the sight of the
> Lord and of men: agreement between siblings, friendship between neighbors,
> and a wife and husband who live in harmony (Sirach 25:1).[1]

First on Sirach's list comes "agreement between siblings." Then the neighbors get the nod. At the end of his list Sirach tips his hat to "a wife and husband who live in harmony."

My intention in this chapter is to demonstrate that for persons in Mediterranean antiquity, marriage took a back seat priority-wise to another more important family relationship—the bond between blood brothers and sisters. Marriages were essentially contractual unions intended to strengthen the larger extended family through alliance-building (with other clans) and the production of offspring.

---

[1] Joshua ben Sira (Hb. for "Jesus the son of Sirach") was a Palestinian Jewish scribe who penned a book of proverbial wisdom c. 175 BC. His work is not part of the Protestant canon but is nevertheless valuable as a source for Jewish thinking and values during the intertestamental years. One could conceivably argue the opposite of what I maintain above, namely, that Sirach saves the closest relationship for the end of his list. The direction established with the first two sets of relations, however (siblings, then neighbors), implies otherwise.

While marriage was important for those reasons, the closest same-generation family relationship was not the one between husband and wife. It was the bond between siblings.

This particular characteristic of the Mediterranean family should markedly inform our understanding of Christian community, since the idea that we are brothers and sisters in Christ constitutes the fundamental conceptual point of departure for coming to grips with God's social vision for His church. No image for the church occurs more often in the New Testament than the metaphor of family, and no image offers as much promise as "family" for recapturing the relational integrity of first-century Christianity for our churches today.

It is imperative to recognize, however, that the way in which Americans do family would have been quite foreign to first-century sensibilities. The early church functioned like an ancient Mediterranean family—not a modern American family. We need to resist the temptation to read our idea of "brother" or "sister" into the biblical text. Instead, we must learn to grasp the way in which "brother" would resonate with a strong-group person, since the New Testament church family model reflects the relational values and priorities of kinship systems in the first-century world.

Family Priorities in the Ancient World

Perhaps the most counterintuitive (to us) aspect of Mediterranean kinship has to do with the way in which family membership is reckoned by members of strong-group societies, that is, how persons in such cultures decide who belongs to their family. In the New Testament world, an individual viewed as family those persons with whom he or she shared a common patriline—a bloodline traced from generation to generation solely through male offspring. The diagram on the following page has been drawn to assume that I am part of an ancient patrilineal family. I belong to the second of four generations represented on the diagram. The patriline (which defines family membership) is marked by the heavy filled-in lines and brackets (the '+' symbol indicates a marriage).

First, observe that only the individuals underlined in boldface type represent my family members. Notice that although my sister and I possess our father's blood, and therefore belong to the same family, only I pass on the bloodline to the next generation. My sister has the blood, but she cannot pass it on (the solid line on her side of the chart ends with her). Follow the solid line from top to bottom and you will notice that it passes from one generation to the next only through sons, not through daughters.

The Mediterranean Family

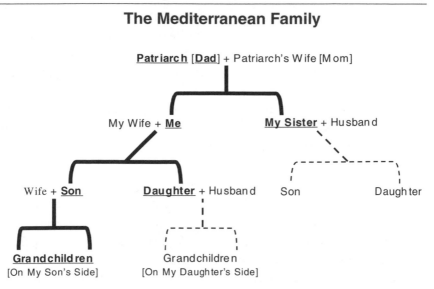

Due to the patrilineal nature of the Mediterranean family, only males pass family membership down to the next generation. Females do not. The diagram illustrates this quite well.

It is for this reason that lineage groups like the one diagrammed above are called patrilineal. Blood is passed down solely through the male line. The result for my grandchildren's generation is that my grandchildren on my son's side are members of my (and my father's) kinship group. The grandchildren on my daughter's side are not, since my daughter cannot pass on my blood. And a person must have the blood to be part of the family.

In the ancient world, a male regarded as immediate family (a) his father (from whom he had received his blood), (b) his brothers and sisters (with whom he shared his blood), and (c) offspring of both genders (to whom he passed on his blood). Females, like males, viewed fathers and siblings as blood kin (the technical term is "consanguine"). Since a mother could not pass on membership in her patriline to the next generation, her children technically belonged not to her family but to the patriline of her husband. Because a husband and wife had different fathers—and therefore belonged to different patrilines—married persons in the world of the New Testament generally expressed primary relational allegiance not to a spouse but to members of their family of origin.

Therefore, this blood-based orientation to kinship directly informed the nature of family relationships. Among those who belong to the same generation in the world of Mediterranean antiquity, the closest family tie was not the contractual relationship between husband and wife. It was the blood relationship between siblings. As is now generally recognized by students of ancient family systems, the strongest ties of loyalty and affection in the New Testament world were ideally those shared among a group of brothers and sisters. The emotional bonding modern Westerners expect as a mark of a healthy husband-wife relationship was normally characteristic of sibling relationships. But marriages were contracted with a view to enhancing the honor or wealth of the extended patrilineal kinship group, so that the relational satisfaction of the couple involved was seldom a key consideration.

What is a woman's role in all of this if she can only inherit, but cannot pass on, her family's blood? Her role is to be married out into another family to produce a son, in order to ensure the future of that family's bloodline. The patrilineal system thus places a woman in a highly tenuous position. She must leave her own family to marry into a family whose blood she can never share. Because blood is such a defining element of family attachment and solidarity, a woman will always sense a closer connection with her brothers and sisters back home (who share her blood) than she will with her husband and his family (who do not share her blood).

In the above diagram the patriarch's daughter (labeled as My Sister) will never feel as deep a sense of loyalty and obligation to her husband and to his family as she does to me and to our father. Note this well. In Mediterranean antiquity, blood runs deeper than romantic love.

Marriage in Strong-Group Culture

The following description of marriage is taken from a recent book about families in the world of the New Testament. I have taken the liberty of numbering the three purposes that the authors offer for marriage in Mediterranean antiquity:

> Marriage, therefore, is a legal and social contract between two families for (1) the promotion of the status of each, (2) the production of legitimate offspring, and (3) the appropriate preservation and transferal of property to the next generation.[2]

Notice what is absent from the above definition. No consideration at all is given to the relational satisfaction or compatibility of the bride and groom. Each of the three reasons has to do with the status or preservation of the family as a whole.

As we saw illustrated in the movie *Titanic* in the previous chapter, the driving question in the collectivist approach to marriage is never "What is best for

---

[2] C. Osiek and D. Balch, *Families in the New Testament World: Households and House Churches* (Louisville: Westminster John Knox Press, 1997), 42.

the couple?" Rather, it is "What is best for the extended families to which the bride and groom belong?" In Rose's case (the heroine of *Titanic*), the benefit of the arranged marriage had to do with augmenting her family's wealth and social status. This is often, but not always, the particular advantage sought. For example, sometimes feuding clans will intermarry in order to avoid future bloodshed by building an alliance. But in each case it is the good of the group—the extended family—that is in view in the arrangement. In each case the happiness of the bride and groom is a secondary consideration.

This is not to suggest that people in descent group family systems are necessarily deprived of relationally satisfying marriages. It is simply to observe that individual marital bliss is generally understood as a secondary by-product, rather than the primary goal, of the institution of marriage. For descent group societies, a good marriage is one that enhances the honor and position of the extended family.

Interestingly enough, things have not changed all that much in rural areas around the Mediterranean even today. I. Whitaker studied the values of the Gheg culture, a rural people group in Albania. He discovered that "romantic feelings between men and women played little part in the expected behavior pattern of husbands and wives." Whitaker concluded, "In brief, I would categorize the marital tie in Gheg society as one based on economic and social factors . . . and containing little emotional dependence."[3]

Whitaker's description of strong-group marriage strikes those of us socialized to embrace the relational values of American culture as less than ideal. So where does a person in a collectivist society find emotional support and solidarity if not in the marriage relationship? Return to the chart one last time and see if you can determine which persons in a given generation share family membership. You will notice that for each generation, siblings, not spouses, are identified on the diagram as belonging to the same family. This reality leads us into an exploration of the most intimate and highly charged relationship for people in the world of Jesus and the early Christians—the bond among brothers and sisters.

Central to this chapter—and to Jesus' vision for authentic Christian community—is the priority of sibling relationships in the strong-group family model. The blood bond between siblings—not between husband and wife—is the most intimate, nurturing, and ultimately satisfying relationship for persons in collectivist cultures. The following is a basic summary of ancient relational priorities:

---

[3] I. Whitaker, "Familial Roles in the Extended Patrilineal Kingroup in Northern Albania," in *Mediterranean Family Structures*, ed. J. Peristiany (Cambridge: University Press, 1976), 198.

- The closest family bond in ancient Mediterranean society was not the bond of marriage. It was the bond between siblings.
- Correspondingly, the most treacherous act of human disloyalty in an ancient family was not disloyalty to one's spouse. It was the betrayal of one's brother.

We simply must grasp these two key principles in order to properly appreciate the relational priorities of ancient Mediterranean people. Only then will we be equipped to fully grasp what it meant for the early followers of Jesus to interact as brothers and sisters in Christ.

A brief comparison with American family values may prove helpful. I am the father of two precious daughters, Rebekah (age 23) and Rachel (age 19). The girls get along quite well (aside from sibling spats) and genuinely enjoy each other's company. I hope that there will always be a close and committed family bond between Rebekah and Rachel, as they begin to chart their different courses as adults and go their separate ways. But over the long haul I am much more concerned about the health of another relationship my daughters will likely experience—the relationship each will have with her future husband.

Now I hope and pray for great communication and ongoing love both between each daughter and each one's future husband *and* between Rachel and Rebekah as sisters. But if I had to sacrifice one for the other, the decision would not be difficult for me, since I am a person whose family outlook reflects Western values. If I were forced to choose, I would rather that my daughters experience healthy marriages than a close relationship with each other. If you are a parent, you probably feel much the same about your children. For most Americans, a healthy marriage comes first.

Not so in descent-group cultures. If my family lived in first-century Palestine, I would be more concerned about Rebekah's and Rachel's relationship with each other than about the health of their marriages. Yes, I would do all that I could to arrange a satisfying marriage for each of my daughters. But if push came to shove, I would far rather have them retain their sense of loyalty and commitment to each other than have them enjoy a meaningful and lasting marriage. This is because sibling solidarity is the highest relational value for collectivist family members. The blood connection is stronger than the conjugal bond.

A Note on Methodology

The balance of this chapter draws upon the Bible and upon extrabiblical literature from antiquity in order to demonstrate the priority of sibling relations among people in the New Testament world. I also offer an example or two from collectivist societies in the Middle East today. But before we begin our journey into the world of strong-group sibling solidarity, a word about methodology is in order.

At this point in the discussion some readers will be tempted to zero in on the distinctions between Mediterranean family values and American family values and to press for a biblical assessment of these two very different ways of doing family. What *is* God's design for family? Does God truly want us to prioritize sibling relationships over the bond of marriage in our natural families?

Such questions are not unimportant, and the Bible clearly contains some rather pointed challenges to the way in which relationships were prioritized in the ancient patrilineal family (for example, Eph 5:22–33). *When the Church Was a Family*, however, is not a book about our natural families. It is about the family of God. Our examination of Mediterranean family systems is not intended as a prescriptive blueprint for natural family relationships. The point of our analysis is to ascertain how the metaphor of the church as a family—especially the image of Christians as surrogate siblings—would have informed social relations in the New Testament church.

Whatever we might think about the way in which God intends our natural families to function—and I will leave it to others to evaluate ancient family values in light of the biblical blueprint for family—it is clear that the early Christians used "brother" as the key image for community in the church and thereby drew on the whole constellation of behavioral expectations and values associated with sibling relationships as they currently functioned in the patrilineal kinship groups of Mediterranean antiquity. We encounter these behavioral expectations and values among traditional peoples in antiquity and around the world today.

Examples of Strong-Group Sibling Solidarity

Our illustrations come from a variety of sources: non-Christian writings from the ancient world, modern ethnographic studies, and the Bible. The first two stories (one from the Jewish side, the other from the realm of Roman family relations) are particularly revealing because both colorfully illustrate the collectivist priority of sibling loyalty over commitment to one's spouse.

Herod and Mariamme

The Jewish historian Josephus was incessantly preoccupied with the intrigues of one rather notorious family from Jesus' day, the family of Herod the Great. Josephus wrote page after page chronicling the scenarios that played themselves out within the walls of Herod's palace. Herod ultimately murdered his own wives and several of his own kids, as well as the infants mentioned in Matthew's Gospel, so the Herodian family is hardly a model of ideal kinship relations. But even in this highly dysfunctional extended family the blood bond between siblings prevailed over other relational attachments.

One point in Josephus' narrative finds Herod in a highly affective, emotionally satisfying love relationship with his wife Mariamme. Again, such relationships are not all that unusual even where arranged marriages prevail. Although Herod's feelings for his wife were not always reciprocated, "the king's love for Mariamme," Josephus informs us, "was beyond all reason" (*Antiquities* 15.207).

Herod's feelings for Mariamme seem almost to mirror American marital values. But we would be misled to assume as much, since Herod's relational affection for Mariamme was not what brought the couple together in the first place. Nor did it prevail in the end. The key reason Herod married Mariamme was not romantic in nature. He contracted the union in order to enhance the honor of his family by marrying into Jewish royalty. Mariamme was a Jewish princess, Herod a despised half-breed. The marriage was a classic alliance arranged for the good of Herod's extended family. It was all about the good of the group. The union just happened to result in a relationally satisfying marriage.

Later, Herod's affection for Mariamme again recedes into the background, as the blood bond between siblings prevails over marital attachment and commitment. At a climactic point in their lives, Herod is forced to choose between his affection for Mariamme and his loyalty to his patrilineal descent group of blood relatives. It seems that Herod's sister Salome (note the sibling bond) had some kind of problem with Herod's wife Mariamme. Herod is caught in the middle, an emotional struggle ensues, and Herod must choose between sibling and spouse. Herod's sister finally convinces her brother to put his beloved wife Mariamme to death (*Antiquities* 15.185–240). Blood "triumphs" over marital affection.

Mark Antony and Octavia

Roman history offers another striking example of what happens when a strong-group person is forced to choose between a spouse and a sibling. Many of us are familiar with the love story of Antony and Cleopatra. Events leading up to the tragic demise of the couple reveal, once again, the priority of the sibling bond for people in the ancient world. A generation or so before Jesus appeared on the scene in Palestine, an epic power struggle in Rome had left two leaders each with half of the imperial pie. Octavian (later known as Caesar Augustus) ruled in the West, and Mark Antony ruled in the East.

Civil wars had torn Italy apart and disrupted life and commerce empire-wide for nearly a century. To satisfy the demands of the people, who were weary of the chaos and who assumed that Octavian and Antony would soon be at each other's throats, the two generals brokered a marriage alliance. Antony would marry Octavian's half-sister (Octavia), thus uniting the two families. The hope was that Octavian would never attack a fellow who was married to his sister, and that Antony would not go to war with his wife's brother.

Antony and Octavia married, but animosity between East and West only continued to increase. Octavia, now married to her brother's mortal enemy (Antony), was caught in the middle. The Roman historian who relates the tragic course of events tells us that Octavia

> appealed to her brother [Octavius] with tears and passionate entreaties not to make her the most wretched of women after having been the happiest. As it was, she told him, the eyes of the whole world were upon her, since she was the wife of one of its masters [Antony] and the sister of the other [Octavius]. "If the worst should happen," she said, "and war breaks out between you, no one can say which of you is fated to conquer the other, but what is quite certain is that my fate will be miserable." (Plutarch, *Life of Antony*, 35)

Notice that Octavia claims to be "the happiest" of women in her present relationship with Antony. We would expect her to stay and support her husband. But what happens in the ensuing narrative is wholly predictable from the perspective of strong-group family values. When Octavia is ultimately forced to choose, she leaves her husband Antony and returns to the side of her brother Octavian. Again, blood runs deeper than marriage, and the bond between siblings must take priority.

Lucius and Antony's Mother (Lucius's Sister)

A related story portrays a member of Mark Antony's family risking her life for a blood sibling. Major changes of rule in Rome often resulted in the deaths of men who had exercised power under the previous administration. At one point in the late history of the Roman Republic, Mark Antony's uncle, Lucius Caesar, was marked out for destruction. It was, in fact, Mark Antony himself who had apparently fingered Lucius. Lucius took refuge in the home of his sister, Antony's mother. Plutarch's description of the ensuing events depicts the sister as a paradigm of what a sibling ought to be in strong-group society:

> When the murderers broke into her [Lucius's sister] house and tried to force
> their way into her room, she stood in front of the door barring their entrance,
> and stretching out her hands, and cried aloud, "It was I who brought Antony,
> your general, into the world, and you shall not kill Lucius Caesar unless you
> kill me first." By this action she succeeded in getting her brother Lucius out of
> the way and saved his life. (*Ant.* 20)

Lucius's sister laid her life on the line for the sake of her brother. This was precisely the behavior expected among siblings when a brother or sister was endan-
gered. Indeed, as one Jewish writer asserted, a person should be "ashamed" of
"rejecting the appeal of a kinsman" (Sirach 41:21).

Augustus, Archelaus, and Family Betrayal

Sibling solidarity may be understood as the archetypical expression of a somewhat broader Mediterranean family value, namely, the undying loyalty a person
owes to his extended patrilineal kinship group. A final illustration from the Greco-
Roman world graphically underscores this nonnegotiable social reality.

According to Matthew's Gospel, shortly after the death of Herod Jesus and
His parents returned to Judea after hiding out for some time in Egypt (2:13–21).
Matthew introduces us at this point in the story to a rather notorious character
named Archelaus: "But when he [Joseph] heard that Archelaus was ruling over
Judea in place of his father Herod, he was afraid to go there. And being warned in
a dream, he withdrew to the region of Galilee" (2:22). Herod had designated his
son Archelaus heir to the throne in his will. Joseph wished to avoid running into a
son of Herod, so he changed his itinerary accordingly.

Joseph was not the only one who had a problem with Archelaus. As it turned out,
Archelaus was a much worse ruler than his father Herod. It was not too long before
some 50 Palestinian Jews sailed clear across the Mediterranean in order to lodge
their complaints against Archelaus directly with the emperor. They were joined by
several thousand of their Jewish kinsmen who resided in the city of Rome. The Jewish embassy finally got a hearing before Augustus, and they proceeded to express in
no uncertain terms their dissatisfaction with Archelaus as a ruler.

Most of them did, at any rate. Among the delegation from Palestine were some
of Archelaus's blood relatives, and they found themselves in a real bind. They
were torn between family loyalty and their disgust with Archelaus as a national
leader. Archelaus's relatives were so vehemently opposed to him as their ruler that
they refused openly to cast their lot *with* him during their audience with Augustus.
But Josephus tells us that Archelaus's kinsmen

considered it reprehensible to cast their vote *against* him with the envoys, for they believed that they would be disgraced in the eyes of Caesar if they were willing to act in this way toward a man who was their own kin. (*Ant.* 17.299, italics added)

This is all quite revealing. Consider the validity of the assumption of Archelaus's family members. Were they correct in their assessment of the emperor's social values? Would Caesar Augustus truly have been angry at Archelaus's relatives if they had cast their vote against their kinsman, given the fact that Archelaus was a totally inept ruler? We follow the story a little further to find out.

Archelaus soon ran to Rome himself in order to answer the embassy's charges in person before Augustus. While he was away from Palestine, a group of Jews took things into their own hands and rebelled against Archelaus. Included among the agitators were some members of Archelaus's own family. The Romans quickly stomped out the insurrection, and Augustus must have been in a particularly good mood because he pardoned every single Jewish rebel (the Romans were seldom so generous)—with the exception, that is, of Archelaus's relatives. Augustus killed off each of Archelaus's family members who had revolted "because they had shown contempt for justice in fighting against their own kin" (*Ant.* 17.298). It appears that the kinsmen of Archelaus who were part of that original delegation to Rome had it right to begin with. Augustus did indeed have a problem with people betraying their blood relatives.

The point of all this is to demonstrate that, according to the family mind-set of the Mediterranean world, it was a disgrace for a person to take sides against a member of his blood family, even if the family member's behavior was totally reprehensible. Disloyalty to one's family is the epitome of impiety in strong-group society. As such, it merits capital punishment. Augustus could indulge a few hundred rebels, but he could not tolerate the betrayal of a kinsman. So he sentenced Archelaus's treacherous relatives to death.

Azize and Mustafa

We return now to the modern world to see collectivist relational priorities working themselves out in a small village on the west coast of Turkey. Strong-group sibling solidarity is colorfully reflected in the lives of a young couple whose marriage and subsequent living arrangements are described by L. Fallers and M. Fallers in a 1976 study of Edremit, a Turkish village.[4]

The couple in view, Azize and Mustafa, interact with each other in typical collectivist fashion. Their relationship through the whole process of betrothal to

---

[4] L. Fallers and M. Fallers, "Sex Roles in Edremit," in *Mediterranean Family Structures*, ed. J. Peristiany (Cambridge: University Press, 1976), 243–60.

marriage, and even afterwards, never assumes a romantic quality. Indeed, wives in Edremit society have no expectations that their husbands will prove to be "a major source of companionship" in this regard.[5] This is hardly attractive from an American standpoint, but it is quite characteristic of a strong-group marriage arrangement.

In contrast to her feelings toward her spouse, the bride Azize's relationship with her brother is highly affective in nature. The authors observe that "frequently brother-sister relationships [have] an almost romantic quality." Even "into later life, the men with whom women feel most comfortable and upon whom they can most depend are their brothers." Brothers remain their sisters' primary source of "companionship, advice, help and defense."[6]

For Azize, marriage to Mustafa necessitates a shift in residence away from her brothers and into the home of her husband's parents in another village (patrilocal residence). After several years of marriage, Azize must still bear the title "bride" in her husband's family, for she has produced no offspring. It is clear that she is not really a full-fledged member of her husband's family although she has been married to Mustafa for four years. Everyday life consistently reflects the priority of sibling relationships over marital ties for both extended families, as the married sisters of Mustafa (Azize's husband) come to the home regularly (almost daily) to visit Mustafa, while Azize returns to her own village to visit her blood family whenever she finds the opportunity.[7]

Sibling Solidarity in Second Temple Jewish Literature

Particularly important for our purposes are the family values held by Jews of the Second Temple period, for we may assume that Jesus and the first Jewish Christians appropriated an understanding of brothers and sisters that reflected the relational priorities of their social world. We gained a window into the world of Jesus' contemporaries in the story of Herod and Mariamme stated above. The Old Testament Pseudepigrapha also contains numerous stories of sibling solidarity and its opposite, sibling treachery and betrayal. The illustrations below represent creative expansions of two familiar Old Testament sibling narratives: the Joseph cycle and the story of Jacob and Esau.

Among Old Testament brothers, the most exemplary representative of sibling solidarity—right in the face of betrayal by his own brothers—is the patriarch Joseph. Joseph's brothers sold him into slavery in Egypt, but then he forgave them and welcomed them back into his arms (Gen 37–50). The Joseph story was partic-

---

[5] Ibid., 253.
[6] Ibid., 254.
[7] Ibid., 249.

ularly appealing to strong-group Jewish readers since it portrayed in a single nar-rative both the best (Joseph) and worst (Joseph's brothers) in sibling relations.

Jews who later wrote colorful expansions of Old Testament stories found the Joseph saga especially amenable to augmentation and adaptation. Among the important Jewish writings coming from the centuries between the Old and New Testaments is a collection of works known as the *Testaments of the Twelve Patri-archs*. In his *Testament* Joseph presented himself as the ideal strong-group brother. He recounted the various times he refrained from retaliation and protected his brothers' honor even in the face of their treachery. Then he concluded:

> So you see, my children, how many things I endured in order not to bring my brothers into disgrace. You, therefore, love one another and in patient endur-ance conceal one another's shortcomings. God is delighted by harmony among brothers and by the intention of a kind heart that takes pleasure in goodness.
> (*T. Jos.* 17:1–3)

"God is delighted by harmony among brothers." Highlight that statement. It epito-mizes ancient Mediterranean family values. As we will see in the next two chap-ters, the statement also epitomizes the relational convictions associated with the idea of Christians being brothers and sisters in the New Testament church.

The rivalry between Jacob and Esau also remained an object of preoccupa-tion for Jewish writers in the Second Temple period. One of the strongest admo-nitions to sibling loyalty found in ancient Jewish literature is contained in Isaac's farewell advice to Jacob and Esau in *Jubilees* (c. 150 BC). The words that the author put in Isaac's mouth first paint a beautiful picture of brother relations at their best:

> Among yourselves, my sons, be loving of your brothers as a man loves himself, with each man seeking for his brother what is good for him . . . and each one will love his brother with compassion and righteousness and no one will desire evil for his brother from now and forever all the days of your lives so that you will prosper in all your deeds and not be destroyed.

But the passage concludes with some rather severe consequences for someone who betrays a brother:

> And if either of you seeks evil against his brother, know that hereafter each one who seeks evil against his brother will fall into his [God's] hands and be uprooted from the land of the living and his seed will be destroyed from under heaven. And on the day of turmoil and execration and indignation and wrath, [then] with devouring burning fire just as he burned Sodom so too he will burn

up his land and his city and everything which will be his . . . and he will not be
written on high in the Book of Life. . . . I am exhorting you, my sons, according
to the judgment which will come upon the man who desires to harm his brother.
(*Jub.* 36:4–11)

As Esau exclaimed to his mother Rebekah a bit earlier in the narrative, "If I do not
love my brother, who shall I love?" (*Jubilees* 35:22). Sibling solidarity was clearly
a highly treasured social value among Jews in ancient Palestine.

Sibling Solidarity in the Bible

The centrality of sibling relations was also assumed by the authors of our
biblical texts. Given the strong sense of closeness and solidarity which obtains
between consanguine family members in descent-group cultures, we should not
be surprised to discover that permanent separation from one's blood relations—
especially siblings—represents a much greater sacrifice for a member of a collectivist society than separation from one's spouse. That is, if my brother is the
closest person in the world to me, then losing him will be my greatest heartache.

Consider the words of Jesus in a discussion with Peter in Mark 10. In this passage separation from one's spouse is apparently regarded as insignificant among
those sacrifices necessary to follow Jesus of Nazareth. It is not even mentioned.
But "brothers or sisters" are right there at the beginning of the list of relations to
be sacrificed:

Peter began to tell Him, "Look, we have left everything and followed You." "I
assure you," Jesus said, "there is no one who has left house, *brothers or sisters,*
mother or father, children, or fields because of Me and the gospel, who will not
receive 100 times more, now at this time—houses, brothers and sisters, mothers and children, and fields, with persecutions—and eternal life in the age to
come." (Mark 10:28–30, italics added)

The same priority is reflected in a different way in a passage from Matthew,
where Jesus reveals the inevitable relational chaos that results from His call to
radical discipleship. Now if, as I have argued, the most important relationship in
Jesus' world is the bond between blood brothers, then it only follows that discord
between siblings constitutes the worst family tragedy imaginable. This is precisely
what we find at the beginning of Jesus' list: "Brother will betray brother to death,
and a father his child. Children will even rise up against their parents and have
them put to death" (Matt 10:21). For Jesus' contemporaries in the ancient world,
the betrayal of a brother—not a spouse—was the greatest of relational disasters.

Of interest here is the fact that the first significant sin recorded after the fall of Adam and Eve is not the break-up of a marriage. Nor is it the murder of a spouse, which is the epitome of evil in American society. The great biblical archetype for all interpersonal sin is the murder of Abel at the hands of his brother Cain. To Cain's query, "Am I my brother's keeper?" the only conceivable answer in descent-group society would be a resounding "Yes!"

There are numerous stories of sibling strife elsewhere in the Old Testament. The Hebrew Scriptures are filled with battles between brothers (and sisters). These stories derive much of their narrative appeal from the theme of sibling rivalry. Jacob steals the birthright and blessing of his twin brother Esau; Joseph is betrayed by his brothers; Aaron, Miriam, and Moses (three siblings) bicker with one another; David and his brothers face off; and chaos erupts among David's children—Ammon, Tamar, and Absalom, and later between Solomon and Adonijah.

The sense of tension and drama surrounding the engrossing theme of sibling betrayal helps to explain why the narratives found in the Hebrew Scriptures merited retelling from generation to generation during Israel's history. Discord between brothers was a most captivating and enduring theme among persons who dearly valued sibling solidarity.

Equally engaging were portrayals of sibling relations that reflected behavior that was expected of brothers in a Mediterranean family. A classic biblical example of loyalty where blood siblings are concerned appears in Genesis 34, where we see that strong-group family solidarity includes the obligation to retaliate when an outsider harms a member of one's family. Dinah, the daughter of Jacob, was raped by a local prince named Shechem. The reaction of Dinah's brothers is predictable:

> Jacob's sons returned from the field when they heard about the incident and were deeply grieved and angry. For Shechem had committed an outrage against Israel by sleeping with Jacob's daughter, and such a thing should not be done. (Gen 34:7)

The story concludes with two of Dinah's brothers, Simeon and Levi, killing all the males belonging to Shechem's city, along with Shechem and his father the ruler. But at first Jacob's sons feigned friendship with the perpetrators. They proposed the following arrangement:

> We will agree with you only on this condition: if all your males are circumcised as we are. Then we will give you our daughters, take your daughters for ourselves, live with you, and become one people. But if you will not listen to us and be circumcised, then we will take our daughter and go. (Gen 34:15–17)

The Shechemites agreed, only to be suddenly attacked and slaughtered by Simeon and Levi while recovering from the painful wounds of circumcision (34:25–29).

The point here is neither to question nor to affirm the morality of the brothers' behavior. It is simply to observe that sibling loyalty—in this case, avenging a wrong done to one's sister—was a paramount family value for persons in the biblical world.

Conclusion

Our survey of sibling solidarity in the biblical world is now complete. Based on what we have learned we can expand our list of key principles:

Principle #1:   *In the New Testament world the group took priority over the individual.*

Principle #2:   *In the New Testament world a person's most important group was his blood family.*

Principle #3:   *In the New Testament world the closest family bond was not the bond of marriage. It was the bond between siblings.*

> *Corollary 1*   *The central value that characterized ancient family relations was the obligation to demonstrate undying loyalty toward one's blood brothers and sisters.*

> *Corollary 2*   *The most treacherous act of human disloyalty was not disloyalty to one's spouse. It was the betrayal of one's brother.*

Our excursion into the realm of cultural anthropology and kinship analysis has not been an end in itself. We have sought to make sense of ancient family systems in order to understand what the early Christians meant when they used family language to encourage healthy relationships in their churches. I trust that you are beginning to see why we cannot simply import our American idea of what it means to be a brother or sister into our interpretation of the New Testament. "Brother" meant immeasurably more to the strong-group authors of the Bible than the word means to you and me—it was their most important family relationship.

At this point you are now prepared, perhaps for the first time ever, to properly appreciate what the early Christians meant when they referred to one another as brothers and sisters in Christ. The most obvious implication of what we have learned is that there would have been no place in the early Christian church for an

American individualist. You and I would have experienced great difficulty fitting in with the first-century church at Ephesus, and the Ephesian Christians would have had a bit of a problem with us as well.

To see just how radically true this is, let's engage in a little culture shock. For the early Christians the church was a family, and since family was the primary group for people in Mediterranean antiquity, the church represented the primary focus of group loyalty and solidarity for a Christian in the first century (see under principle #3 on the list above). This means that we can fairly substitute "church" for the word "group" in a portion of the excerpt from Malina, which I cited in chapter 1. So this is how a New Testament believer would have conceived of his relationship to his church family:

> What this means is, first of all, that the person perceives himself or herself to be a member of a church and responsible to the church for his or her actions, destiny, career, development, and life in general. . . . The individual person is embedded in the church and is free to do what he or she feels right and necessary only if in accord with church norms and only if the action is in the church's best interest. The church has priority over the individual member.[8]

How many of us would sign a covenant of church membership that looked like that? The individual is "responsible to the church for his or her actions, destiny, career, development, and life in general"? The individual person "is free to do what he or she feels right and necessary only if in accord with church norms and only if the action is in the church's best interest"? Really? Do you want me to sign my life away?

Yes, Jesus wants us to sign our lives away—with a qualification or two. First of all, we will probably have to unload the preconceived semantic baggage we attach to the word "church." For the early Christians, the church was not an institutional organization with a mortgage payment. The church was a living organism with a mission. The early church did not even own buildings. They met in homes. Like family. So we will have to begin to think of church in much more organic and relational terms than we are used to doing if we desire to embrace the model outlined in the Malina quote above.

A second qualification relates to the potential cult-like abuses that could arise from a strong-group social model. A church family like the one described above would have to be a healthy group in which authority is ideally (1) shared by several trustworthy leaders who (2) use their power in the community to serve—not control—others. We will see in a later chapter that this is precisely what God intends with respect to the number of leaders and the nature of leadership in His

---

[8] B. Malina, *Christian Origins and Cultural Anthropology* (Atlanta: John Knox, 1986), 19.

family. Finally, commitment to God's group would still have to be made at the individual level. Neither conversion nor commitment can be forced upon the individual by the community.

Given these qualifications, what you see in the Malina citation above pretty much reflects church as it was practiced during the New Testament era at Ephesus and everywhere else Christians gathered in the Mediterranean world. As the early Christians saw it, the individual was indeed "responsible to the church for his or her actions, destiny, career, development, and life in general." And this is what gave early Christianity much of its social power.

I suspect that the intense aversion we feel toward the above description of a strong-group church is a rather telling indicator of just how far our values have strayed from this New Testament ideal. Our reaction demonstrates that there is much work to be done in our American churches if we are someday to recapture Jesus' vision for authentic Christian community. But embracing a genuinely biblical ecclesiology is a challenge that is well worth the effort. The relational and spiritual health of the people in our churches depends on it.

Roberta's story in the introduction is worth considering here. If Roberta had demonstrated the kind of loyalty to God's family that we have seen illustrated in ancient family systems, she would not have abandoned her brothers and sisters to chart her own course as an isolated individual. Roberta would have instead agreed to the conditions for financial assistance laid out by her church leaders, and she would have grown through her grief process in the context of a caring and supportive Christian community. In the end both Roberta and her church family would have been the better for it.

The conceptual and behavioral journey from our individualistic American distortion of Christianity back to the strong-group world of the early Christian church will be a long one. Fortunately, history has left us with an inspiring and informative account of the glorious things that can happen when God's people intentionally embrace His radical alternative for relationships in the church. In the next chapters we will examine the birth and the expansion of the strong-group church during those incredible first three hundred years or so of Christian history—those years when the church was a family.

Chapter Three

JESUS' NEW GROUP

"Who are My mother and My brothers?" And looking about at those who
were sitting in a circle around Him, He said, "Here are My mother and My
brothers! Whoever does the will of God is My brother and sister and mother."
(Mark 3:33–35)

I get involved as a pastor with people who have lost loved ones both young
and old. I help families plan funerals for dearly loved senior saints who
walked faithfully with the Lord for decades. Those are the easy ones. I
have also wept and prayed with the surviving relatives of unbelievers murdered
by enemy gang members and homosexuals ravaged by AIDS. Perhaps most tragic
was the pilgrimage of a young newlywed whose husband died of rapidly spread-
ing cancer.

Moments like these represent the cutting edge of Christian ministry. Surviving family members confront a torrent of deep and conflicting emotions, as they
experience both a sense of personal loss and a sense of their own mortality in the
face of death. To a pastor this presents great opportunities for ministry. It also
demands a degree of sensitivity that is much more exacting than that required of
me in the context of daily church ministry. I must carefully consider the impact
of my words.

Here is something I absolutely would never say to a person who had just lost
his beloved father (an unbeliever), and who came to me seeking support and counsel in order to plan a funeral service: "Forget planning the funeral. Let's just take
off together on a short-term missionary trip. Let the other relatives take care of the

arrangements. Let the dead bury their own dead." I would say nothing of the sort to a grieving son in the situation described above. Neither would you.

But Jesus did. Those of you who are familiar with Matthew's Gospel will recognize the above as a reasonably accurate paraphrase of what Jesus said to a would-be follower who was apparently on his way to bury his father: "'Lord,' another of His disciples said, 'first let me go bury my father.' But Jesus told him, 'Follow Me, and let the dead bury their own dead'" (Matt 8:21–22).

Jesus' response strikes us as a rather insensitive thing to say to a person who has just lost a loved one. In Jewish culture providing a proper burial for one's father was a most sacred and inviolable family responsibility. This gets to the heart of the issue, for there is much more going on here than insensitivity. Jesus' words are not merely insensitive. They are diametrically opposed to first-century Jewish family values; for that matter they fly in the face of any society's family values. Jesus' statement here is not alone in its subversive, anti-family tone among His sayings in the four Gospels.

A Family-Friendly Jesus?

We in evangelical circles make much of the gospel's ability to build healthy families and to restore broken relationships. We regard the good news of new life in Jesus as a truly family-friendly message. But Jesus often emphasized precisely the opposite, namely, the gospel's potential to irrevocably undermine family unity and to divide family members against one another:

> "Don't assume that I came to bring peace on the earth. I did not come to bring peace, but a sword. For I came to turn a man against his father, a daughter against her mother, a daughter-in-law against her mother-in-law; and a man's enemies will be the members of his household. The person who loves father or mother more than Me is not worthy of Me; the person who loves son or daughter more than Me is not worthy of Me. And whoever doesn't take up his cross and follow Me is not worthy of Me." (Matt 10:34–38)

Luke's version is even more troubling. Notice the change in the language. Instead of defining an unworthy disciple as one who "loves" his family "more than Me," in Luke's parallel a person must "hate" his relatives in order to qualify as a follower of Jesus: "Now great crowds were traveling with Him. So He turned and said to them: 'If anyone comes to Me and does not hate his own father and mother, wife and children, brothers and sisters—yes, and even his own life—he cannot be

My disciple. Whoever does not bear his own cross and come after Me cannot be My disciple'" (Luke 14:25–27).

I purposely included the last verse in each excerpt (Matt 10:38; Luke 14:27) to emphasize that the challenge Jesus puts forth in these texts is not peripheral or optional to the Christian life. It is what true discipleship is all about. This is why Jesus concludes the problematic family sayings with His classic statement about the demands of discipleship: "Whoever does not bear his own cross and come after Me cannot be My disciple." According to these passages following Jesus has the potential to seriously compromise a disciple's family relationships—even to the point of severe strife and discord among family members.

But there is more. Not only did Jesus teach His potential followers to reconsider their loyalty to their families. He modeled such behavior in His own family relations:

> Then His mother and His brothers came, and standing outside, they sent word to Him and called Him. A crowd was sitting around Him and told Him, "Look, Your mother, Your brothers, and Your sisters are outside asking for You." He replied to them, "Who are My mother and My brothers?" And looking about at those who were sitting in a circle around Him, He said, "Here are My mother and My brothers! Whoever does the will of God is My brother and sister and mother." (Mark 3:31–35)

These words, spoken in the hearing of a large crowd, were utterly scandalous in the cultural context in which Jesus lived. In the social world of Jewish Palestine, Jesus, as the oldest surviving male in His family (we may presume that His father Joseph had died), was responsible to defend the honor of, and provide leadership for, His patrilineal kinship group. In a single stroke Jesus dishonored Himself and His family by refusing to exercise that crucial family role. And He did so in a public setting.

Bringing Jesus Home

It is informative to see these problematic family passages collected together in one place. They are rather troubling for American evangelicals. I will discuss several of the challenging texts in more detail below. First, I want to offer some comments about how we approach such teachings and then outline a helpful methodology for reading the Gospels.

The way we handle these disconcerting sayings is quite revealing. In our efforts to understand what Jesus said about family, we generally set aside these passages and begin to develop our theology of family from the more positive teachings. We gravitate toward those portions of the Gospels in which Jesus exhorts His followers to honor their parents or to refrain from divorce. Only after we have persuaded ourselves that Jesus is truly family-friendly do we return to the thorny passages cited above and somehow try to fit them into a pro-family reading of the Gospels.

The results are predictable. We convince ourselves that the difficult passages really do not quite mean what they appear to be saying. Jesus does not want us to compromise our loyalty to our families. Jesus was talking about priority of *convictions* and not about *behavior.* His whole point is simply that we are to love God more than the members of our own families. Or so we contend.

Now I am not about to deny the degree of truth reflected in this pro-family reconstruction of Jesus' teachings on family relationships. We are to love God more than we love our families. But there remains a problem with an exclusively pro-family theology of the Gospels. It cannot account for the plain sense of the passages cited above. More than priority of convictions is at stake in these texts. Behavior is involved also. For a straightforward reading of two of the above passages demonstrates that (a) Jesus publicly distanced Himself from His own family and (b) Jesus commanded a would-be follower to abandon his extended kinship group when he was needed the most—to bury his father. To reinterpret such texts in terms of personal priorities is to take the biting edge off of these radical Gospel teachings. There is a phrase for this kind of biblical interpretation. It is called domesticating the tradition.

Think about the word "domestication." Domestication is what we do to otherwise wild animals so that we can bring them home and keep them as pets. The English word "domesticate" comes from the Latin word for home—*domus.* "Domesticate" means to make an animal safe enough to take home.

This is precisely how we treat the stories about Jesus when we reduce what is clearly behavior in the Gospels to priority of conviction. We domesticate Jesus. We "de-fang" the biting edge of Jesus' more radical pronouncements in order to make Jesus safe to take home—to our American Christian homes, that is.

But we cannot domesticate Jesus and remain true to His call to discipleship. The biblical witness will not allow it. Jesus had a very specific reason for challenging the institution of family as it existed in His day. To understand Jesus' intentions in this regard we must situate His anti-family rhetoric in the sociocultural context in which Jesus ministered. Some preliminary reflections on how we interpret the Gospels are in order at this point.

Traditional Christology and the Jesus of the Gospels

Below is the portion of the Nicene Creed that relates to Christology. The creed represents perhaps the most enduring summary of truth about the person of Jesus Christ that has been produced by the Christian church since the writing of the four Gospels:

> I believe in one Lord Jesus Christ, the only-begotten Son of God, begotten of the Father before all worlds, God of God, Light of Light, very God of very God, begotten, not made, being of one substance with the Father; by whom all things were made; who, for us men and for our salvation, came down from heaven, and was incarnate by the Holy Spirit of the Virgin Mary, and was made man; and was crucified also for us under Pontius Pilate; he suffered and was buried; and the third day he rose again, according to the Scriptures; and ascended into heaven, and sits on the right hand of the Father; and he shall come again, with glory, to judge both the living and the dead; whose kingdom shall have no end. (AD 325; revised AD 381)[1]

A friend of mine who teaches New Testament history has his students read the Nicene Creed aloud in class (a rich experience). He then asks them, "What is missing?" Seldom does a student respond with the correct answer: "Only about 30 years!" The creed mentions the virgin birth, jumps to the death of Jesus, but discusses nothing in between. The same is likely the case with your church's statement of faith. I know it is true of mine. In fact, we (like the Nicene Creed) could probably ignore Jesus' entire earthly ministry between His virgin birth and His death on the cross, and our doctrinal statements would hardly be compromised at all.

Our Nicene approach to Christology has profoundly influenced the way in which American evangelicals read Matthew, Mark, Luke, and John. Like the Nicene Creed, we tend to focus much of our attention on the infancy and passion narratives in the Gospels, which inform us about Jesus' birth and about His death and resurrection.

Now it is certainly the case that the stories about Jesus' trial, death, and resurrection take up a disproportionate amount of space in the Gospels. To a degree the creeds appropriately align themselves with the priorities of the biblical texts.

Nevertheless, most of the chapters in the Gospels remain focused on other events in Jesus' life, and these materials seem somehow less relevant to the theological enterprise. When we do turn to those passages that narrate Jesus' earthly

---

[1] As cited by W. Grudem, *Systematic Theology* (Grand Rapids: Zondervan, 1995), 1,169.

ministry, we often continue to reflect upon Jesus along the lines of Nicene Christology. We comb through the Gospels asking questions like, What is Jesus like? Is He divine? Is He human? Is He only human? Is He God?

Such questions are hardly insignificant. They address issues that rightly occupied the church in late antiquity for several centuries during the period in which orthodox Christology was hammered out. Correct answers to these questions remain essential for us today, as we respond to the theological aberrations such as those held by certain cults that deny the deity of Christ. Indeed, as one of my colleagues so aptly put it, "that Jesus is fully and completely God and man is the basis for all of the Christian life."[2]

Most of the debates about Jesus in the ancient church occurred more than three centuries after Jesus walked the earth. Many of us who specialize in New Testament history are not persuaded that the Christological controversies—as the debates that occurred between circa AD 300 to 600 have come to be known—shed much light on events related to Jesus' earthly ministry, a ministry that took place centuries earlier. This is not to suggest that we cannot make a convincing case for the deity and humanity of Christ from Matthew, Mark, Luke, and John. We can. It is simply to observe that the Jesus of the Gospels often seems to be concerned with something quite different than the material typically found in our creeds and statements of faith.

Again, this is not to minimize the core Christological realities of the deity of Christ and His atoning work on our behalf. We will leave these truths securely in our doctrinal statements, right where they belong. My purpose here is to help us view the earthly ministry of our Lord and Savior from another, complementary perspective. The operative question for the first-century Palestinians who were confronted with the miracles and teachings of Jesus of Nazareth was not *What is Jesus like?* The operative question was *What is **God** like?*

The chart below demonstrates that I am not simply wrangling over words here. There is a profound difference between asking *What is **Jesus** like?* and asking *What is **God** like?* The former question leads us to belief and generates a statement of faith. The latter leads us to behavior and provides direction for life together in the family of God. Both are indispensable. But behavior is what this book is all about.

---

[2] The comment came from E. Thoennes in a discussion with me.

JESUS IS LIKE GOD	GOD IS LIKE JESUS
It is indispensable to Christian ORTHO-DOXY that Jesus is the *Christ*, the *Son of God*	It is indispensable to Christian ORTHOPRAXIS that *Jesus* is the Christ, the Son of God
Question: What is JESUS like?	*Question*: What is GOD Like?
Approach: We search the Scriptures looking for CHARACTER QUALITIES unique to God (traditionally referred to as God's "attributes") which are illustrated in the actions of—or statements about/by—Jesus.	*Approach*: We search the Gospels looking for the way in which Jesus RESPONDED to the INDIVIDUALS and the INSTITUTIONS of His day.
Response: Worship and Adoration	*Response*: Act in our world like Jesus acted in His.

The Importance of Orthodoxy

The left side of the chart represents our traditional approach to the person of Jesus Christ as revealed in the Scriptures. Here we ask the question, *What is Jesus like?* We search the New Testament in order to demonstrate Jesus' divinity. As we turn to the Gospels, we zero in on passages in which Jesus overtly asserts His equality with the Father (John 8:58). Or we make note of texts in which Jesus performs works—for example, forgiving sin (Mark 2:10)—that only God can do. From the data that we accumulate come those portions of our doctrinal statements and creeds that assert the deity of Christ and that discuss the relationship between His divine and human natures. The Nicene Creed (AD 325) above and the later Chalcedonian Creed (AD 451) are representative.

The result of this process is what we call "orthodoxy," and the word itself is revealing. The "doxy" part comes from a Greek word meaning "to think" or "to hold an opinion." "Ortho" means "straight" or "right" (an *ortho*dontist is a "tooth straightener"). The two words together mean "right thinking" or, more specifically in our case, "correct doctrine or belief."

As the left side of the chart indicates, it is indispensable to Christian orthodoxy that Jesus is *the Christ, the Son of God.* Notice the emphasis on the predicate. Moving down to the bottom of the left-hand column, we see that the proper response to Jesus' identity is worship and adoration. Now it is not my intention to tamper with this half of the truth. I simply want us to move beyond it to include the other half of the truth.

Turning to Orthopraxis

The right-hand side of the chart approaches the Jesus question from an entirely different angle. Here we are not asking, *What is Jesus like?* We are asking, *What is God like?* Since Jesus claimed to be speaking and acting on God's behalf, we ought to be able to answer this question by observing Jesus in action. If we want to find out what God is like, we simply observe what Jesus said and did. Pretty straightforward.

Yet this is precisely where Jesus' contemporaries in first-century Palestine had a serious problem with Him. As it happened, the Jewish leaders of Jesus' day thought that they had God all figured out. They did not need anyone to tell them what God was like. They already knew. God, so they assumed, wanted clear-cut social boundaries in place between Jews and Gentiles, between "good" Jews (Pharisees and priestly elites) and "bad" Jews (tax collectors and sinners), between men and women, between rich and poor, between educated and uneducated, and so forth.

Putting—and keeping—people in their places gave the Jewish leadership of Jesus' day the kind of security they needed to make sense of their world by preserving social and ethnic distinctions and to safeguard their positions of power and privilege. Unfortunately, the Pharisees' understanding of God automatically excluded a whole lot of people from blessings—both spiritual and material (first-century Jews did not make much of a distinction here)—that God intended them to have with the coming of their Messiah.

Jesus systematically dismantled these "sacred" boundaries between people by warmly receiving marginalized individuals like tax collectors and prostitutes and aggressively attacking cultural institutions that had isolated the unfortunate from the mainstream of Jewish society—institutions like the Jewish purity system of "clean" versus "unclean." By His miracles Jesus authenticated His claim to be doing all these things on God's behalf.

Jewish leaders found themselves backed up against a wall. By behaving in a totally counter-cultural way and by demonstrating His right to do so with stupendous signs and wonders, Jesus was asserting to His contemporaries, "God is not like you think He is—God is like me!" Jesus answered the question *What is God like?* in a way that thoroughly scandalized the power brokers of His day. To return for a moment to the chart (on the right), the Jewish leaders watched the way in which Jesus responded to the individuals and institutions of His day and came to a distressing realization: *If this is what God is like, we've got it completely wrong!*

Tragically, Pharisees, chief priests, and others simply had too much invested in their own view of reality to respond to the prophetic challenge that God brought to their personal lives and precious cultural institutions through the words and ministry of Jesus of Nazareth. So they had Him crucified. But in the stories that are left behind we have the remarkable privilege of watching the perfect God-Man evaluate and respond to a broken and sin-soaked world.

We should, in fact, wrestle with the central question on the right-hand side of the chart on page 59 ("What is GOD like?") before we even begin to engage the more traditional Christological categories found in the left-hand column. Why? Because apart from God's revelation of Himself in Jesus of Nazareth, we really do not know what God is like to begin with!

To do traditional Christology—asking "What is JESUS like?" (left-hand side of chart)—with an unexamined conception of God is to risk investing our affirmation of the deity of Christ with *our ideas* about God, rather than with the *reality* of God's character as revealed in the priorities and activities of Jesus of Nazareth. And this has proven itself to be a dangerous theological enterprise fraught with potentially devastating consequences for Christians and non-Christians alike.

As history has repeatedly demonstrated, the church can hold unequivocally to orthodox Nicene Christology—Jesus is *God*—and nevertheless assume that this "God" somehow affirms or desires the forced conversion of unbelievers (Charlemagne), the destruction of indigenous peoples in the name of Manifest Destiny (American colonists), human slavery (Euro-American enslavement of Africans), or racial apartheid (South Africa)—just to mention a few of the atrocities perpetrated by persons who claimed to be followers of Jesus.

Contemporary Christians would be utterly arrogant to assume that we are somehow immune to similar theological blind spots. No, it will not do simply to cite proof text after proof text demonstrating that Jesus is God. We need to be clear at the outset about what we mean by "God" before we begin to impose our view of God and His character upon the person of Jesus.

But where do we go to acquire an accurate understanding of "God"? It is really rather simple. We go to Jesus. We start with Jesus (the right-hand side of the chart) to get to "God." For as the apostle John so categorically expressed it, "No one has ever seen God. The One and Only Son—the One who is at the Father's side—He has revealed Him" (John 1:18).

This is why those chapters of the Gospels that narrate the events that transpired between Jesus' virgin birth and His atoning death are so indispensable to the Christian life. Only in the incarnation of the Son of God—specifically Jesus'

three-year earthly ministry—did God break into our reality to offer a searing evaluation of human behaviors and cultural institutions as they existed at a particular
point in history.

This simply cannot be overemphasized. The earthly ministry of Jesus of Nazareth constitutes the one time in the history of humanity when heaven fully and
finally came to earth. In Matthew, Mark, Luke, and John, we have the opportunity to see the question *What is God like?* answered in the flesh-and-blood world
in which we live. During His incarnation Jesus not only procured our way to
heaven. He also showed us how to live on earth. Now we can pattern our lives
after Jesus.

Reuniting Belief and Behavior

Regrettably, American evangelicals have not been particularly strong about
patterning our lives after Jesus. Our theological heritage has encouraged us to
focus almost exclusively on the saving significance of Jesus' death and resurrection, while generally ignoring our Lord's evaluations of the sociocultural institutions of His day.

As we will see below, this is particularly the case where Christian community is concerned. Like the Nicene Creed, we tend to leap from the manger to the
cross without touching the ground of everyday human reality—and interpersonal
relationships—in between. It is time to complement our orthodoxy with a robust
emphasis on orthopraxis. Only then will we be able to recapture Jesus' vision for
authentic Christian community.

Much of this is hardly novel. Members of renewal movements throughout
church history have tended to gravitate to the Gospels in order to find direction for
living the Christian life. The recent movement known as the emerging church is a
case in point. Frustrated with current church values and methodologies, emerging
church leaders are turning from the New Testament Epistles to the Gospels for
guidance.

Barry Taylor (of Sanctuary Church in Santa Monica) said, "I needed to stop
reading Paul for a while and instead focus on Jesus." But for Taylor, not just any
Jesus would do. Taylor and his group specifically "focused on the humanity of
Jesus and lost all the categories from church history."[3]

Now it is not uncharacteristic of renewal movements to overreact and generate
false dichotomies in their well-meaning and enthusiastic efforts toward "course
correction." We cannot join Taylor in summarily dismissing "all the categories

---

[3] Quoted by E. Gibbs and R. Bolger, *Emerging Churches* (Grand Rapids: Baker, 2005), 48.

from church history" where Jesus is concerned. Nor can we "stop reading Paul." We will continue to embrace both the formulations of the historic church councils, and we will feed upon the full counsel of God's Word—including both the Gospel stories about Jesus and the letters of Paul—as we navigate our way through the Christian life.

Our emerging brothers and sisters do have something vital to teach us here, and we must not allow ourselves to be put off by the overstatements and rhetoric that often characterizes the reflections of boundary-breaking pioneers like Barry Taylor. Younger generations of Christians have good reason to be troubled by the manner in which traditional Christology ignores our Lord's earthly ministry and generates a picture of Jesus that does little to foster Christian community or to encourage works of social justice. The time has come for us to pursue a more holistic and biblical Christology, one which reunites belief and behavior in a way that is consistent with the teachings and practice of New Testament Christianity.

To summarize our look at the above chart, we must not only peruse the Gospels looking for attributes of God that we can apply to Jesus (left side of chart). We must also carefully observe the various ways in which Jesus responded to the individuals and cultural institutions of His day (right side of chart) in order to learn how to act in our world like Jesus acted in His. This is what orthopraxis—"right behavior"—is all about. We are now prepared to consider orthopraxis, as Jesus understood it, with respect to two important institutions in the ancient world—the natural family and the surrogate family of God that Jesus was gathering around Him during His earthly ministry.

Jesus and Community: A Return to Kingdom Priorities

To adequately grasp what Jesus had to say to His contemporaries about the people of God and, by extension, what Jesus might have to say to us today, we must first understand the world in which Jesus lived. This is why I maintained above that, for orthopraxis, we must consider Jesus' response to the individuals and institutions of *His* day.

What we will discover is that the anti-family passages cited earlier in the chapter are not primarily intended to force us to get our priorities right by elevating our personal relationship with God above our commitments to natural family relations. The loyalty conflict is not about making a choice between God and people. Rather, it is about choosing between one group of people and another—between our natural family and our eternal family.

Recall from the previous chapter the three central social values of the ancient Mediterranean world:

1. In the New Testament world the group took priority over the individual.
2. In the New Testament world a person's most important group was his family.
3. In the New Testament world the closest family bond was the bond between siblings.

As evidenced in the Gospels, Jesus established His followers as a surrogate family. Given the three cultural values listed above, we may assume that one of Jesus' purposes in appropriating the family model was to insure that His followers would exercise primary loyalty to one another as brothers and sisters in the faith. After all, this is precisely how a person in the world of first-century Palestine would relate to a group that he or she viewed as a family.

For Jesus to organize His followers as a strong-group family presented a potentially intractable dilemma. The early Christians suddenly found themselves with not one but two families demanding primary loyalty and commitment: their natural families and their new surrogate family of brothers and sisters in Christ. It is this potential conflict of group loyalties—not simply the issue of deciding between love for God and love for family—that Jesus addresses in the difficult passages cited above.

Jesus radically challenged His disciples to disavow primary loyalty to their natural families in order to join the new surrogate family of siblings He was establishing—the family of God. Relationships among God's children were to take priority over blood family ties. This is the most reasonable way to read the anti-family traditions in the Gospel narratives and still preserve their prophetic thrust.

Jesus' Group: A Society of Surrogate Siblings

Mark 3:31–35 pointedly reveals Jesus' intention for His nascent community of followers to function as a surrogate family:

> Then His mother and His brothers came, and standing outside, they sent [word] to Him and called Him. A crowd was sitting around Him and told Him, "Look, Your mother, Your brothers, and Your sisters are outside asking for You." He replied to them, "Who are My mother and My brothers?" And looking about at those who were sitting in a circle around Him, He said, "Here are My mother and My brothers! Whoever does the will of God is My brother and sister and mother."

The manner in which Jesus publicly distances Himself here from His natural family relations—"Who are My mother and My brothers?"—would have struck those who witnessed this encounter as utterly subversive and counter-cultural. Two central truths in the passage should not be missed: (1) Jesus models the new community He is establishing after the most important group found in the ancient Mediterranean world, the family; and (2) Jesus' faith-family—"Whoever does the will of God"—replaces His natural family at the center stage of Jesus' relational priorities.

Another passage provides additional details about the ways Jesus expected the members of His new group to function in their mutual relations. As we pick up the story in Mark 10:21, Jesus has just carried on an insightful dialogue with a rich young man. The narrative concludes with Jesus challenging the man to sell all of his belongings, give the proceeds to the poor, and become a disciple. The rich fellow cannot bring himself to make such a commitment and soon departs (v. 22).

Jesus then used the encounter as an opportunity to teach His disciples about wealth as an obstacle to entering the kingdom (vv. 23–27). As the discussion draws to a conclusion, Peter contrasted the disciples' behavior with that of the rich young ruler:

> Peter began to tell Him, "Look, we have left everything and followed You." "I assure you," Jesus said, "there is no one who has left house, brothers or sisters, mother or father, children, or fields because of Me and the gospel, who will not receive 100 times more, now at this time—houses, brothers and sisters, mothers and children, and fields, with persecutions—and eternal life in the age to come." (Mark 10:28–30)

Jesus assumed that His followers would relate to one another according to the standards of solidarity shared by families in the Mediterranean world. Jesus promised Peter, who claimed to have compromised his own family loyalty to follow Jesus, that Peter would enjoy family-like relationships with others who have made such a sacrifice ("brothers and sisters, mothers and children"), and that he would also find life's necessary physical resources—such as shelter ("houses") and food ("fields")—in the context of the new community.

The payoff for following Jesus therefore is not only "eternal life in the age to come." It also includes, "now at this time . . . houses, brothers and sisters, mothers and children, and fields." The terms "houses" and "fields" imply that those who become part of Jesus' community will have access to the material goods of the family—just like siblings in a Mediterranean kinship group. The operative mentality among Jesus' followers with respect to their possessions is supposed to be, "What is mine is ours; what is mine is the family's."

The word "fields" in Mark 10:30 is significant. It is hardly a coincidence that just a couple of years later we find Barnabas selling "a field he owned" in order to meet the material needs of the impoverished Jerusalem Christian family (Acts 4:36–37). The passage from Acts suggests that Jesus' earliest followers interpreted His sayings just as I am suggesting. The sharing of material resources was to be a central part of Jesus' new surrogate family.

Hints of such behavior can be found elsewhere in the Gospels. Jesus and His immediate followers traveled together and apparently operated out of a common purse. Luke 8:1–3 suggests this:

> Soon afterwards He was traveling from one town and village to another, preaching and telling the good news of the kingdom of God. The Twelve were with Him, and also some women who had been healed of evil spirits and sicknesses: Mary, called Magdalene (seven demons had come out of her); Joanna the wife of Chuza, Herod's steward; Susanna; and many others who were supporting them from their possessions.

So is John 13:29:

> Since Judas kept the money-bag, some thought Jesus was telling him, "Buy what we need for the festival," or that he should give something to the poor.

Adding the information provided by these texts to that gleaned above, we see that Jesus' concept of the family of God was tangibly realized through the sharing of material resources, as Jesus and certain of His followers traveled together. Here is a group of people, unrelated by blood, who nevertheless spent a significant period of their lives together and who related to each other according to the standards of ancient kinship solidarity. They understood themselves to be a surrogate family.

Elsewhere in the Gospels we encounter other family-like behaviors that are to characterize the community of Jesus' followers. On more than one occasion, Jesus intentionally employed sibling terminology in order to encourage His disciples to treat each other like members of a Mediterranean kinship group. Matthew 18:15–35 is a case in point. Turn to the passage in your Bible, and you will notice that the text is framed with sibling terminology. The word "brother" occurs in the first and last verses of the passage.

In view in Matthew 18 are two related behaviors that (along with the sharing of material resources, as above) would have characterized a properly functioning family in Jesus' day. First, Jesus directed His followers to challenge one another to take responsibility for actions that were inappropriate among people who viewed themselves as family: "If your brother sins against you, go and rebuke him in private. If he listens to you, you have won your brother" (18:15). But Jesus went on to teach that siblings are to remain ever willing to restore a repentant brother to normal family relations:

> Then Peter came to Him and said, "Lord, how many times could my brother
> sin against me and I forgive him? As many as seven times?" "I tell you, not as
> many as seven," Jesus said to him, "but 70 times seven." (18:21–22)

In vv. 23–35 Jesus illustrated His point with the familiar parable of the unmerciful servant who refuses to forgive his fellow-servant despite the fact that his own master has forgiven him an immeasurably larger debt. The master hands the unmerciful servant over to the jailers to be tortured "until he could pay everything that was owed" (v. 34). Jesus concluded (notice the family language), "So My heavenly Father will also do to you if each of you does not forgive his brother from his heart" (v. 35).

The Vexing Problem of Family Loyalty: Some Challenging Gospel Texts

Unwavering family loyalty is a fundamental value of descent-group family systems. As we saw in chapter 2, loyalty to one's siblings was at the center of ancient Mediterranean family sensibilities. Blood ran thicker than marriage as a bond of relational solidarity in Jesus' social world.

We can now begin to see the potential conflict that Jesus' family model posed for His community of followers. Family loyalty was an exclusive commitment. A person simply could not maintain descent-group type loyalty to more than one family. The decision to join God's family invariably meant compromising to some degree the ties of loyalty that connected Jesus' followers to their natural families.

Several passages help us better to appreciate the radical nature of Jesus' call to join the family of God. Mark 1:14–20 reinforces the anti-family orientation of Jesus' challenge to become a disciple:

> After John was arrested, Jesus went to Galilee, preaching the good news of
> God: "The time is fulfilled, and the kingdom of God has come near. Repent
> and believe in the good news!" As He was passing along by the Sea of Gali-
> lee, He saw Simon and Andrew, Simon's brother. They were casting a net into

the sea, since they were fishermen. "Follow Me," Jesus told them, "and I will make you fish for people!" Immediately they left their nets and followed Him. Going on a little farther, He saw James the son of Zebedee and his brother John. They were in their boat mending their nets. Immediately He called them, and they left their father Zebedee in the boat with the hired men and followed Him.

Our familiarity with the story of the call of James and John (vv. 19–20) makes it difficult for us to appreciate the fundamentally counter-cultural nature of the brothers' response to Jesus' request. To abandon one's father ranks right up there with treachery against a sibling (such as Cain's murder of Abel) as the ultimate in betrayal for a descent-group society.

As we learned in the previous chapter, sons (not daughters) carried on the family bloodline. Accordingly, a man's sons would be responsible for ensuring that the honor of the kinship group remained intact during the next generation, when they would inherit from their father the responsibility for providing guidance and oversight for the patrilineal family.

Therefore, while the father remained alive his adult sons stood before him as his tangible, flesh-and-blood hope for the survival and future integrity of his extended family unit. James and John were hardly unaware of this nonnegotiable social reality, so it is all the more remarkable that the two brothers "left their father Zebedee in the boat" to follow an itinerant Jewish holy man.

John Mark, the author of the Gospel, was also quite attuned to the radical nature of the brother's behavior, and it is important in this regard to observe where Mark placed the story in the narrative flow of his Gospel. I have included in the above quotation the two verses preceding Jesus' encounter with the disciples (vv. 14–15). Notice that the story of the call of the four fisherman stands near the beginning of Mark's work, immediately following Jesus' foundational call to repentance and faith in v. 15.

It is no accident that Mark, writing under the inspiration of God the Holy Spirit, placed the material in vv. 14–15 before the story of the call of the fishermen. The two passages are to be read together. The behavior of Simon, Andrew, James, and John is intended to illustrate the proper response to Jesus' message in vv. 14–15. Apparently, leaving one's father and following Jesus constitutes for Mark a paradigmatic example of what it means to "Repent and believe in the good news!" Again, exchanging one family for another is at the very heart of what it means to be a disciple of Jesus.

Luke 14:26 is a particularly hard saying of Jesus: "If anyone comes to Me and does not hate his own father and mother, wife and children, brothers and sisters—yes, and even his own life—he cannot be My disciple." The understandable tendency to want to domesticate Jesus at this point has led some to try to conform the language in Luke to the parallel in Matthew, where the idea is that of loving less instead of Luke's stronger expression "hate." So "hate" simply means "love less."[4]

Recent scholarship, more sensitive both to the first-century background and to our own theological and cultural prejudices, rejects such an interpretation of Jesus' hatred terminology. In fact, the Greek word translated "hate" probably means neither "hate" nor "love less than." I. H. Marshall draws for background upon a Hebrew root that has the sense "to leave aside, abandon."[5] A. Jacobson agrees: "'Hate' here probably does not mean 'dislike intensely' but 'sever one's relationship with' the family."[6]

This makes good sense when we consider the text in light of the other passages cited above. If we interpret Luke 14:26 along the lines suggested by Marshall and Jacobson, the passage finds itself in total agreement with Mark 3:31–35, where Jesus renounces His own family ties, and with Mark 1:16–20, where Jesus challenges the four fishermen to do the same.

But I would want to qualify the above discussion by softening Jacobson's translation somewhat. Joining Jesus' new family did not in every case mean that a disciple had to categorically "sever" his relationship with his family. It is clear that Peter maintained at least some kind of loose connection with his natural family, even after his call to discipleship, since we find Jesus at Peter's house in Matthew 8:14. But we must not overemphasize Peter's ongoing commitment to his family of origin after he became a disciple of Jesus. In the final analysis, the issue here relates to the relative degree of loyalty a follower of Jesus assigns to his new faith-family versus his commitment to his family of origin. Peter's family priorities in this area are quite transparent. Yes, Peter retained some sort of ties to his natural family, but in the passage from Mark 10 discussed earlier Peter claimed to have "left everything" to follow Jesus (v. 28).

In Jesus' response to Peter's claim, He did not contradict or challenge Peter's assertion. On the contrary, Jesus affirmed the truth of what Peter had said, and He proceeded to promise Peter that the family relations he had sacrificed for the

---

[4] W. Hendriksen, *The Gospel of Luke* (Grand Rapids: Baker, 1978), 734–35.

[5] I. H. Marshall, *Commentary on Luke*, in *New International Greek Testament Commentary*, eds. I. H. Marshall and W. W. Gasque (Grand Rapids: Eerdmans, 1978), 592.

[6] A. Jacobson, "Divided Families and Christian Origins," in *The Gospel Behind the Gospels: Current Studies on 'Q'*, ed. R. Piper (Leiden: E. J. Brill, 1995), 362, 364.

kingdom would be restored to him in the church family (Mark 10:30). Whatever
the nature of his ongoing relations with the members of his family of origin
were, Peter's primary family, loyalty-wise, would now be the surrogate family
of God.

The loyalty issue surfaces in an even more radical way in the passage where
Jesus refused to permit a would-be follower to provide for the burial of his father.
Jesus said, "Follow Me, and let the dead bury their own dead" (8:22). Those wish-
ing to blunt the prophetic edge of this pointed saying typically choose one of
several avenues of interpretation.

Some suggest that the inquirer is requesting the delay in order to wait for
an aged parent to die, rather than to bury a father who is in fact already dead.
The father is still alive, and the would-be disciple wants to wait until he is out
from under his father's authority—which would have been the case after his father
died—in order to follow Jesus.[7] Let us assume for the sake of argument that this
interpretation is correct. Let us suppose the father is still alive. This would blunt
the edge of Jesus' exhortation only slightly. For in the strongly patriarchal world
of first-century Palestine, the oldest living male wielded absolute authority over
the members of his extended family. In such a setting, to challenge a person to
exchange his father's authority for that of an itinerant peasant teacher would have
been nearly as scandalous as discouraging a son from attending to his deceased
father's burial arrangements.

A second option takes the passage at face value—the father has just died—but
maintains that the challenge was unique to the individual Jesus addressed. Hendriksen observed,

> As given, [Jesus' challenge] suited this particular person, as, for example, Matt.
> 19:21 answered the needs of "the rich young ruler." Occasions and personalities
> differ, and to conclude from the answer Jesus gave that believers must never
> help to provide for, or attend, funerals of unbelievers, including those of mem-
> bers of their own family, would be completely unwarranted.[8]

Hendriksen is, of course, on target to caution us against misapplying the passage
in the ways he describes, but his individualistic reading of the text fails to come
to terms with the central issue of the passage, namely, the challenge to family
loyalty. Yes, Jesus addressed a specific individual. But the charge to "let the dead
bury their own dead" tells us a lot about Jesus' broader social agenda.

---

[7] Cited by D. A. Carson in *Matthew, Mark, Luke*, vol. 8 of *The Expositor's Bible Commentary,* vol.
8, ed. F. Gaebelein (Grand Rapids: Zondervan, 1984), 209.

[8] W. Hendriksen, *The Gospel of Matthew* (Grand Rapids: Baker, 1973), 409.

More recently, N. T. Wright, in a ground-breaking study of the life of Jesus, asserted that "the only explanation for Jesus' astonishing command is that he envisaged loyalty to himself and his kingdom-movement *as creating an alternative family.*"[9] Wright's interpretation of Matt 8:22 commends itself as the correct one in light of the strong-group cultural orientation of first-century Palestine. It accords perfectly with what we have learned about Jesus' surrogate family program in the Gospel passages discussed above. In a social setting where each and every person found his identity in the group to which he belonged, a call to leave one's primary group—the family—in order to follow an individual would make sense *only if following that individual meant joining his group.*

This is a key point. In the markedly collectivist social setting of rural Galilee, people would not simply have related to a prophet-teacher like Jesus as isolated individuals. Jesus would have been much more than their "personal Savior." They would have joined His group. As the other passages cited above clearly demonstrate, Jesus' group was the new family He was founding, the surrogate family of God.

Wright is therefore quite correct to assume that Jesus' challenge to the man to renounce loyalty to his blood family ("let the dead bury their own dead") implicitly includes the corresponding challenge to become a member of Jesus' new group of followers. As each of the anti-family passages demonstrates—and as the early Christians clearly understood—Jesus did not simply intend for His followers to substitute a personal commitment to Him for ties of blood family loyalty. He intended for them to exchange their loyalty to one family for unswerving loyalty to another—the family of God.

Jesus and Family: Putting It All Together

The diagram on the following page illustrates the various types of family teachings we find in the Gospels. We can sort Jesus' sayings about family into three distinct categories. Most familiar, perhaps, are the Pro-family Teachings (lower left). I have in mind here Jesus' instructions about marriage, divorce, honoring one's parents, and so forth. More troubling are what I have labeled the Anti-family Teachings (lower right), containing admonitions such as "hate" your mother and father, and "let the dead bury their own dead." Finally, we have Jesus' sayings and activities related to His surrogate family of followers, which I refer to in the diagram as His Faith-Family Teachings (top of triangle).

---

[9] N. T. Wright, *Jesus and the Victory of God* (Minneapolis: Fortress, 1996), 401 (italics added).

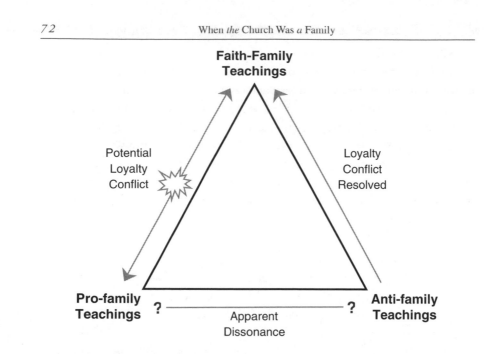

Let us now consider these three kinds of teachings about family as they relate to one another. We begin at the base of the triangle, where the presence in the canonical Gospels of both Pro-family and Anti-family Teachings generates an immediate dissonance in the reader's mind. For example, Jesus strongly affirmed the commandment to honor father and mother. Yet He challenged a potential follower who wished to do precisely that to "let the dead bury their own dead." How do we harmonize these apparently contradictory sayings?

The answer lies in the Faith-Family Teachings, which I have placed at the top of the triangle. Jesus' establishment of His followers as a surrogate family created a potential conflict of loyalties between a disciple's natural family and his new surrogate family of faith (left side of the triangle). A person simply could not express equal allegiance to two families in the social world of Jesus and the early Christians. Those who joined the family of God that Jesus was gathering around Him had to wrestle with their ongoing commitment to their natural families. To which family should they assign priority? The Anti-Family Teachings serve to resolve this conflict in favor of the Faith Family (note the direction of the arrow on the right side of the triangle). When a conflict of loyalty occurred, a follower of Jesus aligned himself with his church family as his primary locus of relational solidarity.

Returning to the Pro-Family Teachings, we can unreservedly acknowledge that, whenever possible, Jesus encouraged ongoing loyalty to natural family relations on the part of His followers. Surrogate family loyalty and natural family loyalty were not necessarily mutually exclusive expressions of relational solidarity for those who belonged to the Jesus movement.

An ideal and not uncommon situation, we might surmise, would see the conversion of a whole household, with the disciple's natural family embedded in, and serving the mission of, the dominant surrogate family of faith. In this case there would be no conflict of loyalties. But even here the natural family existed to serve the designs of the family of God, and not vice-versa. The focus was on the church—not on the family. And where conflict between the natural family and God's family did arise, the faith family was to become the primary locus of relational solidarity.

A New Set of Priorities

It is particularly important at this juncture to grasp the connection in early Christianity between loyalty to God and loyalty to God's group. I use the word "connection" intentionally here, since it has been typical in individualistic American evangelicalism to set up an unfortunate antithesis between commitment to God and commitment to the people of God. We are somehow convinced that we can separate the two. The result is a set of priorities, parroted in church after church in America, which runs as follows:

(1st) God — (2nd) Family — (3rd) Church — (4th) Others

This list of priorities misses the whole point of the above discussion. The strong-group outlook of the New Testament church meant that the early Christians did not sharply distinguish between commitment to God and commitment to God's family. Cyprian of Carthage (c. AD 250) put it like this: "He who does not have the church for his mother cannot have God for his Father." I would express it somewhat differently: "He who does not have God's children as his brothers and sisters does not have God for his Father."

Now most evangelicals would be quick to agree with the above statement theologically, that is, with respect to our position in Christ. Upon conversion we gain both a new Father and a new set of brothers and sisters. Nothing here strikes us as particularly unorthodox. The early Christians, however, would have understood the above assertion to be true not only *positionally* but also *relationally,* that is, as a reasonable description of everyday life in the local church.

This reality cannot be overemphasized. Jesus and His followers did not define loyalty to God solely in terms of a low-group, individualistic "personal relationship" with Jesus. Nor, by the way, did they define it as loyalty to the church as an institutional organization (more on this later). For the early Christians, loyalty to God found its tangible daily expression in unswerving loyalty to God's group, the family of surrogate siblings who called Him "Father."

This is the lens through which we need to read Jesus' variegated teachings about family in the Gospels. People in Mediterranean antiquity had to leave one family in order to join another. If we are truly serious about returning to our biblical roots, where our relationships with our fellow human beings are concerned, our priority list should probably look something like this:

(1st) God's Family — (2nd) My Family — (3rd) Others

This represents a radical reinterpretation of what it means to follow Jesus, and it will need to be carefully nuanced in the chapters to come. But these priorities fairly reflect the way in which the early Christians viewed life together in their local church communities. Later, we will learn more about what this startling shift in values might mean for us in the contemporary church. For now let's summarize what we have learned.

Conclusion

Chapter 1 outlined the collectivist worldview of the Mediterranean world in which Jesus and the early Christians lived. In a strong-group culture, the individual is embedded in, and draws his personal identity from, the group to which he belongs. And the well-being of the group—not the individual—comes first when a member of the group is faced with life-changing personal decisions.

In chapter 2 we studied the most important group in Mediterranean antiquity, the family. We examined the ways in which the collectivist approach to life worked itself out among siblings in the patrilineal kinship groups of Jesus' day. The priority of sibling relations and unswerving family loyalty surfaced as two fundamental characteristics of ancient family systems.

In the present chapter we observed Jesus interacting with the strong-group social world of ancient Palestine, and we watched Him recruit a group of followers. As Jesus evaluated the cultural institutions of His day, He strongly affirmed the "group comes first" orientation of the society in which He lived. And He did so intentionally.

Jesus certainly did not hesitate prophetically to censure those cultural values and behaviors with which He disagreed. He opposed the highly stratified social pecking order of His day. He critiqued the Jewish purity system. He also confronted abuses at the Jerusalem temple. Jesus was hardly slow to denounce cultural practices and institutions that compromised what God wanted to do among His people.

But Jesus did not resist the collectivist outlook on human relationships that characterized life in Mediterranean antiquity. He unequivocally affirmed it, for He established His group as a family. Family served as the primary locus of relational loyalty for persons in the strong-group social matrix of the New Testament world. Those who followed Jesus were to exercise primary allegiance to a new family— just as Jesus Himself had done: "Whoever does the will of God is My brother and sister and mother" (Mark 3:35).

What we have here is transparently clear in light of ancient Mediterranean cultural sensibilities. Jesus wanted His followers to interact with one another like members of a strong-group, surrogate family characterized by collectivist solidarity and commitment on every front. Such was Jesus' vision for authentic Christian community.

You may be tempted at this juncture to jump ahead and envision the kind of cultural critique Jesus might bring to modern America, especially to His people, the Christian church. Contemporary application must wait until later in the discussion. For the present, we will stay among the early Christians to discover what they did with Jesus' model of the church as a strong-group society of siblings.

We discover in the next two chapters that Jesus' followers really "got it." They put collectivist Christian commitment into practice, and their world was never the same. Because the early Christians lived out church as God intended it, the whole Roman Empire ultimately bowed its knees to the King of kings and Lord of lords. Millions were genuinely converted and, for better or for worse, Christianity became the state religion of the empire.

Quite the opposite is happening today in the West. People in America seem to be running from—not toward—the truth of the Gospel. This alone makes it imperative for us to become acquainted with the way in which Jesus' vision for the church as a family found expression in the Christian churches of the early Roman Empire. In chapter 4 we begin our survey with the churches of Paul.

Chapter Four

THE CHURCHES OF PAUL

Instead, brother goes to law against brother, and that before unbelievers!
(1 Cor 6:6)

My formal introduction to the grim reality of individualistic American Christianity occurred during my first months of ministry. I directed a group of about 60 or so high school students. One Wednesday evening before Bible study, two of our teenagers were chasing each other across the church parking lot. Suddenly the girl being chased, a rather rotund young lady named Roxanne (not her real name), ran smack into the side of a small pickup truck that just happened to be the pride and joy of one of our high school students. Fortunately for Roxanne, the truck was not moving. Unfortunately for the truck, Roxanne prevailed in the encounter. She escaped without a scratch. But an ugly dent conspicuously decorated the shiny truck's right front fender.

Ralph (not his real name), the vehicle's owner, was elsewhere on the church campus at the time. When he discovered the damage that had been done to his precious truck, he was rather upset. Ralph had worked long hours at his minimum-wage job in order to purchase the truck. But he was a godly young man, and he wanted to handle the situation in an honorable way. I encouraged Ralph to go to Roxanne's father and tell him what had happened. I naively assumed that the father—a respected church deacon and community leader—would do the right thing and fix the kid's truck.

I had much to learn. So did Ralph. Roxanne's father not only refused to take any responsibility for the damage; he also challenged Ralph to take him to court.

76

This eminent church deacon assured Ralph that he would stand no chance against the older man's lawyers. Ralph was left with a dented fender. Ralph and his high school director were both left with our idealistic picture of God's church—especially church leadership—busted all to pieces.

Attitudes similar to that of Roxanne's father prevailed in the first-century church at Corinth, where litigation among Christians was not uncommon. Paul had spent about 18 months in Corinth planting and growing a brand new church (Acts 18). The Corinthians, however, were slow to buy into the reality that they were now members of the same family. They wanted the experiential benefits of Christian worship, but they were unwilling to put God's group first in their lives. So they apparently spent as much time in court suing one another as they did in church serving one another.

In his first surviving letter to the church, Paul sharply rebuked the Corinthians. He based his challenge of their litigious behavior on the fact that the Corinthians are siblings in the faith. Brothers, Paul admonished his readers, do not sue one another. Brothers would rather be wronged (1 Cor 6:1–8). We will return below to the church in Corinth, but first we need to back up and capture the big picture of life in God's church as Paul envisioned it.

Constant relational struggles among Paul's converts gave the apostle ample opportunity to teach his readers how to live together in community as God's chosen people. Paul often addressed the pressing interpersonal problems confronting his congregations by drawing on the image of the church as a family. He desired his brothers and sisters in Christ to treat one another like good Mediterranean siblings. Like Jesus, Paul viewed the church as a surrogate family.

Terminology

A computer search for family terminology yields the following data for the thirteen letters of Paul in the New Testament:

Greek Root	English Equivalent	Occurrences
adelph-	"brother(s)"/"sister(s)"	139
pater-	"F/father"	63
kleronom-	"inherit"/"inheritance"/"heir"	19
huio-	"sons"*	17
tekn-	"child"	39

*I searched only for plural forms of the Greek root *huios* in order to avoid including usages referring to Jesus as the "Son of God."

The frequency with which Paul used these terms is all the more striking when one considers that the great majority of these occurrences (particularly where "brother" is concerned) reflect the surrogate (church) family model. Paul seldom had occasion to utilize kinship terminology to refer to the natural family, that is, to people who are related by blood.

In 1 Corinthians 1–3 Paul repeatedly drew on the surrogate family model as he addressed his readers (italics added):

> For it has been reported to me about you, my *brothers*, by members of Chloe's household, that there are quarrels among you (1:11).

> *Brothers*, consider your calling: not many are wise from a human perspective, not many powerful, not many of noble birth (1:26).

> When I came to you, *brothers*, announcing the testimony of God to you, I did not come with brilliance of speech or wisdom (2:1).

> *Brothers*, I was not able to speak to you as spiritual people but as people of the flesh, as babies in Christ (3:1).[1]

Paul's other letters reveal much of the same, and the word "brother" is a familiar expression to many of us who have spent time in the New Testament epistles.

Unfortunately, most Western readers treat "brothers" in Paul's letters much as we would a punctuation mark, or perhaps as some sort of aside with little theological import. Such an approach is clearly untenable in view of what we have learned about the importance of sibling relations in the New Testament world. We would do well to assign to Paul's sibling terminology its full semantic weight. For more than terminology is at stake in Paul's employment of family language. Paul views the church family metaphor as an invaluable constellation of symbols for illustrating in a most practical way what it means to live in community together.

Rather than examine Paul's writings book by book, I will treat the material topically to maintain a broader perspective. We examine below Paul's utilization of family imagery under four headings:

1. *Affective Solidarity:* the emotional bond that Paul experienced among brothers and sisters in God's family
2. *Family Unity:* the interpersonal harmony and absence of discord that Paul expected among brothers and sisters in God's family

---

[1] Throughout the New Testament, the Greek word translated "brothers" (*adelphoi*) is generic in its connotations—it means "brothers and sisters"—when used of surrogate siblings in the family of God.

3. *Material Solidarity:* the sharing of resources that Paul assumed would characterize relationships among brothers and sisters in God's family

4. *Family Loyalty:* the undivided commitment to God's group that was to mark the value system of brothers and sisters in God's family

Paul's writings contain numerous references to these four family values. But to apply some methodological constraints to the discussion, I have cited only those passages that contain one or more of these four characteristics along with specific family terms in the same context. This indicates that Paul assumed a church family background for the behavior that he discussed in these texts.

Affective Solidarity

John and Judy (not their real names) are one of my favorite couples at church. John likes to kiss. I assume that John likes to kiss his wife Judy. I know that John likes to kiss me. Please do not misunderstand. There is nothing odd going on with John. John simply takes verses like 1 Cor 16:20 literally: "All the brothers greet you. Greet one another with a holy kiss."

I will be brutally honest here. For months I would cringe every time I saw John walk up close enough to give me a peck on the cheek. Now I have finally convinced John that his kisses are just a bit—make that a *big* bit—out of my comfort zone. I come from a stoic Germanic line of males. The only kissing I do is at home, with the members of my immediate family.

But look at that verse from 1 Corinthians again. Notice the word "brothers." This verse *is* talking about kissing in the family. Maybe my friend John has it right after all! Well, whatever we think about the cultural appropriateness (or, in my case, inappropriateness) of greeting one another with "a holy kiss," it is certainly the case that Paul and his fellow Christians experienced a great deal of brotherly affection in their relationships with one another in those early Christian churches. Emotional attachment was an important part of what being a family was like in the ancient world. And the church was a family.

Chapter 2 explained that in ancient Mediterranean society the most intense emotional bonding did not occur between spouses in a marriage but between siblings who shared the same father. We considered the marriage of Mustafa and Azize, two modern-day persons whose relationship in rural Turkey reflects first-century values. Azize did not view her husband Mustafa as a major source of companionship and emotional support. Instead, her emotional needs were met in her relationship with her brothers and sisters. She journeyed to their homes whenever she found the opportunity, and she experienced her strongest sense of relational affection among her siblings. The Western ethnographer who studied the couple's behavior described Azize's attachment to her brothers as "almost romantic" in nature.

So it was for Paul and his converts. A number of passages reveal that Paul and others in his churches experienced a great degree of affection and emotional bonding with their fellow Christians. And Paul clearly located this affective solidarity in the context of his conviction that the church is a strong-group family of siblings.

First Thessalonians, perhaps more than any of Paul's epistles, reflects the strong affective relationship that existed between Paul and his converts. The letter was written to the Christians in the Macedonian town of Thessalonica. The intensity of Paul's attachment to them is likely due to the brief time that had elapsed between Paul's visit to Thessalonica and the penning of the letter. The gospel had generated both converts and chaos for Paul in Macedonia, and he had to leave town rather suddenly after only a short visit in the province. Paul headed down to Achaia, and ultimately settled in Corinth for about 18 months (Acts 17–18).

Some weeks later, Paul began to worry about the long-term results of his efforts back up in Macedonia. Did those new Christians in Thessalonica have enough grounding to stand firm in the faith? Paul sent his coworker Timothy north to obtain information about the status of the nascent work in Thessalonica. Timothy soon returned with a wonderful report, and 1 Thessalonians is Paul's response to the good news he had received from Timothy.

Paul expressed his emotional attachment to the Thessalonians most pointedly in his first letter to the church. Significantly, the following passage begins and ends with "brothers":

> But as for us, *brothers*, after we were *forced to leave* you for a short time (in person, not in heart), we greatly desired and made every effort to return and see you face to face. So we wanted to come to you—even I, Paul, time and again—but Satan hindered us. For who is our hope, or joy, or crown of boasting in the presence of our Lord Jesus at His coming? Is it not you? For you are our glory and joy. Therefore, when *we could no longer stand it*, we thought it was better to be left alone in Athens. And we sent Timothy, our *brother* and God's co-worker in the gospel of Christ, to strengthen and encourage you concerning your faith, so that no one will be shaken by these persecutions. For you yourselves know that we are appointed to this. In fact, when we were with you, we told you previously that we were going to suffer persecution, and as you know, it happened. For this reason, *when I could no longer stand it*, I also sent to find

out about your faith, fearing that the tempter had tempted you and that our labor
might be for nothing. But now Timothy has come to us from you and brought
us good news about your faith and love, and that you always have good memo-
ries of us, *wanting to see us, as we also want to see you.* Therefore, *brothers*, in
all our distress and persecution, we were encouraged about you through your
faith. For now we live, if you stand firm in the Lord. (1 Thess 2:17–3:8; italics
added)

The close emotional ties that typically characterize Mediterranean sibling relations are evidenced throughout this passage. I have placed in italics both the sibling terminology and the various expressions of affective family solidarity. The
words "forced to leave" in v. 17 are particularly revealing. The NRSV translates
the phrase more literally as "we were made orphans." Paul's language shows that
the emotional attachment that the apostle and the Thessalonian Christians feel for
one another is a very specific kind of attachment—it is a family attachment.

A similar family-like connection apparently existed between the Philippians
and their emissary to Paul, Epaphroditus. There was a three-way family bond
between Paul, Epaphroditus, and the Philippians whom Paul addressed:

But I considered it necessary to send you Epaphroditus—my *brother*, co-
worker, and fellow soldier, as well as your messenger and minister to my
need—since he has been *longing for all of you* and was distressed because you
heard that he was sick. Indeed, he was so sick that he nearly died. However,
God had mercy on him, and not only on him but also on me, so that I would not
have one grief on top of another. For this reason, I am very eager to send him so
that you may rejoice when you see him again and I may be less anxious. (Phil
2:25–28, italics added)

Paul shared the same kind of emotional ties with yet another co-worker and
brother in the family of God:

When I came to Troas for the gospel of Christ, a door was opened to me by the
Lord. *I had no rest in my spirit* because I did not find my *brother* Titus, but I
said good bye to them and left for Macedonia. (2 Cor 2:12–13, italics added)

It is important to notice that in each of the above passages we find expressions of
emotional attachment and family terminology in the same context. This demonstrates that the relational solidarity reflected in these texts should be read in light
of descent-group family values.

A passage from Paul's letter to the Galatians will serve as our final piece of
evidence for the sibling-like affection that existed between Paul and his converts.

By the time Galatians was written, the brother bond between the apostle and the Galatian Christians had been compromised due to the influx of false teachers into the community in Paul's absence. But Paul reminded the readers of better times when the Galatians were willing to do just about anything for their brother and mentor Paul:

> I beg you, *brothers*: become like me, for I also became like you. You have not wronged me; you know that previously I preached the gospel to you in physical weakness, and though my physical condition was a trial for you, you did not despise or reject me. On the contrary, you received me as an angel of God, as Christ Jesus Himself. What happened to this blessedness of yours? For I testify to you that, if possible, you would have torn out your eyes and given them to me. (Gal 4:12–15, italics added)

Here we move beyond affection to the kind of sibling commitment that is ready to sacrifice and suffer for the good of a brother. Paul said to the Galatians, "I testify to you that, if possible, you would have torn out your eyes and given them to me." This leads us out of the arena of emotional solidarity and into other characteristics of Paul's strong-group family model for community organization.

Family Unity

Related to the affective component of sibling solidarity is the theme of family unity. As a pastor, when I want to help my people see why interpersonal harmony in the church is so important in God's eyes, I generally turn to passages like Ephesians 4, where we find the classic theological justification for unity among Christians:

> diligently keeping the unity of the Spirit with the peace that binds us. There is one body and one Spirit, just as you were called to one hope at your calling; one Lord, one faith, one baptism, one God and Father of all, who is above all and through all and in all. (Eph 4:3–6)

The (theo)logic of the passage is quite straightforward. We should be united as one, because God is one. But the oneness of God is not the only biblical source of appeal for encouraging Christians to live together in harmony. Our common family bond in Christ should also cause us to defer to one another and to cease quarreling with one another. And Paul, as we might expect, often drew on sibling imagery to address issues of disunity in the church.

Problems at Corinth particularly caught Paul's attention in this regard:

> Now I urge you, *brothers*, in the name of our Lord Jesus Christ, that you all say
> the same thing, that there be no divisions among you, and that you be united
> with the same understanding and the same conviction. For it has been reported
> to me about you, my *brothers*, by members of Chloe's household, that there are
> quarrels among you. (1 Cor 1:10–11, italics added)

> Finally, *brothers*, rejoice. Be restored, be encouraged, be of the same mind, be at
> peace, and the God of love and peace will be with you. (2 Cor 13:11, italics added)

For Paul, sibling unity in the Christian church is a logical extension of his understanding of the world in which he lived. If there was one place in the ancient world
where a person could expect to encounter a united front, it was in the descent-
group family of blood brothers and sisters. For Paul, the church is a family; as
such, unity must prevail.

A disproportionate number of sibling terms occurs in 1 Cor 6:1–6, where Paul
shamed the Corinthian Christians for engaging in litigation in the pagan courts:

> Does any of you who has a complaint against someone dare go to law before
> the unrighteous, and not before the saints? Or do you not know that the saints
> will judge the world? And if the world is judged by you, are you unworthy to
> judge the smallest cases? Do you not know that we will judge angels—not to
> speak of things pertaining to this life? So if you have cases pertaining to this
> life, do you select those who have no standing in the church to judge? I say this
> to your shame! Can it be that there is not one wise person among you who will
> be able to arbitrate between his *brothers*? Instead, *brother* goes to law against
> *brother*, and that before unbelievers! Therefore, it is already a total defeat for
> you that you have lawsuits against one another. Why not rather put up with
> injustice? Why not rather be cheated? Instead, you act unjustly and cheat—and
> this to *brothers!* (1 Cor 6:1–8, italics added)

This passage benefits greatly from the nearly literal rendering reflected in the
HCSB translation cited above. If you have an NIV Bible to compare with the above
translation, you will notice that the NIV uses the word "brother" only twice in the
passage (vv. 6,8). Although likely done in the service of English style, the NIV's
dynamic equivalency approach is misleading here (using "believers" in v. 5 and
"another" in v. 6), since the Greek term *adelphos* occurs four times in the original
(vv. 5,6 [twice],8). The term is central to Paul's rhetoric in the passage. The NRSV
is even more problematic. In its efforts toward a gender-inclusive translation, the

NRSV has left the masculine term "brother" out of the passage entirely and in each case translated the Greek sibling term *adelphos* as "believer(s)."

Whether done in the interests of stylistic variation (NIV) or gender neutrality (NRSV), the result is much the same. Translations that remove "brother" from the text (or replace it with "believer") deprive Paul's argument of its rhetorical power. Paul has a reason for using "brother" four times in four short verses. The Corinthians were undermining the unity of the church brotherhood in their litigious activities, and Paul was calling them on the carpet for their unfamily-like behavior.

First, Paul challenged his readers to keep their disputes in the family (vv. 5–6). But then he moved his argument to an entirely different level and really got to the heart of the issue. Siblings should not even have lawsuits to begin with: "Therefore, it is already a total defeat for you that you have lawsuits against one another. Why not rather put up with injustice? Why not rather be cheated?" (v. 7).

A person's honor was a highly valued commodity in Mediterranean antiquity, and males were quick to assert and defend their honor in the public arena. The courts, of course, provided a ready setting for such behavior. There was only one social group in the ancient world in which a person would be willing to suffer injustice—a blatant affront to one's honor—and not respond in kind. That group was the family. Paul envisions the church as a family of siblings who would "rather put up with injustice" and "rather be cheated" than to engage in lawsuits with their brothers and sisters in Christ.

Consider the story that began this chapter. How might the outcome have been different if Roxanne's father had responded to Ralph according to the New Testament model of the church as a family? For starters, the father would have offered to repair Ralph's truck. And he certainly would not have challenged Ralph to a court battle. The interesting thing here, though, is that Ralph encountered in Roxanne's dad a person with a lot of Bible knowledge. The man was undoubtedly familiar with what Paul taught about litigation in 1 Corinthians 6, but he chose to ignore it. Why?

The simple answer is that Roxanne's dad sinned. He was disobedient to a clear teaching of Scripture. To be sure, a person who disobeys God's Word in a situation like this will be held morally accountable for his actions. Roxanne's father will answer to God for his sin. But I want us to look beyond the father's unacceptable behavior to the cultural values that generated it.

Simply knowing the commands and prohibitions of Scripture has proven to be an insufficient defense against the powerful socializing influence of radical individualism in the lives of American Christians. Our churches are full of people like Roxanne's father who know their Bibles, but who persist in doing what they perceive to be best for them as individuals rather than what is biblical and most beneficial for the broader family of believers.

Bible knowledge is not enough. A more thoroughgoing resocialization is necessary. Until we truly begin to understand and embrace the strong-group model of the church as a family, we will have neither the theological foundation nor the social capital necessary to act in a manner diametrically opposed to the dominant culture of radical individualism. We will successfully swim upstream against the raging river of personal sin and selfishness only in the context of community as God intends it.

Material Solidarity

Material solidarity refers to the sharing of material resources of food, clothing, and shelter. Paul longed to see this particular Mediterranean family value actualized in his churches, and the collection Paul gathered from his Gentile congregations for the impoverished Christians in Judea beautifully illustrates this aspect of Mediterranean sibling solidarity.

The first Christians in Jerusalem found themselves on the edge of economic disaster. We are not sure why the Jerusalem congregation fell into such financial straits. Some suggest that a relief fund for widows became overburdened as the church grew. Pilgrimages to Jerusalem by Galilean Christians coming to the Holy City to await the return of their Messiah may also have taxed the resources of the Judean churches.[2] External factors certainly contributed to the problem. Luke (in Acts) and Josephus both gave evidence for general economic hardship throughout Roman Palestine, and it is hardly surprising to discover that the "bear market" severely affected a Jerusalem community led by a number of displaced Galileans (Peter, James, and John).[3]

Even before Paul began his missionary journeys, believers at Antioch sent aid to their fellow-Christians in Jerusalem. Note the explicit reference to the family context (v. 29, in italics):

> In those days some prophets came down from Jerusalem to Antioch. Then one
> of them, named Agabus, stood up and predicted by the Spirit that there would
> be a severe famine throughout the Roman world. This took place during the

---

[2] R. Martin, *2 Corinthians*, in *Word Biblical Commentary*, vol. 40, ed. D. A. Hubbard and G. W. Barker (Waco: Word Books, 1986), 256–57.

[3] The literature dealing with first-century Palestinian economics is extensive. M. Goodman's chapter on the subject is a good place to begin; see his *The Ruling Class of Judaea* (Cambridge: University Press, 1987), 51–75.

time of Claudius. So each of the disciples, according to his ability, determined
to send relief to the *brothers* who lived in Judea. This they did, sending it to the
elders by means of Barnabas and Saul. (Acts 11:27–30, italics added)

While the various causes of the Jerusalem church's economic dilemma must
remain somewhat obscure, it is crystal clear that Paul determined to involve his
Gentile churches in alleviating the suffering.

Paul's concern for the brethren in Judea can be traced to his second visit to
Jerusalem, as recorded in Gal 2:1–10. During Paul's visit, the leaders of the Jeru-
salem congregation heartily affirmed Paul's ministry to the Gentiles (vv. 7–9).
The Jerusalem "pillars" (James, Peter, and John) made only one request of Paul:
"[They asked] only that we would remember the poor, which I made every effort
to do" (v. 10).

Paul's assertion that he "made every effort" is a bit of an understatement in
light of the importance that the collection for Judea took on in Paul's later life and
ministry. One writer observed: "Little did the Jerusalem leaders know that their
suggestion would become Paul's *obsession* for nearly two decades."[4] Our earliest
piece of evidence for the magnitude of Paul's efforts is as follows:

> Now about the collection for the saints: you should do the same as I instructed
> the Galatian churches. On the first day of the week, each of you is to set some-
> thing aside and save to the extent that he prospers, so that no collections will
> need to be made when I come. And when I arrive, I will send those whom you
> recommend by letter to carry your gracious gift to Jerusalem. If it is also suit-
> able for me to go, they will travel with me. (1 Cor 16:1–4)

Paul wrote to the church at Corinth to challenge them to contribute their resources
to the collection. The "Galatian churches" are already on board. By the time all is
said and done, Paul had also gathered money from congregations in Macedonia
and elsewhere in Achaia (Rom 15:26).[5] On his way back to Jerusalem Paul vis-
ited with Gentile Christians from Tyre, Ptolemais, and Caesarea Maritima (Acts
21:3–16). It is only reasonable to conclude that Paul encouraged these churches to
participate in the gift as well.

The subject of Paul's collection has preoccupied the imagination of the scholarly community, as Bible students have sought to uncover some underlying theological motivation behind Paul's famine-relief efforts. There must be something

---

[4] S. McKnight, "Collection for the Saints," in *Dictionary of Paul and His Letters*, eds. G. F. Haw-
thorne, R. P. Martin, and D. G. Reid (Downers Grove: InterVarsity, 1993), 143.

[5] At the time Paul gave instructions concerning the collection, there were at least two cities in the
Greek province of Achaia with Christian churches: Corinth and Cenchrea (Rom 16:1). Paul certainly
involved these two Achaian churches in the collection. Perhaps there were others.

more than just poverty relief going on here, since Paul was so passionately committed to the project. What is it?

We do not have to look far. Paul himself revealed that he intended the gift not only to meet practical needs but also to reflect the unity of the church at large, as God's community embracing both Jews and Gentiles: "For if the Gentiles have shared in their spiritual benefits, then they are obligated to minister to Jews in material needs" (Rom 15:27).

Jews and Gentiles had been at one another's throats for decades throughout the Roman world. Mutual hostility led to bloodshed on numerous occasions. For those who became Christians, the gospel broke down the "dividing wall of hostility" (Eph 2:14) and united the two groups into a family in which there was "no Jew or Greek" (Gal 3:28). From Paul's perspective, the freewill offering from Paul's Gentile Christians to their Jewish Christian brothers in Jerusalem was to serve as a practical and tangible picture of that theological truth. It is in this regard that D. Georgi referred to Paul's collection as an "illustrative model of his theology."[6] The gift *from* Gentiles to Jews illustrated the unity *between* Gentiles and Jews.

What I wish to add to the dialogue is the suggestion that Paul's famine-relief effort was also, to adopt and rephrase Georgi's expression, an "illustrative model of Paul's *sociology.*" This means that the collection reflects not only Paul's vision for Jews and Gentiles to be one in Christ, but it also speaks of Paul's conception of God's church as a family of siblings who must make sure that every member's material needs are met through the sharing of the resources of the community. Indeed, the sharing of resources is precisely the way in which Paul's theology—the uniting of Jew and Gentile—is to be tangibly expressed. Jew and Gentile are now siblings in God's eternal family, and alleviating a brother's poverty is, first and foremost, a family responsibility.

Paul wrote most extensively about the famine-relief effort in 2 Corinthians 8–9. These two chapters also happen to contain a disproportionate amount of kinship terminology compared to the rest of the letter. The word "brother" occurs 12 times in all of 2 Corinthians, and Paul used six of those occurrences in the passage in which he describes the collection. The same pattern occurs throughout Paul's letters. There are portions of his epistles (like 1 Cor 6; see above) in which family words like "brother" occur much more frequently than they do elsewhere in the same letter.

The varying frequency with which Paul employed family language is no accident. There is a reason for it. Anthropologists have in fact noted that kinship

[6] D. Georgi, *Die Geschichte Der Kollekte Des Paulus Für Jerusalem*, in *Theologische Forschung* (Hamburg-Bergstedt: H. Reich. Evangelischer Verlag, 1965) 38:79.

terms are employed rather sparingly in most societies. When they do occur, family words are utilized for some very specific reasons. See if Roger Keesing's observations do not describe how things function in your own family:

> A common pattern seems to be to refer to a person's kinship relation to you not in everyday conversation, but in situations when that person is violating the norms of kinship; or in situations when you are trying to manipulate him. ("Lend me a dollar, brother")[7]

In the Hellerman home I seldom make it a point to remind Rebekah and Rachel that they are "sisters" or that they are my "daughters." I only pull these kinship terms out of my linguistic arsenal when I want Rebekah and Rachel to *act* like sisters or daughters.

I cannot recall how many times my wife and I have intervened in sibling spats with the admonition, "Rebekah, you may not treat your *sister* that way!" Or, in a lighter moment, I will be relaxing on the couch with Rachel and I will say, "Rachel, my loving *daughter,* wouldn't you like to go and get your *daddy* a nice cold soda out of the fridge?" Rachel, of course, is not above using the same strategy on me: "Don't you want to be a good *father* and take me to the mall this afternoon?"

This is exactly what Keesing and others who study the usage of kinship terminology have so astutely noticed. We generally reserve family language for those times when we want to do a little social engineering; that is, when we want to get a child or a sibling or a parent to act in a way appropriate to the family relationship. This is how it was with Paul and the Corinthians.

We are now prepared to appreciate the importance of the density of the sibling terminology in 2 Corinthians 8–9, where "brother" functions as the main rhetorical device Paul uses to encourage the Gentile churches to demonstrate their unity in Christ with Jewish Christians by meeting their material needs. Maybe it will help you to think of "brother" as a bullet in Paul's linguistic arsenal. Paul has a 12 shooter—a rhetorical pistol with 12 "brother" bullets to fire into 2 Corinthians (the word occurs 12 times in the letter). Paul used six of his bullets on this single topic (the poverty-relief project). He did so because he viewed his collection for the poor saints in Jerusalem as an expression of sibling solidarity on the part of his Gentile converts.

By the time he gets around to discussing the collection, Paul has written more than five chapters without a single use of "brother." The last time he used the term

---

[7] R. Keesing, *Kin Groups and Social Structure* (New York: Holt, Rinehart, and Winston, 1975), 126.

was in 2 Cor 2:13. Suddenly Paul draws on brother imagery once again as he begins his challenge to his readers to participate in the relief effort:

> We want you to know, *brothers*, about the grace of God granted to the churches of Macedonia: during a severe testing by affliction, their abundance of joy and their deep poverty overflowed into the wealth of their generosity. (2 Cor 8:1–2, italics added)

Paul here attempts to get his readers to *act* like the brothers they are—to share their abundance with siblings in need. In the verses that follow he encourages the Corinthians to join the Macedonians and "excel in this grace of giving" (v. 7). Then Paul spells out his perspective on the sharing of resources among brothers and sisters in the Gentile and Jewish Christian communities. His comments reflect precisely the attitude toward material resources that characterized Mediterranean family relations:

> It is not that there may be relief for others and hardship for you, but it is a question of equality—at the present time your surplus is available for their need, so that their abundance may also become available for your need, that there may be equality. As it has been written: "The person who gathered much did not have too much, and the person who gathered little did not have too little." (2 Cor 8:13–15)

Paul draws on the sibling idea five times elsewhere in the comparatively brief section of the letter that describes the collection (2 Cor 8:18,22–23; 9:3,5). Paul clearly viewed the collection as a prime opportunity for his readers to practice the central Mediterranean family value of sharing their material resources with brothers who were in need.

Family Loyalty

We conclude our study of Paul's social vision for life among the people of God with a consideration of family loyalty. At first glance it does not appear that Paul was as radical as Jesus in his concern for exclusive loyalty among members of God's family. We have no direct parallels to the scandalous sayings of Jesus (for example, "let the dead bury their own dead") in the Pauline epistles.

But a careful reading of Paul finds him quite in harmony with Jesus' conviction that God's group must take pride of place in the life of the Christian. A key passage in this regard is 1 Corinthians 7. You will need to follow along carefully in your Bible, since 1 Corinthians 7 is a long chapter and I have not quoted it in full. I first offer some comments concerning the overall thrust of the passage and then look at a portion of the chapter in some detail.

First Corinthians 7: The Big Picture

I just opened my NIV Bible to 1 Corinthians 7 and found that the editors have placed the heading *Marriage* above the chapter. Aha! This is precisely how we teach this chapter again and again in churches all over America: 1 Corinthians 7 is about marriage. But this is simply another clear-cut example of us reading our priorities—the nuclear family—into a passage that is concerned with God's priority—the church family.

This chapter is not about marriage, at least not about marriage in isolation. It is about the status of marriage as a secondary priority in view of what God is doing to grow his eternal family in the world. The question that the passage addresses is not, "What are God's designs for marriage?" The question is, "How does marriage fit into the overall scheme of things in God's program?"

Along the way Paul did give us some pretty important information about how married people should relate to each other. But a number of Paul's observations suggest that 1 Corinthians 7 is about something bigger than marriage:

> About the things you wrote: "It is good for a man not to have relations with a woman." But because of sexual immorality, each man should have his own wife, and each woman should have her own husband. (vv. 1–2)

> I say this as a concession, not as a command. I wish that all people were just like me. But each has his own gift from God, one this and another that. I say to the unmarried and to widows: It is good for them if they remain as I am. But if they do not have self-control, they should marry, for it is better to marry than to burn with desire. (vv. 6–9)

> About virgins: I have no command from the Lord, but I do give an opinion as one who by the Lord's mercy is trustworthy. Therefore I consider this to be good because of the present distress: it is fine for a man to stay as he is. Are you bound to a wife? Do not seek to be loosed. Are you loosed from a wife? Do not seek a wife. (vv. 25–27)

> And I say this, brothers: the time is limited, so from now on those who have wives should be as though they had none. (v. 29)

> I want you to be without concerns. An unmarried man is concerned about the things of the Lord—how he may please the Lord. (v. 32)

> So then, he who marries his virgin does well, but he who does not marry will do better. (v. 38)

Apparently there is something a little more important to Paul—and to the Spirit who inspired him—than making sure that everyone in the Corinthian church enjoys a relationally satisfying marriage. Our central Western value of emotional intimacy in marriage actually gets no space at all in this chapter. Marriage is instead presented as somewhat of a concession: "it is better to marry than to burn with desire" (v. 9).

I spent my first ten years of vocational ministry as a pastor of singles in a large metropolitan church. I often drew upon the above verses in my work with single adults. But I think I mishandled the text.

I taught these verses as if they were written to encourage singles to be spiritually fruitful during the years before marriage when they have all that extra time on their hands, and to assure singles who might never be married that they still have a place in God's kingdom. Notice that my focus here was still on marriage: what to do until you are married, and what to do if you are not "fortunate" enough to get married.

It is rather revealing that we feel the need to offer special programs (and hire special staff) for single adult ministry in our churches. We struggle somehow to fit single adults into a kingdom plan that we have designed primarily for married folks.

Perhaps the problem is with how we have framed the plan. Paul's concern in 1 Corinthians 7 was not to ask how *singleness* fits into God's kingdom plan. Paul was addressing the issue of how *marriage* fits into His kingdom plan. Single people are already with the program. They are "concerned about the things of the Lord" (v. 32). Married people are the ones who need help sorting out their priorities.

Where marriage is concerned, I believe we can fairly summarize the contents of 1 Corinthians 7 with the observation that for Paul "the things of the Lord" are to take priority over marriage. To conclude otherwise is to unfairly import our own priorities into the text. Additionally, as we learned in the previous chapter, we cannot separate "the things of the Lord" from the Lord's group, the surrogate family of God. So here we may just have a parallel to the teachings of Jesus. For Paul, God's group takes priority over all other claims of loyalty—even family.

The manner in which God's priorities work themselves out in various marriage situations is spelled out in verses 10–16. A detailed look at these verses will underscore the accuracy of the above assessment of Paul's teaching in 1 Corinthians 7.

First Corinthians 7:10–16: Getting at Paul's Priority.

We begin with vv. 10 11:

> I command the married—not I, but the Lord—a wife is not to leave her husband. But if she does leave, she must remain unmarried or be reconciled to her husband—and a husband is not to leave his wife.

Most agree that Paul here is simply paraphrasing teaching that Jesus gave during His earthly ministry. The Gospels were probably not circulating in written form at the time Paul wrote 1 Corinthians. But the early Christians had memorized and retained many of Jesus' teachings, and Paul was familiar with what Jesus had to say about divorce and remarriage.

In the verses that follow, however, Paul introduces a new but related issue, that of marriages between believers and unbelievers. He also reintroduces the word "brother" into his discussion. In fact, Paul suddenly uses sibling words four times within just four verses, after not using the terminology in the previous 23 verses:

> But to the rest I, not the Lord, say: If any *brother* has an unbelieving wife, and she is willing to live with him, he must not leave her. Also, if any woman has an unbelieving husband, and he is willing to live with her, she must not leave her husband. For the unbelieving husband is sanctified by the wife, and the unbelieving wife is sanctified by the Christian husband [lit. "the *brother*"]. Otherwise your children would be unclean, but now they are holy. But if the unbeliever leaves, let him leave. A *brother or a sister* is not bound in such cases. God has called you to peace. (7:12–15, italics added)

Even the HCSB fails uniformly to represent the sibling terminology that is present in the Greek text; thus my recourse to the brackets above. Instead of the HCSB's "Christian husband" (v. 14), we need to keep the brother terminology at the forefront of the text in order to appreciate Paul's argument. Hopefully, you are beginning to ask the right question of passages like these, such as "Why does Paul suddenly use so many family words?" At this point a little background proves useful.

The conversion of whole households to Christianity was not uncommon in antiquity (Acts 16:31–34). In addition, Christians were expected to marry other believers (see 7:39 and 2 Cor 6:14 by implication). The result of these household conversions and Christian marriages was that many Christians were married to others who shared their faith. These are the marriages Paul discussed when he paraphrased the words of Jesus in 1 Cor 7:10–11. Nevertheless, it remained the case that at times only one spouse would convert. The reality of such divided households left Paul and other early Christian leaders with an issue that was apparently not explicitly addressed in the teachings of Jesus.

As explained in chapter 2, loyalty to one's siblings typically took precedence over loyalty to one's spouse in Mediterranean society in situations where one had to choose between them. Tensions were particularly high when serious conflict arose between a woman's family of origin and the family into which she married.

The idea of the church as a strong-group family introduced a whole new factor into the loyalty equation, since the conflict between "God's children" and "the Devil's children" (1 John 3:10) was foundational in nature according to the Christian worldview. Inevitable problems arose in marriages involving parties from both "families."

For Christians who were married to believing spouses, divided loyalty was a moot issue. One's marriage partner was at the same time a sister or brother in the faith. To be loyal to one's spouse was to be loyal to one's brother or sister in Christ. But for believers married to unbelievers, divided loyalties were inevitable. Paul addressed this issue in 1 Cor 7:12–16, drawing on the strong-group value of sibling loyalty by reintroducing "brother" terminology into his argument. In his discussion of "mixed marriages," Paul landed precisely where our studies of Mediterranean family values would lead us to expect him to land. He affirmed the priority of sibling loyalty over spousal loyalty. God's family must come first. Let us see how Paul comes to this conclusion.

In vv. 12–14, Paul forbade divorce in the case of an unbelieving spouse who consents to remain in the marriage. Observe Paul's linguistic strategy here. In v. 12 Paul introduced sibling terminology into the passage, contrasting the Christian (referred to as a "brother") with his wife (referred to as an "unbeliever"). A tension is therefore already introduced here between one family relationship (the man is a "brother" in God's family) and another (the man has a "wife" in his natural family).

According to ancient family priorities, one was expected to exercise greater loyalty toward siblings than toward a spouse. Recall the decision the Roman matron Octavia made to leave her husband Mark Antony and return to her brother Octavian during the war between to two generals (chap. 2).

Paul's first-century readers would have begun to sense a conflict brewing the moment they encountered this "brother"-"wife" contrast in v. 12. Nevertheless, Paul's command remains pretty predictable at this point. Although he had no saying from Jesus' earthly ministry to draw on ("I, not the Lord," v. 12), Paul's admonition for a "brother" to stay married to an unbelieving wife who consents to remain in the relationship is a logical extension of the teachings of Jesus that Paul just cited (vv. 10–11).

But in v. 15 Paul charted some brand new territory. "But if the unbeliever leaves, let him leave. A brother or a sister is not bound in such cases. God has called you to peace." Paul's innovation resides in the phrase "is not bound." Similar terminology in Rom 7:1–6—along with the absence of an explicit prohibition of remarriage here as compared with Paul's instructions for two believers who separate ("she must remain unmarried or be reconciled to her husband," v. 11)—suggests that Paul allowed remarriage for a "brother or sister" whose unbelieving spouse chooses to depart. In allowing remarriage in the case of the departure of an unbelieving spouse, Paul was self-conscious of the fact that he assumed a position not reflected in (but not contradicted by) the teachings of Jesus. Paul faced a problem that Jesus apparently did not address.

What is important for our purposes is to notice how Paul handled the problem. His sudden reintroduction of "brother" terminology into the passage reveals the heart of his convictions. By importing sibling terminology into his argument at precisely this point (four times in just four verses), Paul assumed a paradigm that would have had long-standing implications for Christians in the ancient world: unbelievers are not truly family to begin with. All marriages involving a "brother" or a "sister" with an unbeliever are necessarily and ultimately tentative: "For you, wife, how do you know whether you will save your husband? Or you, husband, how do you know whether you will save your wife?" (1 Cor 7:16).

The Mediterranean family value that demands loyalty to blood relations (especially siblings) over loyalty to one's spouse is thus appropriated and subtly reinterpreted by Paul to apply to a Christian's loyalty to his siblings in the faith. Indeed, Paul expressed his sentiments even more directly, as he summarized his argument later in 1 Corinthians 7. Apparently, even a marriage relationship between believing spouses must take second place to the priority of the broader values and goals of the family of faith. Again, notice the rhetorical tension Paul introduced between "brothers" (the most important relationship in descent-group society) and "wives" (a less important relationship): "And I say this, brothers: the time is limited, so from now on those who have wives should be as though they had none" (1 Cor 7:29).

To conclude our discussion of family loyalty, I find Paul's convictions to be quite in harmony with the priorities reflected in the teachings and actions of Jesus. Neither Paul nor Jesus can be cited in support of a life-priority list that generates a false dichotomy between commitment to God and commitment to His group in order to stick natural family relations somewhere in between:

(1st) God — (2nd) Family — (3rd) Church — (4th) Others

For both Jesus and Paul, commitment to God was commitment to God's group. Such an outlook generates a rather different list of priorities, one that more accurately reflects the strong-group perspective of the early Christians:

(1st) God's Family — (2nd) My Family — (3rd) Others

Ben Witherington appropriately commented on another key Pauline text:

> As Ephesians 5:21–6:9 suggests, the direction of ethical influence moved from the *primary* family (the family of faith) to the *secondary* family, with the physical family being formed and reformed *within* the family of faith.[8]

Witherington's analysis is right on target. We will expand upon it later when we consider in more practical terms the relationship between our natural families and the surrogate family of faith.

Conclusion

The set of values (affective solidarity, family unity, material solidarity, family loyalty) reflected above can only be explained on the assumption that Paul drew directly on the Mediterranean family as the central social model for his churches. The apostle Paul clearly adopted Jesus' model for Christian community, as indicated by the extensive use of family language in his letters. But Paul's vision was not an easy sell, even to people in a collectivist culture.

We might think it would have been relatively effortless for Paul to convince his converts to adopt the strong-group family model for life in God's church. After all, like others in Mediterranean antiquity, the people Paul evangelized had been socialized to believe that the groups to which they belonged took priority over their individual desires, and that these groups defined for them their very place in the world. They understood group solidarity much better than we do.

The problem was that Paul's converts often wanted to be loyal first and foremost not to God's group—the church family—but rather to the pagan interest groups that had held their allegiance before they converted to Christ. The Corinthian church split along the lines of social status. The rich identified with the rich, the poor with the poor. For the Roman Christians, the lines were drawn around the ethnic orientations of Jew and Gentile.

We can be thankful, though, that Paul's converts at times resisted the full realization of Jesus' vision for a church family of united, mutually supportive siblings. For, as we have seen, it was often when Paul wanted to challenge his erring converts to change their ways and engage in proper family-like behavior that he used "brother" terminology. These corrective texts are the very passages that are most enlightening to us as we seek to understand what the church family model meant for Paul and his communities. We would not even have these texts

---

[8] B. Witherington III, *The Paul Quest* (Downers Grove: InterVarsity, 1998), 267–68 (italics added).

if the early church had consistently behaved according to Mediterranean family expectations.

In fact, the Corinthian and Roman churches can be viewed as archetypical examples of the two ways in which human beings have been divided throughout history. Ethnicity divides us at the horizontal level, so that we gravitate toward those of similar racial and cultural backgrounds, and we fear those who are different. Socio-economic inequalities generate a vertical hierarchy of human persons, so that we look down with disdain, or up with desire, at those who stand on different rungs of the social ladder.

The church family model is Paul's divinely inspired solution to these seemingly intractable human issues of race and rank. Ethnicity no longer matters: "There is no Jew or Greek"; social status is now irrelevant: "slave or free"; even gender is a nonissue: "male or female" (Gal 3:28). This is true because we are now members of a family whose social solidarity must transcend all the differences that divide us:

> for you are all *sons* of God through faith in Christ Jesus. For as many of you as have been baptized into Christ have put on Christ. There is no Jew or Greek, slave or free, male or female; for you are all one in Christ Jesus. And if you are Christ's, then you are *Abraham's seed, heirs* according to the promise. Now I say that as long as the *heir* is a *child*, he differs in no way from a slave, though he is the owner of everything. Instead, he is under guardians and stewards until the time set by his *father*. In the same way we also, when we were *children*, were in slavery under the elemental forces of the world. But when the completion of the time came, God sent His Son, born of a woman, born under the law, to redeem those under the law, so that we might receive *adoption as sons*. And because you are *sons*, God has sent the Spirit of His Son into our hearts, crying, "*Abba*, Father!" So you are no longer a slave, but a *son*; and if a *son*, then an *heir* through God. (Gal 3:26–4:7, italics added, except *Abba*)

Notice the family words sprinkled throughout the passage. Paul's point is not simply that God is now my Father and I am now His son. God, in Jesus' great work of redemption, was not establishing a series of isolated personal relationships with His individual followers. He was creating a family of sons and daughters—siblings—who are now "all one in Christ Jesus" (v. 28). The saving work of Christ therefore has a corporate, as well as an individual, dimension. For Paul, the church is a family.

Chapter Five

THE CHURCH IN THE ROMAN WORLD

*Before all things, the Teacher of peace and Master of unity did not wish prayer
to be offered individually and privately as one would pray only for himself
when he prays. We do not say: "My Father, who art in heaven," nor "Give me
this day my bread," nor does each one ask that only his debt be forgiven him
and that he be led not into temptation and that he be delivered from evil for
himself alone. Our prayer is public and common, and when we pray we pray
not for one but for the whole people, because we, the whole people, are one.*
(Cyprian of Carthage, North Africa, c. AD 250)

S ometime around AD 250 a marvelous thing happened at a small town
named Thena on the outskirts of Carthage in North Africa. An actor
converted to Christ. We do not know the man's name, so I will refer to
our actor friend as Marcus. Marcus's conversion created quite a stir among his
brothers and sisters in Thena, and his story paints a delightful picture of the early
church in North Africa functioning at its family best.

Even today people in the entertainment industry convert to Christianity. Not in
droves, but it does happen. And the Christian community often responds by placing such persons on pedestals and proudly displaying them as trophies of God's
grace in the film or television industry in which they work. Many of us take pride
in having our Christian values represented by a celebrity in an area of the public
square that is highly esteemed by the popular culture.

The early church took a rather different approach to the conversion of high-
visibility entertainment personalities. The values and practices surrounding the

theater in the ancient world explain why. The Greco-Roman theater found itself entangled in some highly questionable morality. Most problematic was the close association with pagan religion. Theater performances were typically dedicated to a pagan god or goddess, and the plays often ran as part of larger public religious festivals. Moreover, as is the case in film today, scenes portraying blatant immorality were commonplace in the ancient theater, and this proved most troubling to the early church. In fact, Christian leaders in the second and third centuries were universally outspoken in their opposition to the entertainment industry of the ancient world.

Tertullian, an early second-century Christian leader from the large metropolis of Carthage, drew on the book of Psalms in order to try to persuade his readers that Christians should not attend the theater: "How happy is the man who does not follow the advice of the wicked, or take the path of sinners, or join a group of mockers" (Ps 1:1).

Some people in Tertullian's church apparently found it acceptable for Christians to view immorality on the stage, as long they did not practice the behavior in real life. After all, the Bible does not specifically command, "Do not go to the theater." Tertullian categorically rejected this kind of rationalization:

> Why is it right to look on what it is disgraceful to do? How is it that the things which defile a man in going out of his mouth, are not regarded as doing so when they go in at his eyes and ears—when eyes and ears are the immediate attendants of the spirit? If you are going to forbid immorality, you'd better forbid the theater. If tragedies and comedies are the bloody and wanton, the impious and licentious inventors of crimes and lusts, it is not good even that there should be any calling to remembrance the atrocious or the vile. What you reject in deed, you are not to bid welcome in word. (*De Spectaculis*, 17)

Tertullian would probably not be spending much money at his local movie theater if he were alive today.

If Christian leaders had this much of a problem with believers who attended the shows, imagine how they felt about the actors who made their living in the theater. When an actor converted to Christ in second-century Carthage, the first thing the church demanded of him was to quit his profession. Yes, a born-again actor could be a real testimony to the entertainment industry. How? By cutting all ties and disassociating himself from it forever.

The actor whose conversion I mentioned at the beginning of the chapter did just that. Marcus became a follower of Jesus Christ, so he quit his job. In good strong-group fashion, Marcus bowed to the demands of the Christian community and stopped acting in the local theater. But this new convert now faced an economic dilemma since he was no longer gainfully employed. So instead of acting, Marcus decided to *teach* acting. He opened an acting school.

This apparently created quite a stir among Marcus's fellow Christians. Soon, both the pastor of the small church in Thena and the bishop of the big-city congregation in Carthage found themselves embroiled in the ensuing damage control. The letters exchanged by these two Christian leaders paint an inspiring portrait of the church as a surrogate family.

Marcus's pastor, Eucratius, had a dilemma on his hands that he had not encountered before, and he did not quite know what to do. Naturally, Eucratius sensed a certain contradiction as he considered his new convert's behavior. After all, how could it be acceptable for Marcus to teach others to do what he himself was forbidden to do? Yet Marcus had already made a tremendous sacrifice to follow Jesus, a sacrifice that had cost Marcus his job. So Eucratius wrote to his spiritual mentor, Cyprian of Carthage, to ask "whether such a man [Marcus] ought to remain in communion with us."

Cyprian was one of the most highly respected Christian leaders of his day, and justly so, for he was totally sold out to the Lord and to his church. So intense was his commitment to Christ that in a few short years Cyprian himself would be martyred for his faith before a Carthaginian pagan mob.

Cyprian believed that there was simply no place for moral compromise in the Christian life. Cyprian's convictions about Marcus and his drama academy could not be more straightforward:

> It is not in keeping with the reverence due to the majesty of God and with the observance of the gospel teachings for the honour and respect of the Church to be polluted by contamination at once so degraded and so scandalous. (*Epistulae* 2.1.2)

No compromise. No breathing room. No drama teaching. Marcus must either leave the church or quit his job—again! But the best was yet to come.

Cyprian was not unaware of the hardship that would come upon Marcus if he shut down the academy. He went on in his letter to suggest a way that Eucratius's congregation could assist Marcus in his Christian pilgrimage. As Cyprian's comments clearly demonstrate, the intense emphasis on personal holiness that characterized the North African Christian church had a beautiful complement: a genuine concern for those whose livelihoods might be adversely affected by following the church's demanding moral standards.

In short, Cyprian told pastor Eucratius that the church should support Marcus:

> His needs can be alleviated along with those of others who are supported by the provisions of the Church—on condition, of course, that he can be satisfied with more frugal, and harmless, fare and does not consider that he ought to be bought off by means of a pension, so as to break away from his sins, for he is the one to benefit from such a break, not us. . . . Accordingly, you should do your utmost to call him away from this depraved and shameful profession to the way of innocence and to the hope of his true life; let him be satisfied with the nourishment provided by the Church, more sparing to be sure but salutary. (*Ep.* 2.2.2–3)

And if this is not enough, Cyprian concluded his letter by telling Eucratius that Cyprian's church would foot the bill if the rural church in Thena lacks the resources to meet Marcus's basic needs:

> But if your church is unable to meet the cost of maintaining those in need, he can transfer himself to us and receive here what is necessary for him in the way of food and clothing. (*Ep.* 2.2.3)

There is a phrase for this in English slang. We call it "putting your money where your mouth is." Cyprian did just that. He demanded of those in God's family an uncompromising standard of Christian morality. No theater. No acting. No teaching others to act. God's people would be radically different from the pagans in the dominant culture. But Cyprian made sure that the church would serve as the economic safety net for those whose finances were adversely affected by their willingness to follow Jesus.

The North African Church as a Strong-Group Family

I have used Marcus as our first window into the world of the postapostolic church because his experience aptly illustrates the strong-group model of the church as a family. In chapter 2 we encountered precisely the same thing as here in this third-century North African church. Remember our description of the individual's relationship to the church in a collectivist New Testament setting?

> The person perceives himself or herself to be a member of a church and responsible to the church for his or her actions, destiny, career, development, and life in general. . . . The individual person is embedded in the church and is free to do what he or she feels right and necessary only if in accord with church norms

and only if the action is in the church's best interest. The church has priority
over the individual member.[1]

This is the world of Cyprian, Eucratius, and Marcus in a nutshell. Substitute the
name of our actor friend Marcus for "the person" in the above description, and
the fit is remarkable. Marcus was clearly accountable to the church for the most
important areas of his life.

But more than collectivist priorities are at work here. The church is not simply
a strong group. It is a specific kind of group. The church is a family. In Cyprian's
willingness to undertake Marcus's support we see a central Mediterranean family
value tangibly expressed in the North African church—the sharing of material
resources. In his letter Cyprian referred to fellow-pastor Eucratius as his "dearest brother." Sibling solidarity found practical expression in the incident that
unfolded over Marcus. The Carthaginian church family's moral standards were
high, but everyone in the church who met those standards was entitled to the
financial resources of the community.

There is no surviving letter of reply from Eucratius to Cyprian to let us know
whether Marcus agreed to the church's demands. But we are on solid historical
ground to assume that he did. Why? Because history has shown us that pagans in
Carthage were consistently attracted to—rather than repelled by—the intensely
moral, strong-group family values that characterized the North African Christian
community.

Fifty years before Marcus found the Lord, Tertullian could boast to the North
African Roman pagans:

> Day by day you groan over the ever-increasing number of Christians. Your
> constant cry is, that your state is beset by us, that Christians are in your estates,
> your camps, your blocks of houses. You grieve over it as a calamity, that every
> age, in short every rank is passing over from you to us. We have left you only
> the temples. (*Ad nationes* 1.4; *Apologeticus* 37.4)

Consider the contrast with the church in the West today. The early Christians
made tremendous demands of their converts—demands that affected the most
important areas of their lives. And people came in droves.

But we bend over backward in our churches to accommodate the radical individualism of people who come to us to find a "personal" Savior who, we assure
them, will meet their every felt need. And the overwhelming tide of secular cul-

---

[1] B. Malina, *Christian Origins and Cultural Anthropology* (Atlanta: John Knox, 1986), 19, paraphrased.

ture threatens to suffocate what is left of the spiritual life of our churches, as the West becomes less and less Christian.

The Carthaginian church was a church triumphant. Modern evangelicals are a community in crisis. We have much to learn from Eucratius, Cyprian, and their brothers and sisters in the ancient Christian church.

Lessons from the Past

Sadly, most evangelicals are historically uninformed—even those of us who are highly committed to our local churches and who know our way around the Bible. Events that occurred in church history between the close of the New Testament canon and the modern era strike us as somehow irrelevant to our Christian lives. As a result, few evangelicals have read so much as the equivalent of an undergraduate survey text on the history of the Christian church.

If you find yourself among the historically uninformed, our journey to the past may be a new experience for you. I intend it to be a rewarding one. You will encounter some towering Christian leaders—most of whom were martyred for their faith—whose writings tell us how the second- and third-century church lived out the family model of Christian community and how the early Christians triumphantly multiplied in the face of vociferous opposition.

Consider the obstacles to church growth faced by those first followers of Jesus. Our society is at least nominally Christian. Theirs was passionately pagan. Place yourself back in the first century, in the renowned halls of the mighty Roman senate. How logical would it have been to imagine that a small Jewish sect, originating in a remote and insignificant province at the eastern fringes of the empire, could expand its ranks steadily for more than two centuries in the face of lethal opposition?

"Against All Odds" is the title I gave to a survey course in early church history—and rightly so. The incredible expansion of Christianity during the second and third centuries remains among the most perplexing problems confronting scholars captivated by the study of ancient history. The odds on the books at Caesar's Palace were overwhelming. The Christians did not stand a chance.

At the dawn of the second century, the Christian movement was still but a speck of dirt on the sweeping canvas of Roman dominance in realms both political and religious. Taxes flowed faithfully into Rome from everywhere between Spain in the West and the hinterlands of Palestine in the East. Temples dedicated to Augustus Caesar and his successors, and to a multitude of lesser deities, stood firmly erected throughout the eastern empire. Paganism reigned supreme.

Christianity, meanwhile, was barely significant enough to warrant a few sentences in the works of Rome's great second-century historians, Tacitus and Suetonius—a mere blip on the radar screen of Roman imperial history. Paul and Peter, Christianity's two most charismatic leaders, were now dead, and animosity toward the upstart religion was on the rise in cities throughout the East. Few in Rome would have laid their money on the success of the early Christians.

Well, the emperor's oddsmakers were dead wrong. Little did they know that even Caesar's Palace in Rome would be turned into a church basilica in the not-too-distant future. How delightfully ironic! God must have some sense of humor.

And consider this. In our day and age, the way in which most of us first become acquainted with the name of the first and greatest of all Roman emperors is through a story about the birth of an insignificant peasant boy in rural Judea: "In those days a decree went out from Caesar Augustus that the whole empire should be registered" (Luke 2:1). God truly has used "the world's weak things to shame the strong" (1 Cor 1:27). He has turned the world upside down.

So surprising and significant is the growth of Christianity in antiquity that one of our most eminent historians of the ancient world categorically stated: "The spread of Christianity must indeed be taken as the single most important development which occurred in the period from the reign of Augustus to the death of Constantine."[2] Pretty strong words from a secular writer, and F. Millar is not alone in his convictions. Scholars who study the ancient world are standing up and taking notice.

Explaining the Growth of the Christian Church

Why did the church prevail? The response to this question has traditionally been framed in terms of ideology. It was the belief system of early Christianity that the pagans ultimately found irresistible. The church grew because of the content of its teaching.

This line of reasoning contains a degree of truth. The Christian message was a liberating one for people oppressed by the darkness of a pagan pantheon of gods and goddesses. There were more supernatural beings than you could shake an amulet at.

The ancient world had undergone a tremendous transition during the three centuries before Christianity appeared on the scene. Relatively isolated Greek city-states like Athens in the West and temple-states like Israel in the East were

[2] F. Millar, *The Roman Near East, 31 BC–AD 337* (Cambridge: Harvard University Press, 1993), 21.

gradually united into the vast Greek and Roman empires. This truly world-changing development presented some genuine challenges to the inhabitants of a now expansive empire.

Among these challenges was the daunting task of sorting and choosing from among a whole collage of religious options. As armies and peoples traveled back and forth, the inhabitants of the various areas of the empire were exposed to countless gods and goddesses: Zeus, Jupiter, Mars, Isis, Demeter, Mithras, Asclepius, Dionysus, Artemis, Cybele, Hermes, Axieros—even a goddess of fate, Fortuna. And then there were all those Greco-Roman philosophies to sort through.

After some initial resistance, the official position of the Roman government became one of tolerance. The success and stability of an ever-expanding empire depended upon maintaining the religious cults of the various conquered peoples.

So much for public policy. For the individual, this proliferation of religious options proved more frightening than encouraging. After all, how could a person guarantee that all these gods, goddesses, and other supernatural forces would act in his or her favor? There were just too many gods to placate, too many spiritual bases to cover. One writer noted, "Any account of pagan worship which minimizes the gods' uncertain anger and mortals' fear of it is an empty account."[3]

The early Christians responded with an appealing alternative to the state policy of religious toleration: throw out all the pagan gods and replace them with Jesus. E. Dodds rightly maintained that the exclusive monotheism championed by Christianity strongly appealed to people in the ancient world:

> There were too many cults, too many mysteries, too many philosophies of life to choose from: you could pile one religious insurance on another, yet not feel safe. Christianity made a clean sweep. It lifted the burden of freedom from the shoulders of the individual: one choice, one irrevocable choice, and the road to salvation was clear.[4]

Ideological explanations for the growth of early Christianity clearly have their place in the ongoing dialogue. The early Christians did have a compelling and liberating message to share.

Such explanations, however, remain incomplete. Dodds, who so eloquently summed up the appeal of Christianity's belief system, nevertheless acknowledges that ideological explanations of the phenomenon of the early church ultimately fail to satisfy. To arrive at a truly comprehensive explanation for the expansion

---

[3] R. Fox, *Pagans and Christians* (New York: Alfred A. Knopf, 1986), 38.
[4] E. Dodds, *Pagan and Christian in an Age of Anxiety: The Wiles Lectures* (Cambridge: University Press, 1965), 133.

of Christianity, we must move beyond ideology (beliefs) and enter into the social world (behavior) of the early Christians. We must understand how Christians related with one another and with their pagan neighbors. To posit a strictly ideological explanation for early church growth is to miss perhaps the most convincing reason for the growth of early Christianity.

People did not convert to Christianity solely because of what the early Christians believed. They converted because of the way in which the early Christians behaved. It is not ideology that Dodds ultimately identified as the most important cause of the growth of the Christian movement. It is the social solidarity experienced in the early Christian churches:

> A Christian congregation was from the first a community in a much fuller sense
> than any corresponding group of Isiac or Mithraist devotees. . . . Love of one's
> neighbor is not an exclusively Christian virtue, but in our period (1st-3rd century AD) the Christians appear to have practiced it much more effectively than
> any other group.[5]

The evidence from our sources demonstrates that Dodds is correct. The ancient Christians were known for their love for one another.

The Analysis of a Pagan Intellectual

One way to appreciate the contribution that brotherly love made to the marked expansion of the Jesus movement is to ask someone from the ancient world to tell us first-hand why he thinks the church triumphed against all odds. And we will not ask a Christian. Instead, we will ask a pagan outsider his opinion of the amazing story of early Christianity.

The fellow I am about to quote is a real piece of work. His name says it all: Julian the Apostate. His uncle was Constantine, the first Roman emperor who professed allegiance to Christianity (c. AD 312). Constantine had put an end to the Christian persecutions a couple generations before his nephew Julian walked onto the stage of imperial political history.

Much of the empire was at least nominally Christian in Julian's day, and Julian was provided with the best in theological education. Julian turned his back on the Lord, however, and converted to paganism. Through a series of political intrigues and military victories, he became emperor in AD 361. Julian then embarked upon a mission to turn the Roman Empire back to the gods and goddesses of paganism.

---

[5] Ibid., 136–38.

Julian was a brilliant thinker and a prolific writer, and among his surviving works is a letter to one of his pagan pals, a man named Arsarcius who was high priest of Galatia. Julian recognized that in his efforts to resuscitate paganism, he must first figure out why Christianity has been so successful. Julian's explanation for the rise of Christianity (he calls it "atheism") is crystal clear:

> Why do we not observe that it is their [the Christians'] benevolence to strang-
> ers, their care for the graves of the dead and the pretended holiness of their
> lives that have done the most to increase atheism? . . . When . . . the impious
> Galileans support not only their own poor, but ours as well, all men see that our
> people lack aid from us.[6]

Notice that Julian does not attribute the growth of the church to monotheism or to any other ideological component of the faith. The movement attracted people because of the Christians' behavior toward one another and toward those outside the church. Yes, Christian beliefs were appealing. But for Julian and his pagan peers, the way in which Christians treated one another and their pagan neighbors was the more persuasive explanation for the growth of the early church.

The ancient church was a strong-group family of surrogate siblings who lived out their belief system in a practical and winsome way. Even an avowed pagan like Julian could not deny the power of Christian community functioning at its family best. We turn now to observe Christian community in some detail during the second and third centuries AD.

What follows is a series of vignettes portraying church family life across the Roman Empire. Each scenario depicts some aspect of the strong-group worldview of the ancient church actualized in specific ways in everyday community life. The family ideal reigned supreme as the preeminent model for church organization and social interaction, and the ancient church grew and grew.

Social Solidarity and the Sharing of Material Resources

Several hundred miles east of Carthage on the coast of North Africa was the Egyptian metropolis of Alexandria. This city was second only to Rome in urban renown in the ancient world, and a number of rich and powerful people populated the city. A few of these wealthy folks became Christians.

Among the Christian leaders in Alexandria was a fellow named Clement (c. AD 200). Clement's challenge was to figure out how the rich Christians in his

---

[6] *The Works of the Emperor Julian*, vol. 3, trans. W. Wright, in Loeb Classical Library (London: W. Heinemann, 1923), 17, 69.

church could overcome the apparent stumbling block that Jesus threw in their spiritual pathway with this comment:

> Jesus looked around and said to His disciples, "How hard it is for those who have wealth to enter the kingdom of God!" But the disciples were astonished at His words. Again Jesus said to them, "Children, how hard it is to enter the kingdom of God! It is easier for a camel to go through the eye of a needle than for a rich person to enter the kingdom of God." (Mark 10:23–25)

Clement must have had a number of wealthy folks in his church because he has left us our first surviving commentary on the above Gospel passage, entitled *Who Is the Rich Man Who Is Saved?*

Clement made it clear that the solution to the wealthy Christian's dilemma is not necessarily to be found in simply getting rid of his money. Jesus' challenge to the rich young ruler—"sell what you own, and give the money to the poor"—had quite an impact on the early Christians and a number of elite rich gave away all their money after they converted to Christ. Among them was Cyprian of Carthage, whom we met earlier.

Clement realized, however, that there would be negative repercussions for the church if every wealthy Christian gave away his worldly resources:

> How could we feed the hungry and give drink to the thirsty, cover the naked and entertain the homeless, with regard to which deeds He threatens fire and the outer darkness to those who have not done them, if each of us were himself already in want of all these things? . . . It is on this condition that He praises their [financial resources'] use, and with this stipulation,—that He commands them to be shared, to give drink to the thirsty and bread to the hungry, to receive the homeless, to clothe the naked. (*Who Is the Rich Man*, 13)

The sharing to which Clement referred finds its legitimation in the church family model. For as Clement proceeded to observe, the rich man who shares God's perspective on his riches

> holds possessions and gold and silver and houses as gifts of God, and from them ministers to the salvation of men for God the giver, and knows that he possesses them for his *brothers'* sakes rather than his own . . . [he is] a ready *inheritor* of the kingdom of heaven. (ibid., 16, italics added)

The idea of the rich man sharing his bounty with needy brethren in the context of the Christian surrogate family surfaces again in another passage in Clement's treatise:

> But if we owe our lives to the *brethren*, and admit such a reciprocal compact
> with the Saviour, shall we still husband and hoard up the things of the world,
> which are beggarly and alien to us and ever slipping away? Shall we shut out
> from one another that which in a short time the fire will have? Divine indeed
> and inspired is the saying of John: "He that loveth not his *brother* is a mur-
> derer," a seed of Cain, a nursling of the devil. (ibid., 37, italics added)

By mentioning Cain, the archetypical example of an evil brother (Genesis 4),
Clement essentially demonized any member of the community who would hesitate to practice the central family value of sharing his riches with those in need.
"Love," Clement concluded shortly thereafter, citing the apostle Paul, "seeketh
not its own, but is lavished upon the *brother*" (ibid., 38, italics added).

Clement of Alexandria was hardly alone in his convictions. Throughout the
empire Christian churches pooled their resources and shared them with those in
need. Justin Martyr reflected on practices in the church at Rome:

> We who once took most pleasure in the means of increasing our wealth and
> property now bring what we have into a common fund and share with everyone
> in need; we who hated and killed one another and would not associate with
> men of different tribes because of their different customs, now . . . live together.
> (*1 Apologia* 14)

Later in the same work Justin described the means by which community resources
are collected and distributed on a weekly basis:

> Those who have more come to the aid of those who lack, and we are constantly
> together. . . . Those who prosper, and so wish, contribute, each one as much as he
> chooses to. What is collected is deposited with the president, and he takes care
> of orphans and widows, and those who are in want on account of sickness or any
> other cause, and those who are in bonds, and the strangers who are sojourners
> among [us], and, briefly, he is the protector of all those in need. (ibid., 67)

Back in Carthage, Tertullian (c. AD 200) was in full agreement with the sentiments of Clement and Justin quoted above. Tertullian said,

> We call ourselves *brothers*. . . . So, we who are united in mind and soul have no
> hesitation about sharing what we have. Everything is in common among us—
> except our wives. (*Apologeticus* 39.8–11, italics added)

The common fund is used, Tertullian informed us,

> for the support and burial of the poor, for children who are without their par-
> ents and means of subsistence, for aged men who are confined to the house;

likewise, for shipwrecked sailors, and for any in the mines, on islands or in
prison. (*Apol.* 39.5–6)

Specific examples of the sharing of community resources in early Christian literature could fill a whole book this size.

Meeting the Needs of Imprisoned Confessors

One place where the values reflected in the above quotations found tangible
expression was in the dark musty cell block of a Roman prison. Actually, they
were hardly cell blocks. Some were more like holes in the ground. Prisoners in
the ancient world had no televisions, no libraries, and no weight rooms. Nor did
they have a cafeteria.

Roman elites did not use their tax dollars to feed their prisoners. They used
them to feed themselves. To survive in a Roman prison, a person had to depend on
his family to bring him the necessities of food and clothing, so he could stay alive
long enough to face his accusers. For the Christians the church was their family.
Believers who were imprisoned and awaiting execution because of their confession of Christ had their needs met by their brothers and sisters in Christ.

A persecution broke out in AD 250 in Rome that soon spread across the Mediterranean to Carthage in North Africa. The Roman pastor was imprisoned and
soon lost his life. Cyprian, the pastor at Carthage, wanted to die for his faith,
too. He got his wish a decade or so later, but for now the church needed Cyprian
alive, so they sent him into hiding. But a number of Carthaginian Christians were
thrown into prison. Cyprian wrote to his church leaders to make sure that the
church met the material needs of the imprisoned confessors:

> To the glorious confessors likewise you must devote special care. I know that
> very many of them have been supported by the devotion and charity of our
> *brethren.* Nevertheless there may be some in need of clothing or provisions;
> they should be supplied by whatever is necessary, as I also wrote to you previ-
> ously when they were still in prison. (*Ep.* 14.2.2, italics added)

Cyprian assumed the family context as the background for his admonition. Brothers are expected to take care of brothers who are in prison.

Tertullian's writings indicate that the imprisoned confessors had goods brought
to them both by the church as a whole and also by individual Christians who gave
out of their private means. Tertullian actually thought that for the Christian confessor life in prison is better than life outside:

Let us compare the life in the world with that in prison to see if the spirit does not gain more in prison than the flesh loses there. In fact, owing to the solicitude of the Church and the charity of the *brethren*, the flesh does not miss there what it ought to have, while, in addition, the spirit obtains what is always beneficial to the faith. (*Ad martyras* 2.6–7, italics added)

Brothers care for the needs of brothers. We find this theme appearing again and again in Christian literature when the church faced pagan persecution.

Explaining God's Fiery Discipline

The persecution of AD 250–51 under Emperor Decius highlights in yet another way the high priority assigned by North African church leaders to the sharing of resources with brothers in need. Early Christian literature reveals that Christians did more than just endure pagan persecution. They also tried to explain it.

The suffering under Decius had been quite horrific. Why did God let this happen to His church? How had the church gotten so far off base that God's people needed such a fiery purification? Questions like these are ultimately unanswerable. But it is our human nature to try to figure out how God works, especially during the dark times. Cyprian, on his part, thought that he had a wholly reasonable explanation for the Decian persecution.

As we pick up the story, we are now in AD 251, the pagan threat has subsided, and Cyprian is back in Carthage trying to pick up the pieces of his war-torn congregation. In one of his treatises, he gave a list of reasons the persecution happened in the first place. At the top of the list is the failure of wealthy church members to meet their family obligations to their brothers and sisters in Christ.

During the years leading up to the persecution, the rich members of the North African churches had apparently slacked off in their concern for their needy siblings in the faith. God "wished his family proved," Cyprian claimed, because instead of doing their Christian duty, the wealthy "wandered through the foreign provinces and sought the market places for gainful business; while their brethren in the church were starving, they wished to possess money in abundance" (*Laps.* 6).

The sharing of material resources in the Christian church must have been a pretty important priority for Cyprian to argue that its neglect led to the horrible deaths of numerous Christian saints. For Cyprian, the church is only pleasing to God when its members are engaged in the equitable distribution of the community's resources to impoverished brothers and sisters in the faith family. To ignore this priority is to inevitably open the church up to the fiery discipline of God.

Ransoming the Captives

We stay with Cyprian for a final look at sibling solidarity as it was practically expressed in the early church. Numidia was a rural area to the south of Carthage in North Africa. Numidian towns were always subject to raids by bandits, and the outlaws would often take more than money. They would kidnap people and sell them into slavery.

One day Cyprian received a troubling letter from a group of Christian leaders in Numidia. Bandit marauders had taken captive some Numidian Christians. The church needed ransom money to buy them back from the raiders.

Cyprian's reply deserves a series of extended quotations because it places Carthage's generous response to the Numidians' request squarely in the context of church family behavior. Here is the opening paragraph of Cyprian's letter:

> It has caused us the gravest anguish in our hearts, dearly beloved *brothers*, and indeed it brought tears to our eyes to read your letter which in your love and anxiety you wrote to us about our *brothers and sisters* who are now held in captive hands. Who would not be distressed at such a calamity or who would not reckon the distress which his *brother* feels as his own, remembering the words which the apostle Paul speaks: "If one member suffers, the other members also suffer with it; and if one member rejoices, the other members also rejoice with it" [1 Cor 12:26]. And in another place he asks: "Who is weak and I am not weak also?" [2 Cor 11:29]. We must now, accordingly, reckon the captivity of our *brethren* as our captivity also, and we must account the distress of those in peril as our own distress; for, I need hardly remind you, in our union we form but one body and, therefore, not just love but our religion ought to rouse and spur us on to *redeem brethren* who are our fellow members. (*Ep.* 62.1.1–2, italics added)

The emotional attachment Cyprian expressed toward the Numidian Christians, so characteristic of family relations in ancient Mediterranean society, clearly serves as the driving rhetorical image for the above passage. Cyprian felt a powerful sibling connection with his Numidian Christian brethren.

This should remind us of the affective solidarity that characterized relations among the members of Paul's congregations two centuries earlier. It is not surprising to find that brotherly affection swiftly gave rise to sacrificial action. Cyprian continues,

> And so [our brothers] all forthwith contributed most willingly generous financial aid for their *brothers*. Being of such robust faith, they are ever ready to do

the works of God; but on this occasion they were more than usually fired to
perform such works of mercy by their awareness of these distressing circumstances. (*Ep.* 62.3.1, italics added)

Cyprian proceeds to elaborate upon the specifics of the aid that the Carthaginian
Christians sent to their Numidian brothers:

> Accordingly, we are sending in cash one hundred thousand sesterces which
> have been collected from the contributions of the clergy and the laity who
> reside here with us in the church over which, by God's favor, we have charge.
> This is for you to distribute with your wonted diligence. Our fervent wish is
> indeed that nothing similar should happen in the future and that our *brothers*,
> under the protection of the Lord's majesty, may be kept safe from all such per-
> ils. If, however, in order to test and examine the faith and charity in our hearts,
> anything of the kind should befall you, do not hesitate to write word of it to
> us; you can be fully confident and assured that whilst our church and all of the
> *brethren* here do pray that this should never occur again, yet, if it does, they
> will willingly provide generous assistance. (*Ep.* 62.3.2–62.4.1, italics added)

The relative value of ancient currency is difficult to calculate. But to put the
amount of "one hundred thousand sesterces" in some perspective, it might help to
know that a Roman foot-soldier was paid 900 sesterces for a whole year of service
under Augustus, two centuries earlier.

As the letter continues Cyprian appended a list of the "brothers and sisters"
who participated in the collection so that the Numidians can remember them in
their prayers. He concluded by writing, "We wish that you, dearly beloved *brothers*, may ever fare well in the Lord and be mindful of us" (*Ep.* 62.4.2, italics
added).

What we have seen in the above examples accords perfectly with evidence
cited from the New Testament in previous chapters. Christian communities in
urban and rural areas throughout the Roman Empire tangibly lived out the surrogate family model by sharing their material resources with brothers and sisters
in need.

Family Loyalty

The first followers of Jesus conceived of loyalty to God primarily in terms
of loyalty to God's group. To be committed to God was to be committed to His
family. The inevitable result was that Christians were torn between loyalty to
God's family and loyalty to the natural family. The conflict surfaces often in early

Christian literature, where we find numerous warnings about the spiritual dangers of excessive attachment to one's natural family.

The persecutions forced Christians in various regions of the empire to choose between loyalty to God's family and loyalty to their families of origin. Pagans begged family members who had converted to Christ to denounce their allegiance to the gospel and to God's people in the face of persecution. A choice had to be made.

The confessing Christians understood the challenges that state persecution presented precisely in terms of family loyalty. Here is an excerpt from a letter in which four imprisoned church leaders in Rome described to Cyprian their impending martyrdom:

> To this battle the Lord rouses us with the trumpet call of His Gospel, in these words: "He who loves his father or his mother more than Me is not worthy of Me . . . and brother will deliver up brother to death and father [will deliver up his] son. . . ." (*Ep.* 31.4)

The confessors thus traced back to the teachings of Jesus their conviction that the decision to refuse to worship the pagan gods is closely tied into the issue of family loyalty.

Cyprian himself drew on the anti-family sayings of Jesus in order to encourage confessors from the church at Thibaris, a town in North Africa:

> There is no man who leaves home and land, family and brethren, wife and children for the sake of the kingdom of God who shall not receive seven times more in this present time, and in the world to come life everlasting. (58.2.3; see Luke 18:29–30)

The Christians from Thibaris must remain true to their confession, for they belong to an alternative family with an inheritance which, when received in full, will more than compensate for present sacrifices of family and property. Cyprian thus effectively utilizes the loyalty theme in order to encourage his fellow-Christians to remain committed to their family of faith in the midst of persecution.

Perpetua Trades One Family for Another

Conflicts surrounding family loyalty had already surfaced some fifty years earlier in the North African church, in the pilgrimage of a young mother named Perpetua. In AD 202, Perpetua, who was probably in her late teens or early twenties, suffered martyrdom for her faith in Jesus. Perpetua wrote an intimate and personal diary as she sat in prison during the weeks leading up to her death. The diary offers a revealing glimpse into the conflicts that arose between Christians and their pagan families. There was an increasing estrangement between Perpetua and her earthly father as the story unfolds.

Perpetua was in prison charged with a capital offense because of her profession of faith in Christ. Her pagan father understandably wanted her to recant and return to her family. In her diary Perpetua stated, "While we were still under house arrest my father out of love for me was trying to persuade me and shake my resolution" (*Passion of Perpetua*, 3.1).

Perpetua stood her ground, refused to recant, and the conflict of loyalties was intensified:

> At this my father was so angered by the word "Christian" that he moved
> towards me as though he would pluck my eyes out. But he left it at that and
> departed, vanquished along with his diabolical arguments. For a few days after-
> ward I gave thanks to the Lord that I was separated from my father, and I was
> comforted by his absence. (ibid., 3.3)

Several days later Perpetua was scheduled for a hearing, and her father again attempted to persuade her to deny her Christian faith. Initially, he addressed Perpetua as "Daughter," pleading with her to opt for loyalty to her family of origin:

> Have pity on my grey head—have pity on me your father, if I deserve to be
> called your father, if I have favored you above all your brothers, if I have raised
> you to reach this prime of your life. Do not abandon me to be the reproach of
> men. Think of your brothers, think of your mother and your aunt, think of your
> child, who will not be able to live once you are gone. Give up your pride! You
> will destroy all of us! None of us will ever be able to speak freely again if any-
> thing happens to you. (ibid., 5.2–4)

But Perpetua remained unmoved and claimed that soon her father "no longer addressed me as his daughter but as a woman" (ibid., 5.5). Perpetua's father finally realized that his daughter was no longer a member of her natural family. She had instead made an irrevocable commitment to the family of God; she was no longer his "daughter."

A few more interactions between Perpetua and her father occur in the ensuing narrative. The relationship finally broke down completely in a particularly poignant scene several weeks before Perpetua was martyred. During her imprisonment, Perpetua's father had been in the practice of allowing the church deacons—brothers in Perpetua's new family—to carry her baby to her prison cell on a daily basis so that Perpetua could hold and nurse her son. Now, near the end of the story, her father refused to hand Perpetua's baby over to the deacons, and the family was irrevocably divided.

Before we leave the narrative of Perpetua's diary, I want to draw your attention to one more aspect of her story. Family loyalty is not at the forefront here, but the information provided in this short excerpt tells us a lot about the centrality of the church family model in the behavioral ethos of the imprisoned confessors.

Perpetua was not the only one in prison. Felicitas, her slave from her natural family, was also a Christian confessor awaiting martyrdom. Felicitas was nine months pregnant when the story began, and as the narrative unfolds Felicitas gave birth to a daughter in prison. Because Perpetua had acquired Felicitas as her personal slave long before Perpetua was married, Felicitas technically belonged to the patriarch of Perpetua's family, her father. Upon the death of Perpetua and Felicitas, the slave's infant daughter would therefore have been the legal property of Perpetua's father. So it is remarkably striking that "one of the [Christian] sisters brought [Felicitas' newborn child] up as her own daughter" (ibid., 15.7).

We have now seen that two central Mediterranean family values that characterized the communities of Jesus and Paul—the sharing of material possessions and uncompromising family loyalty—also found tangible expression in the Christian churches of the second and third centuries. We conclude the chapter with two final examples of church family behavior, one from the pen of a pagan detractor, the other written by a godly insider.

The View from the Bleachers

In AD 165, a self-proclaimed philosopher named Peregrinus committed suicide in the presence of hundreds of onlookers by throwing himself on the flames at the Olympic Games. Peregrinus was a wandering soul who had bounced from one belief system to another trying to find himself. At one point in his spiritual pilgrimage he associated himself with a Christian community in Palestine. Peregrinus was initially sincere in his commitment to Jesus, and he became a recognized Christian leader in the area. He even suffered imprisonment for his activities as a follower of Jesus.

But after his release Peregrinus had a falling out with the Christians and went to Egypt where he studied under a Greek philosopher named Agathobulus. A lifestyle of itinerant philosophizing characterized the rest of Peregrinus's life, leading him through Italy and then on to Greece where he publicly took his life in AD 165.

Among those present at the Olympic Games that year was a pagan intellectual named Lucian. Lucian stood there in the crowd witnessing first hand Peregrinus's demise. He was not impressed. Nor did the reaction of the crowds to the sensational event set well with Lucian. Like several rock stars who have committed suicide in our own time, Peregrinus became something of a cult hero to a number of those who watched the fiery spectacle.

Such a response on the part of the public incensed Lucian, who considered himself to be a respectable representative of the philosophical academy. Perhaps Lucian was just a bit jealous of Peregrinus's postmortem notoriety. Whatever the case, Lucian was so turned off by all the hoopla resulting from the suicide that he wrote a whole treatise debunking Peregrinus both as a self-proclaimed philosopher and as a sensationalistic martyr.

In the course of his castigation of Peregrinus, Lucian discusses Peregrinus's fling with Christianity. Peregrinus was not the only object of Lucian's derision. Lucian also ridiculed the Palestinian Christians who were gullible enough to embrace Peregrinus in the first place. Most importantly, in the course of his narrative, Lucian provides some extremely valuable information about how an educated second-century pagan outsider viewed the Christian church.

Lucian utterly disdained the Christian movement. But he could not deny that the church functioned as a surrogate Mediterranean family. Here is Lucian's revealing description of the treatment Peregrinus received at the hands of the Palestinian Christians:

> When [Peregrinus] had been imprisoned, the Christians, regarding the incident as a calamity, left nothing undone in the effort to rescue him. . . . not in any casual way but with assiduity; and from the very break of day aged widows and orphan children could be seen waiting near the prison, while their officials even slept inside with him after bribing the guards. Then elaborate meals were brought in, and sacred books of theirs were read aloud, and excellent Peregrinus—for he still went by that name—was called by them "the new Socrates." (Lucian, *The Passing of Peregrinus,* 12)

Lucian here writes specifically about Peregrinus's experience. The Christians cared for Peregrinus like a fellow-member of a Mediterranean family.

Lucian then broadens his account to include a description of Christian practices in general. Because Lucian traveled widely in the East, he was familiar with Christian activities in Palestine, Asia, and Egypt. His background—along with his obvious lack of sympathy for the Christian movement—makes Lucian a reliable witness to early Christian social solidarity:

Indeed, people came even from the cities of Asia, sent by the Christians at their common expense, to succor and defend and encourage the hero. They show incredible speed whenever any such public action is taken; for in no time they lavish their all. . . . their first lawgiver [Jesus] persuaded them that they are all *brothers of one another* after they have transgressed once for all by denying the Greek gods and by worshipping that crucified sophist himself and living under his laws. *Therefore* they despise all things indiscriminately and consider them *common property*. (ibid., 13, italics added)

For Lucian, the favor extended to Peregrinus is hardly unique. This is how Christians acted toward one another throughout the empire.

This quote reveals why Lucian believed the Christians acted like this. Consider carefully the logic of Lucian's thought in the above passage. It goes something like this:

1. Jesus persuaded His followers that "they are all brothers of one another."
2. Brothers and sisters share material goods with another. This is not explicitly stated but is clearly understood by Lucian and his readers, who live in a society in which sibling solidarity is the norm.
3. "Therefore [the Christians] despise all things indiscriminately and consider them common property."

Lucian drew attention to the sibling mind-set among the Christians. He traced such a conception back to Jesus of Nazareth, and then he identified the surrogate sibling relationship as the logical explanation of the Christian practice of sharing material resources. Christians meet one another's physical needs because "they are all brothers of one another." This much was obvious even to a cynical unbeliever.

Lucian's view of Christianity is worth comparing to what a non-Christian intellectual in modern America might say about the church today. Like Lucian, our contemporary skeptic would probably dismiss Christianity as a faith for the gullible. But would he, like Lucian, find Christians taking the church family model so seriously that they "lavish their all" on their "brothers"?

Lucian was hardly enamored by the sibling solidarity he observed among Christians throughout the second-century Roman Empire. But he could not deny it. For the early Christians, the church was a family—in word and in deed. Even a pagan philosopher like Lucian had to acknowledge it.

Death and Compassion in the Alexandrian Church Family

I saved for last my favorite passage from the church fathers. Around AD 260, a devastating plague afflicted the great city of Alexandria. People were dying right and left, and the church family suffered some devastating losses. The response of the local church to the plague constitutes one of the most powerful examples of Christian brotherhood in the annals of church history.

Here is a section of a letter written by Dionysius, the overseer of the Christian community in the city:

> The most, at all events, of our *brethren* in their *exceeding love and affection* for
> the brotherhood were unsparing of themselves and clave to one another, visiting
> the sick without a thought as to the danger, assiduously ministering to them,
> tending them in Christ, and so most gladly departed this life along with them;
> being infected with the disease from others, drawing upon themselves the sick-
> ness from their neighbors, and willingly taking over their pains. . . . In this man-
> ner the best at any rate of our *brethren* departed this life, certain presbyters and
> deacons and some of the laity. . . . So, too, the bodies of the saints they would
> take up in their open hands to their bosom, closing their eyes and shutting their
> mouths, carrying them on their shoulders and laying them out; they would cling
> to them, embrace them, bathe and adorn them with their burial clothes, and
> after a little while receive the same services themselves, for those that were left
> behind were ever following those that went before. But the conduct of the hea-
> then was the exact opposite. Even those who were in the first stages of the dis-
> ease they thrust away, and fled from their dearest. They would even cast them
> in the roads half-dead, and treat the unburied corpses as vile refuse. (Eusebius,
> *Historia ecclesiastica* 7.22, italics added)

Dionysius began his description with the use of family words: "brethren," "the brotherhood." He closed with a pointed contrast, comparing the behavior of his Alexandrian Christians with behavior among the natural families of pagans in the surrounding community (they "fled from their dearest").

Dionysius clearly viewed his church community as a well-functioning Medi-terranean kinship group, and he was proud that they were living up to their fam-ily ideals, even at the cost of their very lives. As Tertullian had said some years earlier:

> The practice of such a special love brands us in the eyes of some. "See," they
> say, "how they love one another and how ready they are to die for each other."
> (*Apol.* 39.5–7)

Tertullian, Dionysius, and the Alexandrian Christians were only following in the footsteps of their Master: "This is how we have come to know love: He laid down His life for us. We should also lay down our lives for our brothers" (1 John 3:16).

Conclusion

Our journey to the past is now complete. The evidence is conclusive, and the voices are unanimous. For Jesus, Paul, and early church leaders throughout the Roman Empire, the preeminent social model that defined the Christian church was the strong-group Mediterranean family.

God was the Father of the community. Christians were brothers and sisters. The group came first over the aspirations and desires of the individual. Family values—ranging from intense emotional attachment to the sharing of material goods and to uncompromising family loyalty—determined the relational ethos of Christian behavior.

It remains for us now to return to the twenty-first century in order to consider our response to Jesus' vision for authentic Christian community, a vision that in no small way prophetically challenges the radically individualistic version of the Christian faith that so indelibly marks the social landscape of our churches in America today.

Chapter Six

SALVATION AS A COMMUNITY-CREATING EVENT

*You cannot have God for your Father unless you
have the church for your Mother.*

(Cyprian of Carthage,
On the Unity of the Church, 3.1.214)

A friend and mentor unknowingly ignited the flame that led to the writing of this book in a comment he made to me more than a decade ago. Scott Bartchy, who guided me through my doctoral program at UCLA, stopped by my church office one day to connect for a lunch appointment. As he waited in the reception area, Scott picked up a copy of our congregation's "What We Believe" brochure. As I soon discovered, he was not particularly enamored with what he read. In fact, shortly after I emerged from my office, Scott proceeded to take issue with me over our statement of faith.

Oceanside Christian Fellowship is a relatively generic conservative evangelical church. No surprises or theological bombshells jump off the pages of our doctrinal statement. The document that troubled Scott contained pretty standard stuff for a congregation belonging to the Evangelical Free Church of America—statements about the Trinity, the deity of Christ, salvation by faith alone, the kind of simple yet profound summaries of orthodox Christianity that have served the Protestant church as its pillars of theological truth for centuries.

All this made Scott's stinging evaluation of the document even more surprising—until I realized what he was trying to say. Scott made it clear to me that he had no problem at all with what we had put *in* our "What We Believe" brochure. What bothered him was what we had left *out*. He put it something like this: "Joe, a person could read through your statement of faith and conclude that Christianity, as your church teaches it and practices it, has everything to do with how an individual relates to God and absolutely nothing to do with how people relate to one another."

That is a rather profound observation. Scott was right. Our statement of faith contains all the classic cardinal points of doctrine. But none of the twelve paragraphs has anything to say about how people relate to one another in the family of God.

Scott knew that this did not accurately reflect the everyday life of our church family, where we constantly challenge our people to relate to one another in a healthy and nurturing way. To be fair, Scott proceeded to qualify his comments by acknowledging the strong emphasis on interpersonal relations which, I assured him, characterized our congregation. But he remained troubled by the fact that our congregation's most important document (other than the Bible) makes no mention whatsoever of the relational mandate that runs throughout the Scriptures.

I am troubled as well. Our church's doctrinal statement wholly ignores God's design for human relationships, a topic that occupies a great deal of the biblical record. If you request a copy of your own church's statement of faith, you will likely discover that it contains only part of the truth too.

God's "doctrinal statement" has a more balanced perspective. The Bible consistently addresses both dimensions of the relationships in our lives. For example, in the Ten Commandments the first four deal with how we relate to God and the other six speak about our relationships with others.

The same is the case throughout the Scriptures. The apostle Paul generally began his New Testament letters with a discussion of what we might label the vertical dynamic: how humanity relates to God and God to us. Almost invariably, though, the second half of Paul's letters—usually the longer "half"—deals with the horizontal dynamic: how people are to relate to one another in the community of God's family.

There is a good reason why the vertical aspect of our faith appears first in the text in both the Ten Commandments and Paul's letters. Our relationship with God as individuals serves as the indispensable foundation for the community we share with our fellow believers. Unfortunately, however, as Scott insightfully noted, the latter fails to get the attention it deserves when we get around to summarizing what we believe in our statements of faith.

In this chapter my goal is to reunite the vertical and horizontal dimensions of our relational lives in connection with a single aspect of Christian theology, namely, soteriology, the doctrine of salvation. I pay particularly close attention to the way in which evangelicals have traditionally framed the relationship between salvation and the Christian community. As you will see, we have essentially separated the two, both in our theological reflection on these issues and in the way we communicate the gospel.

I will suggest that such an understanding is less than biblical and that it is costing us dearly in our churches in America today. We need to reconsider our approach to evangelism and to rethink the very content of the gospel we proclaim. The biblical model of the Christian church as a strong-group family offers a great tool to help us refine the doctrine of salvation to better accord with the beliefs and practices of the New Testament church.

Salvation to Community

I am one of those who had a rather dramatic conversion experience. I remember it like it was yesterday. I was 22 years of age when my whole world caved in emotionally. I was experiencing what psychologists call an anxiety reaction, and I was desperate enough to try just about anything in order to get my feet back on the ground again. First, I disentangled myself from the drug culture. Then I put the rest of my life on hold while I began a year-long quest for God.

Most of that year was spent dabbling in Eastern religion. But in December of 1975 my search finally led me to Christ. I was fortunate enough at the time to play in a rock band with a guitarist who was a highly committed Christian. I remember spending many late nights after rehearsal talking to Gary about Jesus. Gary assured me that God had a wonderful plan for my life. I just needed to acknowledge that I was a sinner and trust in Jesus' death and resurrection in order to be saved. Gary's goal was to bring me to the point where I was ready to pray "the sinner's prayer." Then I would have a personal relationship with God. Then I would be saved.

Much to Gary's delight—and much more to mine!—I finally prayed the prayer. And I was saved. But not quite in that order. I was actually converted to Christ while reading the Gospel of Matthew on the beach one winter's day near my home in southern California. Then, on the way to a gig our band was playing that evening, I told Gary what had happened to me. I said I knew that Jesus was the truth. Gary immediately pulled the car to the side of the road and led me through the sinner's prayer. This is how my personal relationship with God began.

I have been grateful to Gary ever since then for his boldness and willingness to share Christ with me. But as I recall the discussions I had with Gary, it is now quite apparent to me that I was exposed to only a portion of the truth concerning the biblical picture of salvation. I am not pointing the finger at Gary. Gary was a well-trained Christian who could articulate his faith with the best of them. He knew how to explain with great clarity the plan of salvation—that is, the plan of salvation as it has been formulated in modern evangelicalism.

Gary's problem—like yours and mine—was that Gary had been socialized into an American Christian paradigm that understands salvation to have everything to do with how the individual relates to God and nothing to do with how we relate to one another. This gospel addresses solely the issue of one's personal relationship with God. To become a Christian is to enter into a relationship with a new Father, with little or no emphasis on our relationship with a new set of brothers and sisters. In our typical gospel presentations, we introduce God's family only as a sort of utilitarian afterthought—church is there to help us grow in our newfound faith in Christ.

The Anomaly of an Unchurched Christian

Church was unquestionably no afterthought for the early Christians. A comparison of first-century values to the convictions and behaviors characteristic of modern evangelicalism proves quite revealing. Due to the individualistic tendencies of our culture, and the correspondingly loose connection in our thinking between soteriology and ecclesiology, it is not uncommon to encounter persons who claim to be followers of Jesus but who remain unconnected to a local faith community.

In contrast, we do not find an unchurched Christian in the New Testament.[1] Nor do we find one in the ensuing generations of early church history. It is not hard to see why this is the case in light of what happens from God's perspective when we come to Christ. Paul and the other New Testament writers made it quite clear that getting saved and becoming a member of the people of God are inseparable, simultaneous events: "For we were all baptized by one Spirit into one body—whether Jews or Greeks, whether slaves or free—and we were all made to drink of one Spirit" (1 Cor 12:13).

---

[1] The thief on the cross (Luke 23:42–43) and the Ethiopian eunuch (Acts 8:26–40) might be cited as exceptions. But we should adopt neither as a paradigm for explaining the relationship between salvation and church involvement, since the experiences of these two men are exceptional and not normative. Those New Testament converts whose postconversion activities can be documented invariably find themselves deeply embedded in a local Christian community.

In the New Testament era a person was not saved for the sole purpose of enjoying a personal relationship with God. Indeed, the phrase "personal relationship with God" is found nowhere in the Bible. According to the New Testament, a person is saved *to community.* Salvation includes membership in God's group. We are saved "into one body," as the above passage from 1 Corinthians indicates. Or, to draw on the family metaphor that has occupied our attention throughout this book, when we get a new Father we also get a new set of brothers and sisters. In Scripture salvation is a community-creating event. As Cyprian of Carthage expressed it using yet another pair of family metaphors, "You cannot have God for your Father unless you have the church for your Mother."

This is only reasonable in view of what we learned in chapter 3 about Jesus and the community of followers He established. In the Gospels we often find Jesus challenging people to leave their families and follow Him. But following Jesus in the first century could never be reduced to a subjective, individual experience like a "personal relationship with God." In the collectivist mind-set of antiquity, following an individual had a distinctly social dimension—it meant joining his group. For Jesus' disciples this meant loosening the bonds of loyalty to one's natural family in order to unite with God's eternal family.

Paul and others in the early church accurately replicated Jesus' teachings about God's group when they shared the gospel in the eastern Roman Empire. To follow Jesus meant to join Jesus' community. The thought that one could somehow acquire a "personal relationship with God" outside the faith family—and remain an "unchurched Christian"—was simply inconceivable to those whose lives had been defined from birth by the groups to which they belonged. To become a Christian was to change groups, plain and simple.

Jesus as Personal Savior

I mentioned above that the phrase "personal relationship with God" never occurs in the Bible. Neither does the phrase "personal Savior." In and of themselves these omissions are not particularly determinative. A number of important expressions for biblical truths—the word "Trinity" comes immediately to mind—do not appear in Scripture either. But it is instructive to note that of the 23 times in the New Testament that "savior" is used in conjunction with some person or group being saved, only once does it refer to the Savior of an individual (Luke 1:47). Elsewhere the word refers to Jesus as Savior of a group of persons or a collective entity, for example, "Christ our Savior" (Titus 3:6) or "Savior of the world" (John 4:42). And when Paul used a first-person possessive pronoun with the word

"Lord," he chose the plural 53 times ("our Lord") and the singular only once ("my Lord"). The point here is that the New Testament focus, as we would expect of a collection of strong-group documents, is upon Jesus as Lord and Savior of a group—not only of the individual.

This strong-group perspective runs throughout both the Old and New Testaments. It has been God's design from the beginning. The one-sided emphasis in our churches on Jesus as "personal Savior" is a regrettable example of Western individualism importing its own socially constructed perspective on reality into the biblical text. Our individualistic culture encourages us to assume that God's main goal in the history of humanity consists of getting individual people saved. Salvation is all about what God has done for *me* as an individual.

I suggest instead that we view God's work in human history as primarily group-oriented. S. Grenz put it like this: "According to the Bible, God's ultimate desire is to create from all nations a reconciled people living within a renewed creation and enjoying the presence of the Triune God. This biblical vision of 'community' is the goal of history."[2]

I would only want to qualify Grenz's assertion by observing that "this biblical vision of 'community'" as "the goal of history" is not an end in itself. Rather, God's plan for His people ultimately serves a much greater and more encompassing aim—that through His people our great God and Savior would fully and finally receive the glory that is His due. As Peter expressed it: "you are . . . 'a people for His possession, so that you may proclaim the praises' of the One who called you out of darkness into His marvelous light" (1 Pet 2:9).

Putting It All Together

Now hear me well on this. I am not dispensing with personal salvation. God's Holy Spirit lives in His church. An individual human being, sinful and separated from God, cannot be a part of a community of believers inhabited by the pure Holy Spirit of God. One who has not trusted in Christ can enjoy neither a (vertical) relationship with the Father nor (horizontal) relationships with others in a family of surrogate siblings. Each individual must therefore be saved *to the family of God* by an act of personal repentance and faith in the atoning work of Jesus. But notice the italics in the previous sentence. We are not saved only to enjoy a personal relationship with God. We are saved to community. We are saved to God's group.

---

[2] S. Grenz, *Created for Community: Connecting Christian Belief with Christian Living* (Grand Rapids: Baker, 1996), 38.

A couple of diagrams should prove useful. The first diagram represents the view of salvation that has traditionally characterized modern evangelicalism. It should be quite familiar to you:

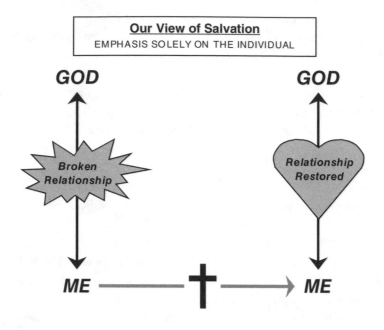

This model looks exclusively at the effect of salvation upon my individual relationship with God. Before trusting in Christ, I was at enmity with God. Through the cross, I have been restored to a right relationship with my Creator.

As far as it goes, the diagram is certainly biblical, but like our doctrinal statements it tells only part of the truth. It may very well be the most important part, but it remains incomplete. For nothing whatsoever is said or even implied in the model about the impact of the cross of Christ upon our relationships with our fellow human beings. The emphasis is solely on the individual.

The diagram on the next page illustrates the more complete biblical perspective. Here the emphasis is placed not on the individual but on the community—God's family. I must still do business with God as an individual. I must come to terms with Christ's work on the cross. But note carefully that where salvation is concerned, the cross of Christ is the doorway to the community of faith. God's goal is not simply to usher me into a personal relationship with Him. God's goal is to

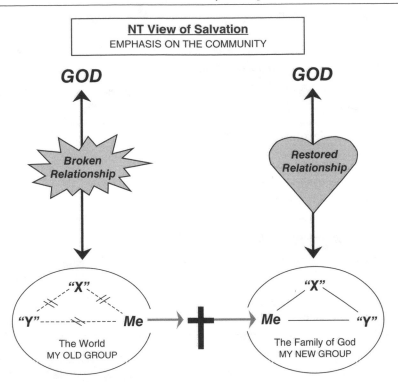

transfer me from one group to another, from "the world" to "the family of God" (see on Acts 2 below). *From the dominion of darkness to the Kingdom of His dear Son Col 1:13*

A look inside the circles reveals that the cross restores me to a right relationship with God *and* to a right relationship with others ("x" and "y" on the diagram). Here is an aspect of salvation that is rather foreign to American evangelicalism but crucial to biblical soteriology. Apart from Christ, I have no solid basis on which to build healthy relationships with my fellow human beings. But as a child in God's family I belong to a group where relational integrity and wholeness are to be the norm. Salvation thus has tremendous sociological as well as theological ramifications.

Salvation and Community in the Bible

Both the Old and New Testaments attest to the above reality. Genesis and Exodus document the birth of the nation of Israel. The earliest concentrated usage of salvation terminology in the Hebrew Scriptures occurs in the context of Israel's deliverance from Egypt by the mighty hand of God. This deliverance from slavery is consistently associated in the Old Testament narratives with the establishment of God's people, the nation of Israel. The descendents of Abraham were saved to community.

Salvation to Community in the Old Testament

Here are just two of many Old Testament passages where salvation is associated with Israel's exodus from Egypt:

> That day the LORD saved Israel from the power of the Egyptians, and Israel saw the Egyptians dead on the seashore. (Exod 14:30)

> The LORD is my strength and my song;
> He has become my salvation.
> This is my God, and I will praise Him,
> my father's God, and I will exalt Him. (Exod 15:2)

This close association of salvation terminology with the Israelites' escape from the bonds of slavery is not unique to the early narratives in Exodus and Deuteronomy. The connection surfaces throughout the Old Testament. Salvation for the Israelites was quintessentially deliverance from Egyptian bondage.

But the exodus was to be more than simply deliverance *from* slavery. God also intended the Israelites' exodus experience to function as a deliverance *to* community. This is precisely what happened at Mount Sinai. The exodus is identified as the specific point in history at which God established Israel as His group:

> I will take you as My people, and I will be your God. You will know that I am Yahweh your God, who delivered you from the forced labor of the Egyptians. (Exod 6:7)

> But the LORD selected you and brought you out of Egypt's iron furnace to be a people for His inheritance, as you are today. (Deut 4:20)

Notice what is happening here. Each of the passages quoted above combines the two themes of the Israelites deliverance from Egypt and the birth of the nation Israel. The historical event that the Israelites most dearly associated with the idea of salvation—deliverance from Egypt—was the very act that established them as the people of God.

What this means is that salvation in the Old Testament is a community-creating event. God saved the Israelites not just so they could relate to Him as individuals but, most importantly, "to be the people of his inheritance" (Deut 4:20). God saved the Israelites to community.

Salvation to Community in the New Testament

Acts 2. In Acts 2, Peter proclaims Jesus as Messiah to a multitude of Jews gathered in Jerusalem for Pentecost. We would do well to pay close attention to Luke's narrative because this first Christian sermon can serve as an instructive blueprint for all subsequent preaching of the gospel:

> When they heard this, they were pierced to the heart and said to Peter and the rest of the apostles: "Brothers, what must we do?"
>
> "Repent," Peter said to them, "and be baptized, **each of you**, in the name of Jesus the Messiah **for the forgiveness of your sins**, and you will receive the gift of the Holy Spirit. For the promise is for you and for your children, and for all who are far off, as many as the Lord our God will call." And with many other words he testified and strongly urged them, saying, *"Be saved from this corrupt generation."* So those who accepted his message were baptized, and that day *about 3,000 people were added to them.* (Acts 2:37–41, emphasis added)

The key words are highlighted. The boldface text shows that personal repentance was the indispensable prerequisite to being involved with God's program. Each person must respond individually to the claims of Christ. This is at the heart of Peter's message.

But notice the result of this individual repentance as given in italics in vv. 40–41. We read nothing of a personal relationship with God that results from conversion. This does not exclude the reality of relating to God at the individual level. It just shows us that Peter and Luke are concerned to highlight another, more immediately relevant (for them) aspect of salvation. The italicized text shows that for early Christianity individual salvation was understood as deliverance from one group to another—from "this corrupt generation" to the family of God (identified as "them" in the above passage).

Peter's sermon establishes a principle that can be traced through the New Testament and into the first three centuries of early church history. People are saved to community. To be sure, our sins must be forgiven or we cannot enter a community inhabited by the Spirit of the living God. But God's overarching goal since Pentecost (as was also the case in the Old Testament) is the creation of His group. And under the new covenant, God's group is His church—a society of surrogate siblings whose interpersonal relationships are to be characterized by all the family attributes encountered in the previous chapters of this book.

The above interpretation of Peter's sermon is decidedly confirmed by Luke's Spirit-inspired commentary in the ensuing verses in Acts 2. What excited Luke was not the fact that the three thousand converts could now experience personal relationships with God at the individual level. What set Luke's heart aflame was the community that resulted from Peter's gospel presentation. Here are the next four verses:

> And they devoted themselves to the apostles' teaching, to fellowship, to the breaking of bread, and to prayers.
>
> Then fear came over everyone, and many wonders and signs were being performed through the apostles. Now all the believers were together and had everything in common. So they sold their possessions and property and distributed the proceeds to all, as anyone had a need. (Acts 2:42–45)

Here we have the first church in Jerusalem living together like family.

The miracle of deliverance from Egypt was the establishment of God's group, Israel. The miracle of Pentecost was the reestablishment of God's group as a surrogate family that would soon include all the nations. Salvation, at Sinai and at Pentecost, was a community-creating event.

The writings of Paul. I have already cited 1 Cor 12:13 (see p. 122) a text that clearly demonstrates the close connection between salvation and membership in God's group. Ephesians 2:14–18 is another passage demonstrating that more is involved in salvation than reconciliation between the individual and God:

> For He is our peace, who made both groups one and tore down the dividing wall of hostility. In His flesh, He did away with the law of the commandments in regulations, so that He might create in Himself one new man from the two, resulting in peace. He did this so that He might reconcile both to God in one body through the cross and put the hostility to death by it. When Christ came, He proclaimed the good news of peace to you who were far away and peace to those who were near. For through Him we both have access by one Spirit to the Father.

This passage describes the uniting of Jew and Gentile into one body, the church. From the mid-second century BC onward, Jews and Gentiles were at one another's throats to the point of bloodshed in Greco-Roman cities throughout the eastern Mediterranean. The fighting at times became so vicious that Roman magistrates had to intervene and enforce the peace. Paul insists that the cross of Christ has put an end to such "hostility" once and for all.

Just as Acts 2, Ephesians emphasizes both the vertical aspect of the cross (individuals reconciled to God) and the horizontal aspect of the cross (people—in this case Jews and Gentiles—reconciled to one another). God's purpose in the death of Jesus was "to create in Himself one new man." The phrase "one new man" is, of course, a collective expression referring to the church. Again, salvation is a community-creating event.

Look carefully now at the verses that follow Paul's description of what happened at the cross:

> So then you are no longer foreigners and strangers, but fellow citizens with the saints, and members of God's household, built on the foundation of the apostles and prophets, with Christ Jesus Himself as the cornerstone. The whole building is being fitted together in Him and is growing into a holy sanctuary in the Lord, in whom you also are being built together for God's dwelling in the Spirit. (Eph 2:19–22)

The expression at the beginning of v. 19 is significant: "So then." It is the signal that what Paul is about to say sums up everything in the immediately preceding context. Yet Paul's summary here says nothing about the individual relationships with God that resulted when all these Jews and Gentiles got saved (the vertical dimension).

It is certainly not the case that Paul fails to appreciate the vertical aspect of salvation. After all, he ended the previous section with the assertion that through Jesus "we both have access by one Spirit to the Father" (v. 18). Paul highly valued the individual dimension of the work of Christ. But that is not what gets him excited in the present context. Instead, Paul was compelled by the Spirit of God to zero in on the sociological ramifications of the cross. We are now, to put it into Paul's words, "members of God's household." As Paul maintains in another of his letters, Jesus "gave Himself for us to redeem us from all lawlessness and to cleanse for Himself a special people, eager to do good works" (Titus 2:14). The death of Jesus is a community-creating event.

Maintaining a Healthy Balance

I have taught the above model of salvation in various church and seminary settings for more than a decade now. At about this point in the presentation I often begin to sense my students' discomfort. "Joe," they will say, "what about all the verses in the Bible that talk about the individual's relationship with God?" The parable of the lost sheep is often cited as a challenge to my understanding of the doctrine of salvation:

> "What man among you, who has 100 sheep and loses one of them, does not leave the 99 in the open field and go after the lost one until he finds it? When

he has found it, he joyfully puts it on his shoulders, and coming home, he calls his friends and neighbors together, saying to them, 'Rejoice with me, because I have found my lost sheep!' I tell you, in the same way, there will be more joy in heaven over one sinner who repents than over 99 righteous people who don't need repentance." (Luke 15:4–7)

"There, do you see that, Joe? God cares dearly about the individual!"

Of course He does. And it is certainly the case that we become regenerated one person at a time. After we are saved to God's group, moreover, we continue to relate to God as His individual children. We approach Him directly, as individuals, without the mediation of any ecclesiastical institution or priest—except, of course, for our great high priest Jesus Christ, who intercedes on our behalf. As children of a heavenly Father, we relate to God in an intimate and personal way. But preoccupation with individual spirituality remains an incomplete and inadequate picture of the Christian life. This is the point in the present connection.

It may help at this juncture briefly to adopt a more traditional theological approach to the issue. As I have emphasized above, there is both a vertical and a horizontal dimension to our position in Christ. We make much in our doctrinal statements and our preaching of the vertical aspect of salvation: the fact that we are justified—declared righteous and put into a right relationship with God—when we are saved. And we encourage new believers (just as we encourage one another) to live out of our position in Christ, that is, to increasingly actualize the positional reality of our justification in our daily lives, as we are gradually—often painfully—conformed to the image of Christ in the sanctification process.

But something else happens when we are saved, which is just as real in God's eyes, on God's positional ledger sheet, so to speak, as our justification, something I like to call our "familification." Just as we are *justified* with respect to God the Father upon salvation, so also we are *familified* with respect to our brothers and sisters in Christ. And this familification is no less a positional reality than our justification.

It would follow from this that just as we need to increasingly actualize the positional reality of our *justification* in the spiritual formation process, so also should we long to increasingly actualize the positional reality of our *familification*, as we grow into the image and likeness of Christ. Indeed, as we have seen throughout our discussion, we simply cannot separate the two. To be sold out to God (and thereby actualize our *justification*) is to be sold out to God's group (and thereby actualize our *familification*). We need to cultivate both the vertical and the horizontal dimensions of what happened to us at salvation, as we seek to mature in the Lord.

The purpose of this book is not to dismiss the familiar truths of orthodox Christianity as erroneous. We should leave them in our doctrinal statements right where they belong, and we should continue to teach them in our churches. The Bible itself encourages us to delight in God's love and care for each of His individual children. But we cannot stop with the vertical aspect of salvation. We must also embrace the horizontal dimension of New Testament soteriology. American evangelicalism is a community in crisis, and it will remain such as long as we fail to recapture the biblical understanding of salvation as a community-creating event.

The State We Are In

I am hardly alone in my increasing dissatisfaction with the way the gospel is understood and presented in modern evangelicalism. Our approach is simply not working. We are not making disciples as Jesus intends us to.

D. Willard, in his book *The Divine Conspiracy*, wrestled with the spiritual and relational poverty resulting from the "disjunction between faith and life" that characterizes evangelical Christianity today. As Willard so perceptively observed, our "bar-code faith" approach to evangelism deals solely with the issue of "sin management"—the forgiveness of sins. It says nothing about the life of discipleship to which Jesus calls His followers.

We pray the sinner's prayer, or perhaps we mentally assent to some doctrinal creed. We receive in return God's spiritual "bar code" of divine forgiveness indelibly stamped upon our souls. Someday, when we die and cross the threshold of eternity, God's scanner will read our "bar-code faith," and we will be admitted to heavenly bliss—irrespective of our behavior or lifestyle during the period in between our conversion and our translation to glory. Or so we assume. After all, as the bumper sticker happily proclaims, "Christians Aren't Perfect, Just Forgiven."

D. Willard's response to this kind of teaching is unequivocal:

> The real question, I think, is whether God would establish a bar code type of arrangement at all. It is we who are in danger: in danger of missing the fullness of life offered to us. Can we seriously believe that God would establish a plan for us that essentially bypasses the awesome needs of present human life and leaves human character untouched? . . . Can we believe that the essence of Christian faith and salvation covers nothing but death and after?[3]

---

[3] D. Willard, *The Divine Conspiracy: Rediscovering Our Hidden Life in God* (San Francisco: HarperSanFrancisco, 1998), 38.

The obvious answer, of course, is "No." "Bar-code faith" is but a caricature of biblical Christianity. D. Zander stated, "In this scenario, the gospel is informing how we die. Instead, the gospel ought to be about how we live!"[4]

Actually, it ought to be about both. We should avoid false dichotomies. Willard's stinging indictment of American evangelicalism must not be read as a clarion call to jettison the great Pauline doctrine of justification by faith. Willard, in fact, finds nothing inherently wrong with Paul's theology, nor with the manner in which Paul was later understood by the Protestant Reformers. Willard affirms the Protestant Reformation, referring at one point to "its truly great and good message of salvation by faith alone" (p. 301). Instead, he locates the problem in "the distant *outworkings* of the Protestant Reformation," which have now left us with a truncated understanding of the New Testament gospel of whole-life discipleship.

Willard is right on target. In fact, it may surprise you to discover just how strong-group the Protestant Reformers were in their thinking about the church and its role in salvation and spiritual growth. We would be hard-pressed to find support among the Reformers for the wholesale separation of ecclesiology from soteriology that has become so characteristic of popular American evangelical thought. We will let J. Calvin speak for himself:

> But because it is our intention to discuss the visible church, let us learn even from the simple title "mother" how useful, indeed how necessary, it is that we should know her. For there is no other way to enter life unless this mother conceive us in her womb, give us birth, nourish us at her breast, and lastly, unless she keep us under her care and guidance until, putting off mortal flesh, we become like the angels [Matt. 22:30]. . . . Furthermore, away from her bosom one cannot hope for any forgiveness of sins or any salvation, as Isaiah [37:32] and Joel [2:32] testify. . . . God's fatherly favor and the especial witness of spiritual life are limited to his flock, so that it is always disastrous to leave the church. (Institutes 4.1.4)

Apparently the problem is not with the early Reformers. They maintained a much closer connection between salvation and church involvement than they are often credited with in less-informed treatments of Reformation history. The problem lies in our popular American interpretations of Reformation thinking.

---

[4]   E. Gibbs and R. Bolger, *Emerging Churches* (Grand Rapids: Baker, 2005), 55.

American Individualism and Personal Salvation

Only as Protestant theology took root in American soil, and radical individualism began to sweep the American evangelical landscape, did Christians increasingly dismiss the role of God's group in the process of individual salvation. The community-oriented approach to Christianity characteristic of the European Reformers—and of seventeenth- and eighteenth-century American Puritanism—slowly gave way to a version of the faith that has focused almost exclusively on personal salvation.

Nineteenth-century American revivals, for example, were noted for their emphasis upon emotionalism and individual decisions for Christ. This understanding of conversion solely in terms of a relationship between God and the individual later found expression in the twentieth-century evangelistic crusades of Billy Sunday and Billy Graham. Moreover, the evangelistic tracts that were popular in our churches and parachurch ministries up until just recently invariably presented salvation solely as the acquisition of a personal relationship with Christ. The reader had to turn to the last pages of these booklets to find any mention of God's group, the Christian church.

The reason? According to popular American evangelicalism, the church has nothing to do with salvation. God's group only comes into the picture as a sort of utilitarian aid to individual growth in the Christian faith. The goal in sharing Christ is not to get a person to join God's group. The goal is to get him to pray the sinner's prayer or to respond in some way to the evangelist's invitation. Only after he is saved in this way is he encouraged to find a church to help him grow in his personal relationship with Christ.

As long as America's traditional social glue of relational commitment and integrity continued to hold people together in their marriages, their churches, and their communities, an individualistic "bar code" gospel could be preached and little damage done. In fact, great good was accomplished as converts took their "personal relationships with God" back into their church and family settings.

Until the late 1960s, social pressure alone was sufficient to keep people married, and it was sufficient to keep church members committed to one another in local community life. Society frowned upon divorce, and it highly valued commitment to church and civic organizations. We could preach an individualistic gospel, ignore the sociological aspects of biblical soteriology, and rely on the pressures of society to keep people in community. And for a season it worked.

But in recent decades the inherent weaknesses of such an approach to the gospel have become increasingly apparent. As we are now painfully aware, the social values that once exerted pressure in favor of relational commitment are gone. The glue that held American society together for nearly two centuries is irredeemably cracked and brittle. Now that American society has become relationally disconnected, the poverty of our "group-less" gospel is glaringly manifested.

The practical ramifications of all this for our lives and for our churches are enormous. By separating salvation from church involvement, in a culture that is already socially fragmented and relatively devoid of relational commitment, we implicitly give people permission to leave God's family when the going gets rough—to take their "personal relationships with Jesus" with them to another church down the block or, worse, to no church family at all. And this is precisely what they do. W. Roof observed, "With *believing* disjointed from *belonging,* it amounts to a 'portable' faith."[5]

So here is the tragic result of driving a wedge between soteriology (salvation) and ecclesiology (church). We have removed from the gospel what the Bible views as central to the sanctification process, namely, commitment to God's group. In doing so, we invariably set ourselves up for the relational shipwrecks that happen in the lives of countless Sunday attenders who opt for individual satisfaction over loyalty to God's group. After all, "I can leave my church—or my marriage—and my personal Savior will happily accompany me wherever I go."

The biblical picture forcefully underscores the spiritual bankruptcy of this incomplete understanding of the gospel. So does everyday life in the local church. Thirty years of church ministry—combined with constant immersion in the conceptual world of the early Christian church—has convinced me of an important truth. To leave God's family is to leave the very arena in which God manifests His life-giving power and hope to human beings in the world in which we live.

It has been common in our teaching to outline salvation chronologically as follows:

1. Past: We *have been* delivered from the *penalty* of sin.
2. Present: We *are being* delivered from the *power* of sin.
3. Future: We *will be* delivered from the *presence* of sin.

As a colleague of mine insightfully noted, past and future salvation rest solely upon the response of the individual to the atoning work of Christ. Present salvation (from the power of sin), however, is necessarily mediated in the context of

---

[5] W. Roof, *A Generation of Seekers: The Spiritual Journey of the Baby Boom Generation* (San Francisco: HarperCollins, 1994). 200.

Christian community.[6] Calvin had it right after all: "it is always disastrous to leave the church."

The idea of salvation cannot be reduced to a personal relationship with Jesus. God's plan is much more encompassing. God intends for salvation to be a community-creating event. Any convictions we might have about how we relate to God as individuals must stand as subordinate to this overarching biblical reality. B. Witherington eloquently put it this way: "The community, not the closet, is the place where salvation is worked out."[7]

Among the early Christians, salvation involved both a new relationship with God and a new relationship with God's group. If we wish to be faithful to biblical soteriology, we must communicate these truths when we share the gospel with unbelievers. For as we share the gospel in this way, we will help our converts make professions of faith that embrace both halves—individual and corporate— of the biblical teachings about salvation. Their Christian lives will be immeasurably richer for it. Let us consider how we might go about sharing a more holistic version of the gospel in the broken and fragmented world in which we live.

Evangelism and the Ministry of the Church

Church ministry has traditionally been framed as a discipleship process that includes evangelism, the assimilation of newcomers, and the ongoing education and training of believers. During my earlier years in the pastorate, I conceived of this process as a linear one: (1) conversion, followed by (2) involvement in a local church, where (3) biblical education would characterize the continuing life of the believer. After all, this had been my own experience when I became a follower of Jesus at 23 years of age in 1975.

I am now discovering that the "1→2→3" of discipleship often looks more like "2→1→3" in twenty-first century southern California where I minister. In other words, non-Christian newcomers to Oceanside Christian Fellowship first tend to establish relationships with our church members. Then they make decisions for Christ months or even years later. In this process of spiritual formation, it is the quality of the relationships our newcomers make with our regular attenders—and the quality of the relationships they observe among the members of God's family— that ultimately leads these folks to give their lives to Jesus. Our new converts learn from the outset that the Christian life is preeminently a community endeavor.

---

[6] I am grateful to Erik Thoennes for this observation.
[7] B. Witherington III, *The Paul Quest* (Downers Grove: InterVarsity, 1998). 277.

Reconciliation and the Church as a Family

The "2→1→3" of modern discipleship makes perfect sense when we consider it in view of what I like to call "the many-faceted jewel of the atonement." The New Testament writers assembled a variety of images from the Old Testament and from the world of their day as they sought to picture the manifold fullness of salvation in Christ. From the temple and altars come images of sacrifice and propitiation. From the courts of law comes the idea of justification. From the marketplace comes the metaphor of redemption. In other contexts the victory won at the cross over the powers of darkness is the particular aspect of Christ's death that is emphasized, a picture taken from the battlefield.

Each of these portrayals of the atonement is important because taken together they help us to grasp the almost inexpressible magnitude of what God has accomplished for us in the work of Christ on the cross. But as our cross-cultural missionaries will tell us, the impact of these different images of the atonement varies considerably from time to time and from culture to culture.

For example, in traditional strong-group societies where moral guilt is generally not internalized, there may be little sense of personal sin (what we might call *internal* evil) on the part of the individual. Such cultures often exhibit a profound dread of *external* evil, as people desperately employ a variety of religious rituals and practices to protect themselves from unseen forces of evil in the spiritual realm. In settings like these, it is the good news of Jesus' victory over the powers of darkness through His atoning death that profoundly resonates with those who hear the gospel, and an effective evangelistic ministry will intentionally highlight this aspect of the atonement.

Contrast this traditional setting with the more introspective, individualistic orientation of modern Western society where, until recently, the New Testament image of individual justification through the forgiveness of sins—a message dealing specifically with *internal* evil—has proven to be the key "facet of the jewel of the atonement" drawing men and women into the kingdom. I included the phrase "until recently" in the previous sentence because I believe that we have observed a shift in our culture that renders yet another biblical image of salvation more relevant for contemporary society. The image I have in mind is the New Testament picture of the atonement as reconciliation—an image drawn not from the temple, the marketplace, the courtroom, or the battlefield, but one drawn instead from the family.

As cultural analysts will tell us, people in our relationally fragmented, increasingly isolated techno-culture are highly sensitive to the need for healthy relationships with their fellow human beings. We long for community, but our own family experiences have often left us painfully aware of the tremendous difficulties involved in cultivating such relationships with the resources the secular world has to offer. We are left wholly unequipped to satisfy our deepest relational longings and needs.

The biblical picture of reconciliation, with its hope-giving promise of lasting and meaningful relationships, just may be the key "facet of the jewel of the atonement" for the age in which we live. We can define reconciliation as the restoration of a right relationship with Father God and the restoration of right relationships with our fellow human beings who, through conversion to Christ, become our brothers and sisters in the faith.

No biblical image of the atonement has greater potential to resonate with our relationally broken culture than the good news that we can be reconciled to God and to our fellow human beings through the death of Jesus on the cross. But the gospel of reconciliation must take on incarnate form, and here is where the New Testament idea of the church as a surrogate family comes in.

The Church as a Family: An Obstacle to Evangelism?

A recent denominational leader made an observation that struck me as rather counterintuitive, to say the least. He claimed that one of the most damaging things we have done to the evangelistic enterprise of our local churches has been to convince our people that the church is a family.

Now I can understand this brother's passion and even, to a degree, his reasoning. He is a leader who rightly longs to see our churches outwardly focused. He assumes that the family metaphor will encourage precisely the opposite set of priorities and values, that a church which views itself as a family will turn in on itself and ignore those who are not part of the family.

Apart from the obvious fact that our denominational leader's assertion summarily dispenses with the primary metaphor for Christian community in the whole New Testament (and early Christian literature), the well-intentioned observation fails to consider the potential that a healthy church family has for encouraging the unchurched to make a commitment to our Lord Jesus Christ.

A Christian community that seeks to live out the surrogate family model can serve as a living metaphor for the reality of reconciliation with God and others in Christ. Unbelievers who attend such a church begin to get a taste of the hope God provides for right relationships in Christ as they live among us and develop friendships with church members. Some months later, God willing, they give their lives to Christ. In such a pilgrimage, regeneration often follows, rather than precedes, association with God's children in a local Christian church.

To be sure, this assumes that the local church effectively functions according to the surrogate family model outlined earlier in this book. It also assumes (to take into consideration the concerns of the denominational leader mentioned above) that the church adopts an inclusive—rather than an exclusive—approach to church family life. All of this demands a significant degree of intentionality on the part of church leaders and members alike. But we are not charting new territory here. Thankfully, the history of the Christian church has left us with some remarkable precedents for a connection of this kind between church family life and effective community evangelism.

The Moravians

The Moravian communities of eighteenth-century Europe offer us a remarkable example of the "2→1→3" approach to evangelism and spiritual formation. The Moravians preached a whole-gospel message that embraced both the individual and corporate aspects of salvation. These pioneering Christians attributed their remarkable achievements in mission and personal evangelism directly to their conviction that commitment to God's group constitutes an indispensable aspect of genuine conversion.

The outreach success of the Moravian house-church movement, which began among German Lutherans, was truly remarkable. R. and J. Banks assert:

> Proportionally, the missionary dimension of the Moravian life exceeded that of any Christian group from the first century. Never has a single expression of the church had so many of its members involved in mission, traveled so many places, reached out to so many different peoples, or influenced so many other churches to follow its example.[8]

What was the secret of such effective evangelism? How did the Moravians pull it off?

Moravian leaders tended to shy away from extensive theological discussion, so we have to read between the lines a bit to reconstruct their soteriology. We can easily discern from their writings the Moravian approach to evangelism. For the Moravians the preaching of the gospel clearly involved much more than just helping an individual find a personal relationship with God through Jesus. A person was not genuinely converted in their judgment until he or she evidenced a strong-group commitment to one of the small, home-based, Moravian church families.

---

[8] R. and J. Banks, *The Church Comes Home* (Peabody: Hendrikson, 1998), 58.

Moravians made sure that their potential converts understood from the outset that commitment to Jesus meant commitment to His group.

The degree of theological sophistication with which the Moravians articulated their soteriology must remain somewhat of a mystery. They were quite aware, however, of the pragmatic advantages of their strong-group evangelistic strategy. The Moravians made the corporate aspect of the gospel absolutely central to their outreach strategy because they recognized that, in their particular cultural setting, the best way to convert an unbeliever was to expose him to the group to which he was about to be converted. N. von Zinzendorf, the founder of the Moravian movement, put it like this:

> We must establish the principle that the happy, fruitful, and almost irresist-
> ible calling in of many thousands of souls, supposes a little flock in the house,
> cleaving to our Savior with body and soul, . . . in such a manner that we may as
> it were point to such a people with the finger, when we are inviting others; that
> is an advantage, a blessing, a preaching of the gospel to purpose, if we can say:
> "Come, all things are ready, I can show you the persons, who are already there,
> but do come and see.". . . This is simply that thing called preaching the gospel.[9]

These observations call for some qualification. Exposure to Christian community is not, in and of itself, "preaching the gospel." Zinzendorf's enthusiasm may have gotten the best of him here. But let us not miss the point of the Moravian approach to outreach. What better way to bring our friends up to speed on what Christian community is all about than to invite them to experience it for themselves like the Moravians did? And what better context in which to proclaim the gospel than a healthy Christian community—one which by its very relational integrity and social solidarity attests to the truth of the message of salvation that is being proclaimed?

The Story of the Brown Family

I have had the privilege of observing the "2→1→3" of spiritual formation work itself out again and again in the pilgrimages of a number of individuals and families at Oceanside Christian Fellowship. A living example of the community-creating power of the gospel serves as an appropriate conclusion to the chapter.

Brian and Rose Brown [not their real names] began attending our church with their two children back in 1998. Our church family received them with open arms, and it was not long before they had made friends with a number of our people. The kids soon received Christ, and Rose followed shortly thereafter. It took Brian a

[9] Ibid.

bit longer to embrace the gospel. For nearly a year Brian played his guitar on our worship team and vicariously enjoyed the benefits of Christian community before he finally became a child of God.

It happened like this. One Sunday Brian approached me to let me know how much he was enjoying our church and to express his appreciation for how much Oceanside Christian Fellowship had done for his marriage and for his family. I was greatly encouraged. But then Brian remarked that he needed answers to some intellectual questions he had about Christianity before he himself would join the party. Here is how Brian expressed it: "It sure is warm and cozy in this hot tub here, Joe, but I just want to make sure the water's clean before I jump in." Well, as God's timing would have it, I was about to begin a four-week apologetics series titled *Tough Questions* on the following Sunday, and I encouraged Brian to pay close attention.

The first sermon in the series tackled the thorny issue of origins. I chose not to deal that morning with the scientific evidence for and against evolution, nor did I delve into the details of Genesis 1. (Either task would have proved all but impossible for a thirty-minute Sunday morning time slot.) Instead, I outlined for our congregation the alarming moral implications of adopting the worldview that underlies the theory of evolution (metaphysical naturalism) as a foundation for relating to our fellow human beings.

Brian's reaction was, how shall I say, quite encouraging but rather unorthodox. He found me among the crowd in the lobby after the service, gave me a big bear hug, and proclaimed at the top of his lungs (so everyone in the lobby could hear), "Joe, that was the best *%!&@# talk I have ever heard!"

Shortly thereafter Brian joined his wife and kids as an eternal member of the family of God. We baptized them together as a family at the beach the following August. The Browns recently relocated to the East Coast, and now Brian serves as a worship leader in a church in North Carolina.

Conclusion

There are good reasons, biblical and practical, to revisit our understanding of soteriology and retool our evangelistic strategies in light of the New Testament model of the church as a strong-group family. Our spiritual lives and the health of our congregations depend on it.

It has become increasingly difficult for church leaders to encourage our people to stay long-term in their congregations so that we can grow together in a healthy context of familial support and relational accountability. The ever-present challenge of Christian consumerism, endemic to many of our densely-populated urban settings, deludes some into thinking that another church down the street will somehow better "meet their needs."

For others the temptation to leave becomes acute when discord erupts in the church family. Quarreling Christians often find it much easier to abandon a local congregation in order to escape the immediate pain of the conflict. This is easier than staying and doing the hard work of cultivating those potentially redemptive relationships that God has provided for their spiritual growth and development.

We can trace such tendencies to the radical individualism that so pervasively characterizes the American social landscape. It will remain difficult to convince our people that the group comes first—and that staying with the group is, in the final analysis, in the best interest of the individual—while our culture continues to socialize us to believe that our personal desires and felt needs should determine the course of our daily lives.

But we cannot lay full responsibility at the feet of the surrounding society for the relational poverty that characterizes much of the church in America today. We are at fault as well. American evangelicals have allowed the dominant culture to skew our approach to the Christian life in ways that have contributed significantly to the current state of affairs.

Consider our fixation upon Jesus as personal Savior, so central to the evangelistic strategies of the previous generation. Such privatization of the Christian faith turns out to be little more than a regrettable accommodation to a pagan culture's unbiblical obsession with individual determinism and personal subjective experience. And we are now paying the price for peddling a less-than-holistic gospel. Framing conversion to Christ in solely individualistic terms has left us with little social capital to draw on in our churches as we try to encourage our people to stay in community and grow together as brothers and sisters in Christ.

The good news is that the gospel of Jesus Christ has always contained the inherent power victoriously to resist the trends of the dominant culture. We do not have to be conformed to this world. It is time to return to our biblical roots by emphasizing both the corporate and the individual aspects of salvation.

It is time to inform our people that conversion to Christ involves both our *justification* and our *familification,* that we gain a new Father *and* a new set of brothers and sisters when we respond to the gospel. It is time to communicate the biblical reality that personal salvation is a community-creating event, and to trust God to change our lives and the lives of our churches accordingly.

Chapter Seven

LIFE TOGETHER IN THE
FAMILY OF GOD

*Now the multitude of those who believed were of one heart
and soul, and no one said that any of his possessions was his
own, but instead they held everything in common.*

(Acts 4:32–33)

What would Christianity look like if we truly recaptured Jesus' vision for authentic Christian community? It would likely vary considerably from person to person and from church to church, since the surrogate family values we observed among the early Christians would manifest themselves in different ways in different church environments. The values themselves—group loyalty and the sharing of material resources, for example—would remain much the same. But these fundamental expressions of social solidarity would surely express themselves in our churches in a myriad of ways.

Much of what follows narrates my own pilgrimage with Christian community. I have been privileged to enjoy the reality of New Testament family life over the years in some rather unique ways. My story, of course, will not be your story. Each person and each church must write their own stories where Christian community is concerned. But perhaps some specific examples of the way in which the church family model has taken on tangible form in my own experience as a brother and a pastor will stimulate your thinking along these lines.

Four New Testament family values will serve as our roadmap:

1. We share our stuff with one another.
2. We share our hearts with one another.
3. We stay, embrace the pain, and grow up with one another
4. Family is about more than me, the wife, and the kids.

We Share Our Stuff with One Another

Perhaps most basic to Christian brotherhood is the sharing of material resources. We share our stuff with one another. The theme is a familiar one from the New Testament. The family context for such activity is crystal clear in this familiar passage:

> We know that we have passed from death to life because we love our broth-
> ers. The one who does not love remains in death. Everyone who hates his
> brother is a murderer, and you know that no murderer has eternal life residing
> in him. This is how we have come to know love: He laid down His life for us.
> We should also lay down our lives for our brothers. If anyone has this world's
> goods and sees his brother in need but shuts off his compassion from him—how
> can God's love reside in him? (1 John 3:14–17)

The apostle John simply cannot conceive of brotherly love—or love for God—apart from the sharing of material resources with those in need among the church family.

The socioeconomic setting of my church family is such that we do not have a whole lot of people who are dependent on their siblings in Christ to meet their daily needs. Most of our members and regular attenders are white-collar professionals who lack for little in the way of material possessions. But we do have a handful of people who live on the margin economically, so to speak, and who run into tough seasons financially.

Our church does a pretty good job of ministering to such people in practical ways. We have an elders' fund to meet pressing material needs, and our people are remarkably generous with the resources that God has provided for them. More often than not we share our stuff with one another in informal ways, as people in our church become aware of a need and seek to meet it outside of official church channels.

My wife Joann and I often have the joy of being both on the giving and the receiving end of the sharing of material resources among our church family. As it happens, our financial situation is a rather comfortable one because I inherited the house we live in, and we have a very low mortgage and minimal property taxes. One of the things Joann and I enjoy doing is to drop little monetary gifts into the lives of people we know are in need in our church family—a hundred dollars to a single mom over here, another hundred to a struggling student or unemployed brother over there. But what little Joann and I have been able to do on the giving end of our church family utterly pales in comparison to what we have experienced on the receiving end. A most amazing tangible expression of church family love happened to the Hellermans in the summer of 2004.

The house I inherited (and in which I was raised) is a little two-bedroom, 750 square-foot cottage in Hermosa Beach, California. Joann and I have lived in the house with our two daughters now for more than two decades. It has been a bit of a challenge over the years, with three women in the house and only one bathroom, but as I tell my friends, it is 23 years and running, and I have not had to use the backyard yet, so we have actually managed quite well.

Most of the credit for keeping life simple goes to Joann, who has always been content with very little and who thankfully does not feel the need for a big house and all the fancy stuff that so many women in our culture cannot seem to do without. At any rate, to continue with the story, our house was built back in 1950. I am an absolute idiot with any mechanical device except for a laptop computer and a fishing reel. As a result, our little house has become more than a bit shabby over the half century of wear-and-tear.

Every year, Joann and I and the girls go up to the mountains—to Mammoth Lakes in the Sierras—for several weeks in August. I take a box of books and my fishing equipment, Joann enjoys an extended break from her normal routine, the girls get to watch cable television for the only time during the year, and we all benefit from some great family time together. Back in March of 2004, long before we went to the Sierras that year, totally unknown to us, a group of about 20 people from our church family began to meet together to plan how *they* were going to spend the Hellermans' vacation time that summer.

As we discovered later, these dear brothers and sisters spent five months meeting and planning an extreme home makeover. They picked out paint colors, chose floor tile, selected furniture, and designed cabinetry. When we returned home from our three weeks in the mountains in August of that year, we discovered—totally to our surprise—that these wonderful people had completely remodeled our kitchen and our living room, along with portions of the rest of the house as well.

We arrived home to all new top-drawer Pottery Barn furniture, professional interior decorating, a beautiful hardwood floor, a pantry that had not been there before, and a complete reorganization and cataloguing of all our belongings. And as if that were not enough, our brothers and sisters completely rewired the house— from two circuits to nine circuits—so that we could use all the new gadgets (like the new lighting and the ceiling fan) that they had included in the remodel. They even installed outdoor lighting in our backyard so that we could barbecue after dark!

Before the remodel we could not run our blow dryer and microwave at the same time without overloading a circuit and shutting off the power. The first thing Rachel (my youngest) did when we got home was to go around turning on every electrical appliance in the house to see if she could flip a breaker. She found that she could not.

I will never forget the following Sunday. The Hellermans were not supposed to know who was involved in the remodel, and we were, in fact, taken totally by surprise when we arrived home after our vacation. But in a church of 250 or so people, you know who the cabinet guy is, you know the electrician, and you know who has the financial resources to drop more than $20,000 into a project of this magnitude.

We played along, though, pretending not to know who was involved. That Sunday I stepped up on the platform in our church auditorium, took my place behind the podium, and began to say thanks to my brothers and sisters for what they had done for my family. Well, I tried to, at any rate. Actually I just lost it. I stood there and wept before my people. Who are the Hellermans that we had the privilege of being on the receiving end of such an incredible work of God? The church is a family. We share our stuff with one another.

Sharing our stuff with one another within the context of a given local church only begins to scratch the surface of the implications of the surrogate family model for the church at large. Recall for a moment that aspect of the sharing of material resources among Christian siblings that consumed much of the later years of Paul's life and which, in fact, accounts for his most extensive teaching on giving (2 Cor 8–9).

I have in mind here Paul's collection from his Gentile congregations for the poor brothers in Jerusalem—a biblical model (indeed, a biblical mandate) for sharing our stuff not just with our brothers and sisters in our own congregations, but also with Christian siblings in less fortunate socio-economic settings throughout our city and around the world. Getting our arms around the idea that the church is a family has the potential to greatly inform our perspective on the stewardship of our material possessions.

We Share Our Hearts with One Another

A second way in which the New Testament church experienced its surrogate family values in everyday community life relates to what psychologists refer to as affective solidarity. We share our hearts with one another. This is the emotional attachment, the affective sense of closeness and intimacy that the Holy Spirit weaves into the lives of brothers and sisters in Christ who spend time together and share life and ministry together. We have all experienced it at times, and we certainly see affective solidarity evidenced in Paul's relationships with others in the family of God.

Paul apparently felt particularly close to those in his Macedonian congregations. This is the way he expressed his affection toward the Philippians: "Therefore, my brothers and sisters, whom I love and long for, my joy and crown, stand firm in the Lord in this way, my beloved" (Phil 4:1, NRSV). The sentiments in this verse are almost syrupy sweet when viewed according to our standards. But as we have learned, this is precisely how siblings in traditional cultures relate to one another.

Let us consider in a bit more detail Paul's relationship with his brothers and sisters in Thessalonica:

> But as for us, brothers, after we were forced to leave you for a short time (in person, not in heart), we greatly desired and made every effort to return and see you face to face. So we wanted to come to you—even I, Paul, time and again— but Satan hindered us. For who is our hope, or joy, or crown of boasting in the presence of our Lord Jesus at His coming? Is it not you? For you are our glory and joy.
>
> Therefore, when we could no longer stand it, we thought it was better to be left alone in Athens. And we sent Timothy, our brother and God's co-worker in the gospel of Christ, to strengthen and encourage you concerning your faith, so that no one will be shaken by these persecutions. For you yourselves know that we are appointed to this. In fact, when we were with you, we told you previously that we were going to suffer persecution, and as you know, it happened. For this reason, when I could no longer stand it, I also sent to find out about your faith, fearing that the tempter had tempted you and that our labor might be for nothing. But now Timothy has come to us from you and brought us good news about your faith and love, and that you always have good memories of us, wanting to see us, as we also want to see you. Therefore, brothers, in all our

distress and persecution, we were encouraged about you through your faith. For now we live, if you stand firm in the Lord. (1 Thess 2:17–3:8)

We situated Paul's comments in their historical context back in chapter 4. Here I want to make a couple of additional observations about Paul's relationship with the Thessalonian Christians.

First of all, the emotional solidarity in the Thessalonian correspondence is not simply touchy-feely community for community's sake. This is important. The affective bond Paul shared with his Christian siblings cannot be separated from the profound concern Paul had for the spiritual well-being of his brothers and sisters in the faith. The emotional connection Paul experienced was, therefore, a very purposeful and focused kind of affective solidarity. Paul's joy and sorrow were deeply connected to the spiritual status of his siblings in the family of God: "For now we live, if you stand firm in the Lord" (3:8).

Secondly, Paul's bond with his fellow Christians was an emotional connection that generated a corresponding action. Paul did not merely feel concern for the Thessalonians, though he certainly did that. He actually did something about his concern for the well-being of his brothers and sisters in Christ. He sent his very best. Paul sent Timothy to the Thessalonians to find out how they were doing.

It seems like all big things—good and bad—happen to the Hellermans while we are on vacation in Mammoth Lakes. In 2004, we had our house remodeled while we were in Mammoth. In 1989, I almost died while we were on vacation in the Sierras. It was the July 4 weekend, and I was doubled over with pain in my abdomen, lying on the floor of our condominium and unable even to button up my pants I hurt so badly.

Mammoth Lakes is a famous winter ski resort, so the doctors in the Sierras are experts with broken bones and the like. Apparently, they are rather clueless when it comes to internal medicine. Such was my experience, at any rate.

I ended up in a little ten-bed high-tech hospital in town, where the staff kept me high on morphine and poked around at me for a couple days. Finally, they sent for a country surgeon from the valley below to try to figure out what was wrong with me. When Dr. Sheldon cut me open he discovered that my appendix had burst two days earlier. I was full of peritonitis and just about ready to be absent from the body and present with the Lord.

After the doctors took out what was left of my appendix and cleaned out my abdomen, they kept me in the hospital for another week on high-powered intravenous antibiotics trying to kill off a stubborn infection. As the days passed, this regimen appeared to have little positive effect, so the doctors began to talk about taking me back into surgery to treat the problem more directly and aggressively. I was physically and emotionally devastated. I can honestly say that I was more discouraged and despondent at that point in my hospital stay than I have ever been during my 33 years as a believer in Jesus.

That very day I received a call from a brother on staff at our church, our youth pastor, Craig Cooper. Now I am normally a pretty upbeat person, and Craig immediately picked up on the sadness and sense of hopelessness in my voice. Mammoth is about 300 miles from the church in Manhattan Beach, and a good portion of the journey runs along crowded southern California freeways. But that did not stop Craig from jumping into his car with his wife and two toddlers and driving 12 hours that day round-trip just to spend a half-hour with me in that hospital room in Mammoth Lakes so that he could pray for me and encourage me as a brother in the Lord.

Craig's affective connection with me as a brother in Christ was such that he apparently could not do otherwise, and I have been forever grateful for it. During a moment of utter darkness, when God seemed so far away, Craig became my lifeline to Jesus. Indeed, Craig proved to be the very hands and feet and voice of Jesus at that critical point in my life. So it was for Paul and the Thessalonians: "We cared so much for you that we were pleased to share with you not only the gospel of God but also our own lives, because you had become dear to us" (1 Thess 2:8). We share our hearts with one another. Affective solidarity is a key part of what being family is all about.

We Stay, Embrace the Pain, and Grow Up with One Another

As the story goes, one day God sent a couple of His angelic messengers to planet Earth, to see how we were doing. The two angels went through city after city, country after country, and brought back a less-than-happy report to their Creator. The angels told God that 99 percent of the people they encountered were selfish, obnoxious sinners, and only 1 percent was doing well. Only this small minority of the human race stayed on the straight and narrow path, consistently doing what God wanted them to do.

God was more than a little discouraged by the angels' report, and His first inclination was to deal severely with the 99 percent who had turned their backs on Him. He considered unleashing a flood but then remembered that He had promised not to do that again. God thought for awhile and finally came up with a more positive approach to the dilemma.

God decided to withhold His anger against the majority and, instead, to send an e-mail to the 1 percent—the good people—to challenge them to continue in their faithful and obedient way of life. So God composed and sent His e-mail, which contained the kind of affirmation and encouragement that only God Himself could provide.

Do you know what that e-mail said? You don't? *You mean to say that you didn't get one either?*

Well, as it turns out, none of us gets that e-mail, do we? Because not one of us stays on the straight and narrow path, always doing only what God wants us to do. No, as we are all so painfully aware, not 99 percent of us but all 100 percent of us have sinned and fallen short of the glory of God. And we continue to wrestle with sin and selfish behavior in our lives long after salvation. This is precisely what makes it so very difficult to live as family, to stay together, to embrace the pain, and to grow up in community with one another.

Here is the kind of hurt, heartache, and frustration so often encountered in our relationships with people in our natural families and, by extension, in our church families. One of the dangers in all this talk about community is the temptation to idealize the concept of the church as a family and to fail to embrace the reality that doing family right is tough stuff—at church and at home. It was difficult for Paul, and it is difficult for us. We will likely experience as many failures as victories along the way.

In fact, I have to chuckle inside this morning as I am editing this chapter. I am fighting off a raging sore throat and was unable even to shave today because stress-related cold sores are breaking out all over my face. And I know exactly what it is that has lowered my resistance: a relational hassle at church in which I have been deeply engaged because, for better or worse, it involves my whole natural family as well as several other key people in our congregation. It is not always easy to share life together as a church family.

Nor should we expect it to be. We do not choose our natural families, and neither do we choose our church families. We might initially choose the particular church we attend. But once we commit to a local congregation, we invariably find ourselves among a group of brothers and sisters, some of whom we gravitate toward and some of whom we probably do not even like very well. But that is quite typical of family, is it not?

In the Hellerman family we remind ourselves that there is a difference between "like" and "love." There are times when Joann does not like me very much. And for good cause, since I can be quite unlikable in certain situations. The same is true, of course, for Joann and our daughters. We all have our moments. The commitment to love, to stay, to embrace the pain, and to grow together prevails among the Hellermans, and no one has left the family yet simply because one of us decided for a season that he or she did not happen to like another member of the family.

If someone did get mad and leave the Hellerman family, we would all be the worse for it. For it is in the context of our families that we grow up and hone the relational skills necessary to interact as mature adults with people in the world around us. As our therapists know so very well, people who leave their families due to conflict often take their dysfunctional relational strategies and behaviors to another family, where—surprise, surprise—they encounter all over again the very issues that they thought they had left behind.

The same dynamics characterize life together in our church families. Yet church culture in America tends to discourage—rather than encourage—ongoing loyalty and commitment to a local family of believers. More than a decade ago, sociologist and pollster George Barna offered an arresting summary of the typical attitudes of Christians in America today toward the local church. Given the picture of the New Testament family of God outlined in the previous chapters, I believe you will find Barna's bullet points more than a little disconcerting:

American Christians . . .

- prefer a variety of church experiences, rather than getting the most out of all that a single church has to offer.
- think that spiritual enlightenment comes from diligence in a discovery process, rather than from commitment to a faith community and perspective.
- view religion as a commodity that we consume, rather than one in which we invest ourselves.
- are transient—15 to 20 percent of all households relocate each year.[1]

Barna's research reveals that American evangelicals have increasingly moved away from maintaining long-term commitments to their local churches. We have chosen, instead, to focus on experiencing God at the individual level. The trends enumerated above unfortunately reflect a broad paradigm shift that characterizes much of the evangelical church, one that contrasts markedly with the church family model as we have observed it functioning among the early Christians.

But as our theologians wisely remind us, we cannot compromise biblical truth in one area without affecting other doctrines also. The various truths of the Bible

[1] G. Barna, *The Second Coming of the Church* (Waco: Word, 1998), 18–19.

are profoundly and perfectly intertwined. In the present case, exchanging the New Testament's community-centered approach to the Christian life for our own culture's individualistic view of spiritual formation has, in turn, subtly skewed our conception of God. God has now been recast in the role of a divine therapist who aids the individual Christian in his or her personal quest for spiritual enlightenment and self-discovery. And Jesus, in the final analysis, has become little more than a "personal Savior."

Such a truncated image of God does little to encourage us to stay, to embrace the pain, and to grow up with one another. As a result, when a person with this view of God encounters conflict with others, he generally feels the liberty to take his "personal Savior" from church to church and from marriage to marriage, desperately hoping that he can somehow improve the quality of his life by escaping the immediate pain that often clouds the potentially redemptive relationships in which God has placed him.

All of this blatantly betrays the strong-group New Testament image of the church as a surrogate family of brothers and sisters. A person does not grow up by running from family to family. This is self-evident in our natural families, and we know it to be true of our church families too.

The common practice of running from church to church is rather silly when viewed in light of New Testament relational priorities. I am not suggesting that there is never a legitimate reason for leaving a local church, but I find it rather striking that neither in the midst of the Galatian heresy nor in the context of divisiveness and immorality at Corinth did Paul instruct his readers to leave the community in order to find a healthier group of brothers and sisters. Instead, he challenged them to stick it out and partner with God to make things better.

Fortunately, Jesus gave His church some direct and challenging guidance for hanging together and working through conflict, and it is hardly a coincidence that the density of family language in the New Testament spikes once again in Matthew 18, where Jesus gave instructions about what to do when a "brother" sins against you:

> If your brother sins against you, go and rebuke him in private. If he listens to you, you have won your brother. But if he won't listen, take one or two more with you, so that by the testimony of two or three witnesses every fact may be established. If he pays no attention to them, tell the church. But if he doesn't pay attention even to the church, let him be like an unbeliever and a tax collector to you. (Matt 18:15–17)

Most of our churches struggle with exercising church discipline. We are overly hesitant to deal with sin in the church. And when finally we do attempt to correct a hurtful person, we often bumble around and handle the confrontation in a less-than-loving manner.

Perhaps we need to begin with the social context in which Jesus expects us to work through our conflicts and disagreements. The people involved in Matthew 18 are not simply members of an impersonal institution that assembles for a large meeting on Sunday, which we happen to call "church." They are brothers—brothers who share their stuff with one another and brothers who share their hearts with one another. The point here is that Jesus assumes an intimate relational context for the exercise of church discipline. He assumes a family context.

The elders at Oceanside Christian Fellowship came to grips with the family context for church discipline several years ago, while engaged in a rather intense discussion about a thorny situation in our church. A man in our congregation—I will call him Bill—had decided to divorce his wife with no biblical grounds whatsoever for such action. As the process of attempted restoration unfolded, Bill stubbornly refused to be dissuaded from his intentions, and we found ourselves at the end of the progression outlined in Matthew 18. It was time to "tell the church" (v. 17).

The debate at the elder meeting that morning centered on the definition of "church." Precisely whom do we "tell"? The answer to this question seemed rather self-evident to one of our elders, and it may seem self-evident to you. Church is our Sunday morning gathering. We need to share Bill's sin with the congregation as a whole. The rest of us saw things a bit differently and took what I would suggest is the more biblical approach to the exercise of church discipline.

Bill and his wife had been members of the same small group for nearly a decade. It was quite obvious to us that this group was the place where they experienced the tangible reality of being part of the family of God. For all practical and relational purposes, Bill's group members were his brothers and sisters in Christ. The small group, therefore, was Bill's "church" in the New Testament sense of the word.

So we proceeded to "tell the church." We lovingly, but painfully, informed Bill's small group of the unrepentant determination of one of their brothers to divorce his wife. Sadly, Bill proved unwilling to reconsider his destructive behavior, even when confronted by people he knew loved him dearly. So his brothers and sisters asked him not to return to the group until he had a change of heart. We all grieved about the unfortunate outcome of the process. But I believe that we handled the situation with integrity and in a manner faithful to Jesus' teaching in Matt 18:15–17.

Thankfully, some relational dilemmas see a more positive resolution. Several Sundays ago I sat in a two-hour meeting with our sound men and our worship team, where we discovered that one of our sound men was highly indignant about a perceived injustice he had experienced in the hustle and bustle of setting up for an outdoor church service. Apparently, our keyboard player had crossed that invisible but very real boundary line between musician and sound technician when he jumped in to help set up the sound system in the park that day.

The amazing thing about all this was that the incident had happened quite some time ago, and here our sound man was still nursing his wounds—three years later! Now to these brothers' credit, we all sat down, put the cards on the table, and worked through the problem in a transparent and humble way. The fellows in our worship ministry are quality people who are determined to stay, to embrace the pain, and to grow up in community together. Fortunately, their commitment to one another as brothers in Christ prevailed over petty hurts and perceived injustices at the meeting that afternoon. But sometimes I think there must be an easier way to do this thing called church.

This point is a simple one. Do not be surprised to discover that it is hard and often downright painful to live out the church family model. After all, look at how much frustration and even failure Paul himself encountered trying to get the members of his congregations to live in harmony together as brothers and sisters in the Lord. We set ourselves up for great disappointment if we overidealize the concept of the church as a surrogate family.

Even the warmest blessings of living out the church family model do not come without their own challenges. This was certainly the case with our surprise house remodel that year, for Joann at any rate. My wife has struggled for years with obsessive compulsive disorder. One of the ways in which Joann's OCD manifests itself is that she collects stuff, and she has trouble throwing things away. In addition, Joann is in a number of ways a very private person. As a result, our remodeled house left Joann with a set of painfully conflicting emotions.

Naturally, Joann was utterly overwhelmed with joy and gratitude for the sacrifice that had been made on our behalf. She delights in her new kitchen, and she is crazy about her new living room. But our church family did not only upgrade our house; they went drawer-by-drawer, cupboard-by-cupboard, through every bit of our stuff in our kitchen and living room.

Our brothers and sisters now know exactly how much of their hard-earned money Pastor Joe spends on fishing equipment. More troubling, from my wife's perspective, was the fact that these dear folks went through and reorganized every one of Joann's possessions. And they threw out all the stuff that *they* did not think Joann needed.

It was a good thing that we had nothing to hide because all our stuff was out there, where about 20 of our brothers and sisters could see it in living color. As much as she appreciated all that was done for us, this aspect of the remodeling was very difficult for Joann. But that's family, isn't it? And being family is what God has called us to do.

Family Is about More than Me, the Wife, and the Kids

We considered the place of singles in the church family when we examined 1 Corinthians 7 in chapter 4. God desires us to subordinate the particulars of our various social stations in life—single or married—to our overarching common bond as brothers and sisters in Jesus' kingdom family. The Hellermans have been fortunate to experience firsthand how singles and marrieds can transcend the typical life-stage categories that often pigeonhole us into various social niches in congregational life.

Joann and I moved to our present church in 1996. We knew that the change would involve making a new set of Christian friends. After all, we were about to join a whole new church family. Little did we suspect that we would be adding a new member to our own family. No, Joann did not have another baby. The family member I am talking about is a full-blown adult—Margy Emmons, our director of Worship and Administration at Oceanside Christian Fellowship.

Margy is a single adult in her fifties who is one of the most delightful, intelligent, gifted human beings I have ever known. Margy and I hit it off immediately as partners in the ministry, and it was not too long before Margy and Joann became best friends. On top of it all, our two daughters absolutely adore Margy. We all feel very strongly that Margy is a full-fledged member of the Hellerman family. She shares several meals a week with us, spends her days off with Joann, and does a whole lot more stuff to spruce up our house than I do. She also joins us on our yearly vacation in the Sierras. Twelve years ago the Hellermans never envisioned being a five-some. Now we cannot imagine life otherwise.

God works in deliberate ways and His timing is impeccable. I regard it as no coincidence that Margy became part of our family during the very years of my life when I researched and wrote my UCLA dissertation about the church as a family.

I am not sure just how open I would have been to welcoming another member into the Hellerman family if I had not been immersed in the collectivist model of early Christian community when Margy came into our lives.

The results of integrating Margy into our family have been nothing short of marvelous—truly a win-win situation for all involved—and I have spent a good deal of time reflecting on just why this has been the case. In what follows I have attempted to articulate what I have learned in my own pilgrimage in this regard about the roles of singles and marrieds in the context of the larger family of God.

Until Margy came along, Joann had not had a close girlfriend since high school. Although I was relatively unaware of it during the early years of our marriage, Joann has certain needs as a woman that I as a male simply cannot meet. I believe Joann would tell you that I am pretty thoughtful, expressive, and supportive, as husbands go. I love my wife dearly, and I make it a priority to spend time with Joann and to be involved in her world to the best of my ability. But there is a part of Joann that I can never quite seem to reach. The emotions she experiences as a woman, the cares and concerns that consume her in a unique way as a mother—these are just not "guy things."

The deluge of books that address the topic of relationships between the sexes has certainly helped husbands come to grips with the fact that "men are from Mars and women are from Venus." We have gained some important pointers about "his needs and her needs," and we have become more skilled at employing "the language of love" when we converse with our wives.

Men's movements like Promise Keepers have prophetically and rightfully rebuked us for our tendency to isolate ourselves, physically and emotionally, from our wives and families. As a result, many of us have now come a long way in our ability to understand and serve the wonderful women God has placed beside us. All this is good.

But there is a downside to this emphasis on emotional empathy: the erroneous impression husbands sometimes get that leads us to believe that we can somehow meet *all* of our wives' relational needs. As marriage after marriage has demonstrated, we cannot. Try as I might, there will always be a part of Joann that I as a male cannot touch. And for my marriage to function at its best, I must come to grips with this reality. To assert otherwise is to romanticize marriage into the surreal stratosphere of dreamland and to set ourselves up for inevitable relational disappointment.

This is not summarily to reject the recent emphasis upon male empathy and sensitivity toward our wives. The challenge to intentionally engage in meaningful relationships with our spouses serves as a much-needed correction of our macho male tradition. The problem with a lot of the recent prescriptions for healthy relations between the sexes is the family model on which such advice is based. Most well-meaning attempts to help men communicate with women, and women with men, assume as their point of departure a Western, nuclear family model: husband plus wife plus kids.

For most cultures throughout history, family has included more than just a nuclear family living together in the same residence. We spent some time discussing the extended family of the ancient Mediterranean world in chapter 2. As family system theorists are recognizing today, there are some tremendously practical and relational benefits to having more than one adult male and one adult female participating in the family unit.

I have observed this very dynamic operating firsthand in the Hellerman family. A marvelous thing happened as Joann's friendship with Margy blossomed. My relationship with Joann blossomed also. Joann and I had a good marriage to start with, and we have our typical share of struggles today. But our marriage is richer now that Margy is involved in meeting relational needs in Joann's life that only another woman is equipped to meet. I offer just one example of an area in which this dynamic has become apparent to me.

Joann is an at-home mom. As Tony Campolo has observed, she is accomplishing the eternally significant task of "socializing two homo sapiens into the dominant values of the Judeo-Christian tradition so that they can become the eschatological change-agents God has designed them to be for all of eternity."[2] Memorize that quote! It is what Tony's wife (a stay-at-home mom) used to reply to her working friends who would imperiously ask, "And what do *you* do for a living?"

We chuckle at Mrs. Campolo's reply. But the statement is a serious one, and Joann takes her role as a parent as seriously as that quote implies. In fact, like most moms, much of Joann's personal identity is tied up in the well-being of our two daughters, Rebekah and Rachel. This is typically true of women much more than it is true of men.

This means that there has always been much more at stake emotionally for Joann in the parenting process than there has been for me. Do not misunderstand. I am passionately concerned and deeply involved with my daughters' lives. But Joann is the one who typically rides the emotional roller coaster of ups and downs

---

[2] This is a paraphrase of a statement I heard Tony Campolo make at an Urbana Conference about 20 years ago.

in dealing with the kids' problems, whether medical or otherwise. I am somehow able to maintain a more detached perspective.

Because Joann expends so much emotional energy on the kids, there is often little left for me. In the past, the result of all this was that much of our date night together was spent with me trying to encourage Joann, affirming her and cheering her on to face yet another challenging day or week as a mom—until Margy came along.

Margy is not a parent. But Margy knows a whole lot about parenting because she was closely involved in raising her God-daughter Alisha from childhood through adolescence. So when Margy talks Joann listens. And because Margy is a woman, Joann listens to Margy in a way that she does not listen to me. As she does, Joann finds herself thankfully relieved of the responsibility of bearing the maternal half of the parenting burden alone, as Margy confirms (or helps Joann to reconsider) key decisions about how to raise our girls.

Because Margy is a woman she can touch a part of Joann's motherly instinct in a way that I as a male cannot. The result of all this is that Joann finds her emotional tank full more often, and this overflows into my relationship with Joann. Now, when Joann and I get away for a date night together, Joann has more to give emotionally, and our time together is even more enjoyable than before Margy came into the picture.

From a kinship perspective, what is going on in the Hellerman family is a transition from a nuclear family model to a social system more closely approximating the extended family model of the ancient world. In extended family societies women partner with other women (as well as their husbands) in the raising of their children. This interchange of wisdom and support provides a context in which no mother bears the emotional burden of parenting her children alone in isolation from other women. This is what has happened in the Hellerman home, as Margy's friendship with the Hellermans has grown into a family relationship.

And what a remarkable affect the arrangement has had on our daughters! Neither Rebekah nor Rachel ever dreamed that we would add another person to the family— especially another parent. But they are the real winners in all this because now my daughters have yet another godly woman around to serve as a role model for life in the kingdom of God.

Again and again, when Joann and I "run out of ears" in our efforts to listen attentively to the seemingly infinite—but important—ramblings of our now college-age daughters, Margy appears on the scene with a fresh attention span, and she ministers to the girls during some truly teachable moments. And this has been going on consistently now for nearly a decade.

But all of the above represents only half the story. Not only have the Hellermans greatly benefited from adding Margy to the family. Margy has been blessed as well. Here is Margy's perspective on her relationship with the Hellermans, expressed in her own words:

> For most of my fifty-some years I have been single. And though I hope to have many more years ahead, I can already look back at a pretty rewarding and successful life. In the fields of music, ministry, and graphic arts, I have done pretty much what I wanted to do as the opportunities arose. That's not to say I haven't prayed about my decisions or sought counsel. I just don't have a husband or children who play a part in deciding whether I should stay put or move on. But while I am by nature comfortable with a good amount of solitude, too much independence can be pretty lonely.
>
> For twelve years, I lived with Alisha (my God-daughter) and her parents. Their home was of the old Victorian design with a semi-private apartment on the 2nd level. The book you are reading hadn't even been written yet, but Alisha's family and I somehow knew that we were living together according to a biblical model that had many benefits (as well as a steep learning curve!). When Alisha went away to college, circumstances led me to move to another part of suburban Los Angeles.
>
> When the Hellermans came to my church, I knew instinctively that I had found some great friends. As our relationship developed, Joe and Joann frequently commented on how unusual it was for them to welcome outsiders into their home as more than just "company." I know I am more than "company"—I can tell the minute I walk in the back door! I get caught up in Rebekah's (age 23) and Rachel's (19) hugs and chatter before I even sit down! This is the kind of welcome that can't be faked, and it does wonders for me when I've had a tough day.
>
> Joe and I enjoy a level of camaraderie that is a special treasure to me. His hunger and thirst for a growing spiritual life combined with his accomplishments as a theologian and pastor make it possible to probe the deep things of God— something we both enjoy—and I learn so much from him! We also share the privilege of ministering together as part of our church staff. That doesn't mean we spend 8 hours a day working together—but it does mean that a mutual trust, accountability, and support exists that is crucial to successful ministry.

Joe has described my friendship with Joann quite well above. Joann and I trust each other enough to share our rock-bottom confidences, needs, worries, and hopes. We pursue being godly women together. We face growing gray together! We are secure enough in our friendship to be able to kindly say "that swimsuit doesn't look real good on you. . . ." We talk a lot, which I imagine reflects a bit of that men are from Mars, women are from Venus stuff.

As part of the Hellerman extended family, I am often involved in running errands, picking up the kids, and so forth. I am there to debrief school-life tragedies and to guide ethical decisions. I have been there to celebrate birthdays, school plays, and art awards. And I have been there to watch two lovely and unique girls grow up—this is a great gift to me as a single. I am happy to know that I have a family among whom I am welcome just as I am, to spend time with them just as they are.

Being included in the Hellerman family means I'm not so independent anymore. But I don't struggle with loneliness as I did before either! My life is very rich. I am learning that it is in the context of our receiving and giving love that we learn so much about our Lord's love for us.

As you can see, the relationship between Margy and the Hellermans constitutes much more than just a supporting and encouraging friendship. It is based on a church-family model that goes all the way back to the earliest days of the Christian church. And all five of us are the better for it.

I spent the first 15 years of vocational Christian service involved in specialized ministry to single adults. Now I find myself with increasing reservations about the wisdom of compartmentalizing God's family into separate fellowship groups according to life stages. I readily acknowledge the different needs of different age and interest groups in the church. Paul targeted instructions in his letters to specific groups of people, such as husbands and wives. Perhaps at some level there is a legitimate place for a life-stage approach to ministry.

But it is clear that for Paul and the other early Christians there existed a focus of personal identity that was much bigger than one's life stage or marital state, namely, membership in the eternal family of God:

for you are all sons of God through faith in Christ Jesus.

For as many of you as have been baptized into Christ have put on Christ.
There is no Jew or Greek, slave or free, male or female; for you are all one
in Christ Jesus. And if you are Christ's, then you are Abraham's seed, heirs
according to the promise. (Gal 3:26–29)

If Paul penned those words today, I suspect that he would have no reservations about adding "married or single" to his list in verse 28.

The congregation I serve is presently too small to offer specialized programs addressing the unique needs of people at each stage of life. And I like it that way. For I am convinced that Margy and the Hellermans have gained much more by engaging with one another according to the church family model than we ever would have gained if we had been isolated from one another in the "singles" (Margy) and "marrieds" (the Hellermans) groups that define the social landscape of the typical evangelical church.

Conclusion

We have examined four important values that should characterize a church that longs to recapture Jesus' vision for authentic Christian community:

1. We share our stuff with one another.
2. We share our hearts with one another.
3. We stay, embrace the pain, and grow up with one another.
4. Family is about more than me, the wife, and the kids.

The list is hardly exhaustive. We could surely add other values and behaviors gleaned from our survey of surrogate family activities in the ancient Christian church.

Each of these church family values will manifest itself in a myriad of tangible ways in congregational life. Your pilgrimage in community with your brothers and sisters in Christ will differ from mine, but I trust it is clear that doing church as family can make a tremendous difference in our everyday experience of the Christian life. God has designed us to go through life together. We are family in God's eyes, and we must begin to live accordingly.

One of the most beneficial aspects of the church family model surfaces in the area of personal decision making. We considered in chapter 1 the challenges that individualistic Americans face when making key life decisions alone, apart from any meaningful input from a broader village or family community. The concept of the church as a surrogate family of brothers and sisters in Christ has great potential to ameliorate the emotional angst associated with individual decision making and to assist God's people in making wise and lasting decisions when we arrive at the key crossroads of life. We turn now to consider decision making and the will of God through the matrix of the church family model.

Chapter Eight

DECISION MAKING IN THE FAMILY OF GOD

He replied to them, "Who are My mother and My brothers?"
And looking about at those who were sitting in a circle around
Him, He said, "Here are My mother and My brothers! Whoever
does the will of God is My brother and sister and mother."

(Mark 3:33–35)

*N*ick and Tina (not their real names) attended a church where I served in the late 1980s. They came to see me on a Wednesday evening in mid-October, having just finished their weekly ministry in our children's department. The couple had met at a church softball game a couple of months earlier. Now they wanted to get married in December. I did the math. Nick and Tina would have just four months together from acquaintance to the altar. The way that Nick and Tina wrestled with this major life decision helpfully illustrates what can happen when the church family functions as God intends it to.

I knew the couple's background, but I asked them to tell their stories again, together and in my presence. Both Nick and Tina had been divorced, and Nick was a single parent doing his best to raise a young son and daughter alone.

The match-up had much in its favor. Nick was a responsible, caring father. And I sensed that Tina would be a great mother. Perhaps most important, Nick's kids loved Tina already, and it was quite clear that the affection was mutual. Things seemed solid spiritually as well. Nick and Tina were deeply committed to Christ and to the ministry of His church. Finances would pose no obstacle to the health of the relationship, since both of them held well-paying jobs. I saw a lot of positive signs.

Nick and Tina's past marital failures concerned me deeply, however, and their relationship seemed to be moving much too fast given the complexities of what would be a blended family arrangement. I told the couple that I wanted to discuss their situation with another pastor on our church staff so that we could pool our wisdom to help them make this important life decision.

My colleague was a trained family therapist, and I was not surprised to discover that Pastor Steve was as troubled as I was about Nick and Tina's rush to the altar. We put our heads together and formulated a plan. At my meeting with the couple the following week, I informed Nick and Tina that Steve and I would be happy to marry them in December—but not this December. Rather, the wedding would occur a year from December.

We wanted Nick and Tina to get into counseling and to nurture their relationship with one another over the course of a year, under the loving and guiding direction of one of our church leaders. I told Nick and Tina that we would then be happy to bless their union with a grandiose church wedding, assuming that no major obstacles arose during the year of intensive therapy.

As I shared our feedback, Tina's face began to redden, and her body language communicated to me in no uncertain terms that she was not at all happy with our feedback. Nick was troubled also. They wanted time to think it over.

When the couple left my office, I was not sure how it would all turn out. I caught their eyes on the way out the door and gave some final words of encouragement. I gently insisted that what we offered was God's best for Nick and Tina and for the kids. I hoped to discourage them from taking a shortcut by trying to find someone outside the church to perform the wedding.

I assured Nick and Tina that even if they ignored our input and rushed ahead with a wedding, we would continue to consider them part of our church family, and we would do our best to help them make their marriage work by providing postmarital, instead of premarital, counseling. I suppose I expected Nick and Tina to do the American individualistic thing and run off and get married in December.

Put yourself in Nick or Tina's place. How would you respond to such an apparently heavy-handed approach on the part of your church leaders? You are in your mid-thirties. You are madly in love. And you are absolutely convinced that the relationship is God's will for your lives. Then a church pastor tells you that you must wait another year to get married.

Decision Making in the Family of God

Nick and Tina's decision offers us a practical, real-life situation to consider in view of the strong-group surrogate family values that have surfaced in the course of this study. Recall the challenging redefinition of relational priorities that I introduced in the overview of Jesus' vision for community (chap. 3). As we saw, during His earthly ministry Jesus at times portrayed the natural family in a rather negative light. In some cases Jesus went so far as to present ongoing family loyalty and becoming a disciple as mutually exclusive options.

Jesus publicly disowned allegiance to His own blood family (Mark 3:31–35). He called James and John to leave their natural families (Mark 1:18–20). He commanded a man who wished to provide for his father's burial, in accordance with traditional Jewish family piety, to instead follow Him and "let the dead bury their own dead" (Matt 8:22).

Jesus warned His followers that as far as the natural family was concerned, He came not to bring peace but rather "a sword"—to set blood relatives so severely against one another that "a man's enemies will be the members of his household" (Matt 10:34–37). A fair assessment of the Gospel evidence uncovers as much anti-family sentiment as pro-family sentiment in the public ministry of Jesus.

Passages like these, along with the strong-group orientation of the world in which Jesus lived, suggest that Jesus demanded of His followers a radical exchange of loyalties. The issue for Jesus was not simply commitment to God versus commitment to our natural families. Rather, Jesus challenged His disciples to transfer their primary family allegiance from one group (the natural family) to another (the family of God).

In a social setting where each and every person found his identity in the group to which he belonged, a call to leave one's primary group—the family—in order to follow Jesus would make sense only if following Jesus meant joining His group. As Jesus said of His followers, "Here are My mother and My brothers! Whoever does the will of God is My brother and sister and mother" (Mark 3:34–35).

The result of all this is that we can no longer drive a wedge between commitment to God and commitment to God's family, as we do when we prioritize our lives according to the traditional lines of thinking that characterize modern evangelicalism:

(1st) God — (2nd) Family — (3rd) Church — (4th) Others

Jesus and His followers viewed things quite differently. For the early Christians, loyalty to God was tangibly expressed in loyalty to God's family. According to biblical thinking, commitment to God cannot be divorced from commitment to God's group, and our priority list should read something like this:

(1st) God's Family — (2nd) My Family — (3rd) Others

Now consider Nick and Tina's important decision in light of these two very different ways of prioritizing our relational lives.

Nick and Tina's Big Decision

A week or so after the couple left my office, I received a call from Nick. He was a broken man. He said that our counsel was a "tough sell" for Tina, but that he had convinced her to receive the input and assent to the guidelines provided. Nick acknowledged that he had already experienced the chaos that results from trying to live life—and make marriage work—apart from the relational accountability provided by God's family. This time Nick wanted to do it right. He wanted more for himself, he wanted more for Tina, and he desperately wanted more for his children.

By God's grace, Nick recognized in our counsel the hand of God reaching out and offering him another chance to make marriage work. Nick had tried to do family on his own before. He had learned the hard way that a family functions best in the relational context of the larger surrogate family of God. Now he was ready for a change.

Tina soon got with the program too. Their counseling went so well, in fact, that I married Nick and Tina in June, just eight months after our initial encounter. And the marriage really "took." Nick and Tina face their challenges just like any other couple, but now, more than 15 years later, they remain faithfully married and they have done a wonderful job raising their two kids to love and serve Jesus.

Nick and Tina put God's group—the guidance and support they received through church accountability—at the top of their priority list. They took the biblical approach. This is why they were able to say no to their strong emotional desires in a family-related decision. They put the wisdom offered by God's family ahead of any feelings they had concerning the immediate future of their own natural family.

Consider the alternative. What if Nick and Tina had done the opposite? What if they had taken the standard evangelical approach and somehow convinced themselves that they could separate their commitment to God as a couple from commitment to His group? Recall the list of relational priorities with which our own church culture is so familiar:

(1st) God — (2nd) Family — (3rd) Church — (4th) Others

Working from this list, Nick and Tina could have reasoned just like so many other couples do when they are faced with the same dilemma: "How dare the church [3rd] tell us what to do! We each have a personal relationship with God [1st]. And God is in our relationship with one another [2nd]. We can ignore Pastor Joe's and Pastor Steve's advice [3rd] without being unfaithful to God [1st]. After all, family [2nd] is more important than church [3rd]. We need each other, and the kids need a mother. Let's just get married in December."

Fortunately, Nick and Tina did not respond like this to the input of their church family. The interesting thing for this particular couple is that the outcome may have been the same in either case. Now I do not want to minimize the peace, security, and joy that Nick and Tina enjoyed as a result of holding their wedding at their home church and having the union blessed by their church leaders. The affirmation of a loving church family constitutes a key ingredient in a meaningful wedding ceremony, and it serves as a solid foundation for a lifelong marriage also. But Nick and Tina had so many things going for them as a couple that I suspect they would have had a successful marriage even if they had not listened to Steve and me and waited those extra months.

Yet life in the family of God is not just about Nick and Tina—or any one individual or couple for that matter—and it is absolutely crucial to grasp this point. The payoff for making right decisions goes far beyond the boundaries of the lives of those immediately involved. As it turned out, Nick and Tina's decision to put God's family first in their lives influenced other people in our church family in ways the couple could never have imagined.

As a singles pastor I officiated at well over a hundred weddings for couples who had met in our various groups. Along the way I inevitably encountered situations similar to Nick and Tina's. And now, thankfully, I had a referral to give.

Nick and Tina's experience was ultimately such a positive one that they soon gave me permission to give their phone number to other couples who had been told by the church to "cool their jets" and to readjust the timetable for their race to the altar. What Nick and Tina could tell these young men and women was that God does work through His people to guide and direct in a way that benefits both the group and the individuals involved. Several of these couples heeded Nick and Tina's advice and they waited. At least one of them split up during the premarital counseling process, and a potentially disastrous marriage was avoided.

Nick and Tina would likely have had a good marriage even if they had rejected our counsel. But because they put God's group first at a crucial point in their own relational pilgrimage, the couple soon found themselves in a position to minister wisdom to others in the church. Nick and Tina put God's family before their own family timetable, and the fruit remains—in their lives, in the lives of their children, and in the lives of several couples who have heard and heeded their advice. This is how God often works when we put His family first, where it belongs, on our priority list.

The lesson to be learned from the story of Nick and Tina is that big decisions are best made in community, in the context of the church family—especially big family decisions. Sadly, many of us choose to ignore this principle and isolate our families from the context of relational accountability—and input on decision making—offered by the people of God. But we do so at great risk when it comes to the relational health and spiritual development of those we most dearly love and cherish. It really does take a village to raise a child or to nourish a marriage. But only a special, supernatural kind of village will do: the surrogate family of God.

Recall, once again, Malina's striking description of a strong-group approach to church family life:

> The person perceives himself or herself to be a member of a church family and responsible to the church for his or her actions, destiny, career, development, and life in general. . . . The individual person is embedded in the church family and is free to do what he or she feels right and necessary only if in accord with church family norms and only if the action is in the church's best interest. The church family has priority over the individual member.[1]

Modern evangelicals will surely struggle with the idea that we ought to be responsible to God's family for our individual "actions, destiny, career, development, and life in general." Nick and Tina's decision was not an easy one for them to make. But as we have seen in both the New Testament and in later church history, the above description is much more than a conceptual abstraction from the pen of a cultural anthropologist. It quite accurately reflects the way in which the early Christians conceived of their relationship to their local church families.

An example is the story of the acting instructor from third-century North Africa. Marcus found himself answering to the church for his whole vocational and financial future. Marcus was teaching acting. The church said, "Quit your job." And the church family offered the material resources necessary to alleviate the financial hardship that could result for Marcus should he decide to fully fol-

[1] B. Malina, *Christian Origins and Cultural Anthropology* (Atlanta: John Knox, 1986), 19.

low Jesus. Marcus was, in short, responsible to God's family for his individual "actions, destiny, career, development, and life in general." So were Nick and Tina. God honored Nick and Tina and their church for the couple's commitment to strong-group family values.

The "Cobus" Group and Wise Decisions

I was fortunate enough to be first a member, then the pastor, of a college group that operated as a church-within-a-church. We called ourselves "Cobus" because both college students and business people in the 18-to-25 age bracket filled our ranks.

The church itself was a fairly typical suburban congregation. We held our services in a large auditorium, with the result that a lot of people showed up only on Sunday and had little or no interpersonal connection with others in the church. At the church-wide level, people did not experience a whole lot of community in the New Testament sense of the word.

Cobus was another story entirely. We averaged around 50 to 60 members during the years I was involved with the group, and the participants were highly committed to God and to one another. We spent hours and hours sharing life together as we met on Sundays, interacted in midweek small groups, and traveled as a group on weekend outings. During my first 15 years of ministry, this college group was the closest thing I experienced to the New Testament church. In many ways, Cobus operated like a strong-group surrogate family.

The college years are, of course, a time for making big decisions. During my tenure with the group I saw literally hundreds of life-changing decisions made by Cobus persons. Time and again, young people would meet with me, or with another adult sponsor, in order to wrestle through major life decisions together. Group members also spent a lot of time interacting with their peers when choices loomed large.

Numbers of collegians sought advice about the kind of job that might fit their particular gifts and temperament. Others just out of college discussed with us the direction that their romantic relationships were taking. "How do I know if she's the one, Joe?" Again and again, these young adults involved their spiritual shepherds—and their peers—in the process of decision making.

Chapter 1 addresses the major decisions facing young people in Western society today:

- **Vocation**　　What am I going to do with my life?
- **Spouse**:　　Who am I going to spend my life with?
- **Residence**　　Where am I going to live?

As noted earlier, we pay a tremendous emotional price for the freedoms in decision making that we exercise in our radically individualist society. God has not equipped us to operate as isolated individuals, especially where the most important decisions of our lives are concerned. God has created us for community, and it only makes sense to think that we will be healthier psychologically if we make important decisions in the context of a loving and caring church family.

This is hardly rocket science. After all, life works precisely in this way in our natural families. Because people from healthy families have a support network from which to tackle life's big decisions, they experience less stress and emotional heartache than those who must go it alone. We should expect the same to be the case in our church family.

There is another reason for making life decisions in the context of the broader church family. Not only will we experience less angst and emotional upheaval. We will also make better decisions—decisions that are better for us, and decisions that are better for the expansion of God's kingdom.

In my 25 years of church ministry, I have observed a general principle that I believe we can take to the bank when it comes to making major life decisions. I have blocked it off in the text in order to emphasize its importance:

> The closer a Christian group approximates the strong-group, church family model that characterized early Christianity, the better the decisions that are made by the group's individual members and nuclear family units.

This is a rather bold statement, but it is true. Experience bears it out again and again.

The young men and women whose lives were deeply embedded in the Cobus group made great decisions—eternally meaningful decisions—again and again. Precisely because the group functioned in a way that approximated the New Testament model for the church as a family, the members generally made wise decisions that greatly benefited them as individuals and significantly contributed to the mission of God's group, the church, in the world today.

Community Guidance as a Way of Life

More than mere advice-seeking is at work here. It will not do simply to challenge American evangelicals, who otherwise live life as isolated individuals, to seek counsel from others only when they come to a defining fork in the road of life. In the strong-group church family model, input from others is a way of life, not a resource to occasionally draw on as one of several items on a checklist that purports to tell us how to find God's will for our lives.

Many of our Cobus members were involved for years in the group, in an ongoing context of commitment, relational warmth, and interpersonal accountability. When these young people were faced with vocational and romantic options that would determine the very course of their future lives in the kingdom, the strong-group network was already securely in place to bear the life-giving fruit of eternally significant—and personally beneficial—decisions.

This is quite important because what I am advocating here is not an institutional program. To be sure, the context for wise decision making can be a formal one, like a meeting with a pastor to plan a wedding (Nick and Tina) or the calling of a "wisdom council" of church leaders to receive input for making an important decision (Pastor Martin below). More often than not, input comes in a less structured, much more organic way, as long-term relationships with brothers and sisters in the church family provide a natural context for speaking wisdom into one another's lives in a variety of settings.

This is not to say that our collegians invariably took the advice of their leaders and peers. Nor was our advice invariably good! But more often than not, God used His family to guide these young people to godly decisions in the vocational and romantic realms, decisions that continue to prove their worth even today.

The Fruit of Wise Decisions

More than a dozen people from this college group chose to enter full-time vocational Christian ministry. They are all over the world serving God in various capacities, from church planting to Bible translation. Their decisions to enter the ministry did not come as individual emotional responses to a sermon or to a highly charged camp message. The decisions were hammered out in the context of a community of peers and leaders who were well aware of the strengths and weaknesses of the individuals. So far, only one couple has returned stateside to choose an alternative direction for their life's work. The rest have had the wisdom of their vocational decisions confirmed in the crucible of Christian ministry in some real tough places.

Moreover, just as in the case of our actor friend Marcus from North Africa, Cobus members put their money where their mouth was in support of the decisions made by fellow group members. To this day, former Cobus persons who are now on the mission field are supported to a significant extent by their brothers and sisters who belonged to that college group back in the 1980s. Joann and I send monthly checks to a halfdozen missionaries who once belonged to Cobus. Others in the group who have remained stateside and have pursued secular employment give much more generously than we are able to give.

Not too long ago one of our Cobus missionaries stopped by to see me during furlough from his ministry with Wycliffe Bible Translators. I asked him about his financial needs and he replied, "Our support is at 100 percent." Much of the financial resources this couple enjoys can be traced to connections made during their college days. The Cobus group thus further exemplifies first-century surrogate family values, as members continue to share their material resources with their brothers and sisters in Christ.

Finding a Life Partner

I performed wedding after wedding during my decade-long tenure with the Cobus group. For the most part, these young people made the wisest of decisions in choosing their life partners. They married other members of their Cobus family, and most of these marriages are still solid today, more than a decade later.

Others chose instead to go outside the group and operate on their own in their search for a mate. Sadly, those collegians who married outside the Cobus group experienced a higher rate of failed marriages than those who found a mate within the group. And the trend is not limited to those who married outside the faith. Even those who married believers from outside the group have tended to find themselves in less-satisfying or less-healthy relationships. A number of these marriages have already ended in divorce. In contrast, Cobus members who chose their spouses within the group have generally experienced genuine spiritual and relational life in their marriages.

The closer a Christian group approximates the strong-group church family model of early Christianity, the better the decisions that are made by its individual members. Cobus was a living demonstration of this principle. The group was in many ways similar to the New Testament church. And lasting, life-giving commitments to God's kingdom and to significant others were made by Cobus members who chose to receive the input of God's family when they came to the crossroads of life's key decisions. My wife Joann and I can testify firsthand to this truth. We are a Cobus couple who first met in the group and who have now been serving Jesus, happily married, for more than 28 years.

The Paths of Jerry and Kristen

As Cobus leaders, Joann and I occasionally saw the contrasting paths of spiritual (and relational) life and death illustrated in the experiences of members of a single family. A brother and a sister attended our group whom I will refer to as Jerry and Kristen. Jerry was highly committed to the group and deeply engaged with his peers and with our Cobus staff in his pilgrimage as a young Christian. Jerry opened up his life to us in the context of the relational accountability that the group provided.

We had the opportunity to help Jerry make those key life decisions that invariably face a young collegian. Jerry proceeded to marry a young woman who was a solid Christian and who, most importantly, had similar convictions about her commitment to church family life. Jerry's biggest relational decision was made in the context of the Cobus family, and Jerry and his wife Claire continue to enjoy a quality Christian marriage nearly two decades later.

But Kristen, Jerry's sister, never really came under the care and shepherding of her peers and leaders in Cobus. She attended the larger Sunday meetings and enjoyed our activities, but she seldom involved herself on an intimate level with others in the group. A traditional assessment of Kristen's spiritual condition would perhaps conclude that she was not as committed to God as her brother Jerry.

As you have learned in the course of this book, commitment to God cannot be separated from commitment to God's group. And it was the latter—Kristen's reluctance to live out her Christian faith in the context of relational accountability—that proved to be her undoing. Most telling was the fact that Kristen's dating relationships usually involved men from outside the Cobus group. These relationships were invariably disappointing.

The friendships that my wife Joann and I established back in the 1980s with young people in that Cobus group continue even today. Amazingly enough, after nearly a decade of trying to make life and relationships work apart from the input and guidance of God's family, Kristen called Joann on the phone. She set up an appointment to seek Joann's advice on a marriage prospect.

Kristen's hindsight vision was 20-20. She saw the fruit of group accountability in her brother Jerry's life. So now, nearly a decade later, Kristen wanted it for herself. She came for counsel from Joann. Kristen's dilemma was not an uncommon one. She had become involved with a man who, due to work demands, suddenly had to relocate from southern California to Atlanta. Kristen's question was a simple but profoundly important one: "Should she move to Atlanta and join her prospective spouse?"

Joann is a highly skilled listener with genuine gifts of wisdom and insight, and she saw too many red flags to encourage Kristen in her desire to move out of state. Except for the meeting with Joann, Kristen was still operating in total isolation. She showed up in church now and then, but Kristen had no ongoing connection of personal accountability with any Christian community.

But Kristen was in a great position to begin to develop meaningful relationships in the context of God's group. She had been raised in the church that she occasionally attended, and there were many opportunities to develop a network of supportive friendships should she choose to do so. Kristen's parents, both committed Christians, also lived in southern California. Both her potential church family and her natural family beckoned Kristen to begin to profit from the benefits of making decisions in a strong-group setting. A move to Atlanta would only isolate Kristen further from the very benefits that God's group could bring into her life.

Joann also discovered that the track record of Kristen's boyfriend was, at best, unknown. He may have been a superb young man. But because he had lived his own life pretty much in isolation from the family of God, his true character would only be revealed later, in the crucible of marriage, after the big decision had already been made.

This situation was a recipe for deep marital disappointment, as Joann and I have discovered again and again. So Joann gently but firmly counseled Kristen to stay in southern California and to get involved with other Christians in a responsible network of church-family accountability. If Kristen's relationship with her prospective husband were solid, Joann informed her, it would survive a temporary geographical separation.

Kristen wanted the benefits of group input, but she was ultimately unwilling to integrate Joann's wise counsel into the process of decision making. She chose instead to ignore the advice and move to Atlanta. Several years have gone by now, and I recently heard that Kristen has returned to California with the scars of an unhealthy and failing marriage. Her brother Jerry, on the other hand, continues to enjoy a thriving relationship with his wife of 14 years.

Jerry and Kristen came from the same solid Christian home. They had the same relational opportunities during those formative Cobus years. Their radically different experiences in the relational arena can likely be attributed to a single factor: the degree to which they were willing to submit their individual desires and aspirations to the guidance and input provided by God's group. Jerry chose for the group, and he prospered. Kristen chose to go it alone, and her heart has been broken again and again.

Calling a Wisdom Council

Much of the advice-giving and wisdom-seeking that went on in the Cobus class occurred in rather informal ways as we interacted with one another on a regular basis during our years together as a group. Some churches adopt a more intentionally structured approach to communal decision making. A friend named Michael Martin pastors a church a few miles down the road from my church. Michael has devised what I consider a brilliant idea for helping to turn the church family model from an abstract concept into a tangible reality in the lives of his people. When individuals in Michael's church face heart-wrenching decisions, they are encouraged to call a wisdom council.

It works like this. On one occasion a single mother in Michael's church was forced to make a tough decision about her son, a decision that would significantly shape the young man's future for years to come. The boy's teacher and school administrators had informed the woman that her son would benefit academically from being held back a year to repeat sixth grade.

But there was a trade-off. The boy would suffer socially from such a move. School officials implied that the decision was a bit of a "toss up," and they left our single mother with the daunting responsibility of deciding which way to go. Mom asked Michael to call a wisdom council.

The council has standing members, including Michael and several deacons. Individuals who might bring particular insight to the situation under review fill out the rest of the group on an *ad hoc* basis. In the present case, Michael invited people in the church with backgrounds in education and psychology, as well as another single parent or two.

No formal structure is employed. The group simply shares a meal together and openly discusses all the pros and cons associated with each option, so that an informed decision can be made with the kind of wisdom that can only come from community input. And then they pray together. *I would pray before discussion!*

I do not recall the specific outcome of the situation outlined above. But we can assume that mother and son both went away assured that all options had been considered and that their church family would be there to support them whatever the decision and whatever the outcome. This, after all, is how the church as a family works.

Transitioning to a Family-Oriented Church Model

Much has been written in recent years about creating community in the local church. The good news is that we do not need to create community. Indeed, we could not do so even if we wanted to. God has already created His community by saving us into His eternal family. We already are, for better or worse, brothers and sisters in Christ. Sharing a Common life in Christ by the Spirit

Our problem is that we do not often enjoy the kind of community that we sense we should as people who are family in God's eyes. To reframe the issue in theological terms, our relational reality falls far short of our positional reality, where the horizontal aspect of the Christian life is concerned. Indeed, given the present state of some of our churches, recapturing Jesus' vision for authentic Christian community may seem like a nearly insurmountable challenge.

I find it immensely encouraging to remember that this is God's project, not ours, and to remind myself that the Holy Spirit truly longs to knit us together in community as God intends it. God is more than ready to come alongside those who are willing to do the hard work of living life as the new covenant family of God. More often than not, we simply need to figure out how to get out of God's way in order to let Him do His community-creating work in our lives.

What follows are some suggestions for putting the church family model into practice. Contextualization of the family metaphor differs from congregation to congregation in the modern world, and I offer the following observations and directives with a good deal of reservation, since actualizing the surrogate family values that we have encountered in the course of our study constitutes a way of life—not another set of church programs. The kind of change I am advocating will not occur without a significant degree of intentionality, so it is vital to consider, at least in general terms, how we might establish and cultivate New Testament church family values and behaviors among our people.

Churches of less than 200 members may be able to live out the family model as a single group. Larger churches will need significantly to retool their ministry priorities to facilitate such a social reality. But it seems to me that those of us in church leadership must begin the change process by critically evaluating both the content of our teaching and the various social contexts in which this teaching takes place.

The Content of Our Teaching

Right thinking constitutes the foundation for life change, and solid teaching is needed about the New Testament model of the church as a family, including specific instructions detailing the biblical responsibilities of brotherhood. The time is past for preaching and teaching that serve only to reinforce, rather than to challenge, the unbiblical assumption that Christianity is to be conceived of as some sort of an individual path to spiritual enlightenment or, worse yet, a commodity to be consumed.

We can also teach our people much about New Testament community through our worship ministries. Paul used the expression "our Lord" 53 times in his letters. He wrote "my Lord" only once. It's all in the pronouns! And pronouns are a powerful teaching vehicle where worship is concerned.

Given our cultural environment, it is only to be expected that much of our contemporary worship music continues to be produced by people who are quite unaware of the influence of Western individualism on their work. The result is a multitude of wonderful songs that reflect on our personal relationship with Jesus but tend to ignore the connection between God and His people as a group.

We would do ourselves well, I think, where copyright laws and "singability" permit, to replace a lot of the first-person singular pronouns in our worship songs (I, me, my, mine) with their corresponding plurals (we, us, our, ours). There is something about congregational singing that weaves biblical truth deep into the tapestry of our lives in ways that nothing else is able to do. We should take advantage of the power of corporate worship to teach our people that the church is a family.

As the pastor-teachers of God's family, we must lovingly immerse our people in the eternal truth that the Christian faith is preeminently a community endeavor to partner with God to further His kingdom program. And we must teach our people how to live as brothers and sisters in community together.

Reconsidering the Social Context

But teaching our people about the church as a family will not suffice to alter deeply ingrained patterns of behavior. We must also reevaluate the social contexts of church life, the ways in which our ministries are executed. The priority most churches place upon the success of the Sunday service subtly but powerfully communicates the message that this impersonal, once-a-week social environment is quintessentially what "church" is all about. After all, this is where most church leaders count heads, and this is where we collect the money.

As a result, the one event preeminently identified with the word "church" in most congregations finds our people seated side-by-side, facing forward, with little or no interpersonal interaction with persons to the right or to the left. A fellow sitting next to me in Sunday church might have lost his job—or his spouse—that very week. Tragically, however, I would never know it.

We have discovered, moreover, that a highly successful approach to evangeliz-ing a whole generation of people (baby boomers) who attend these large-group meetings is to assure our listeners that God desires to meet their felt needs. Now it is certainly the case that God often does meet us at our point of need. But a teaching ministry that overemphasizes this reality runs the risk of promoting an individualistic, anthropocentric view of the Christian life. We give our people the wrong impression that God's primary objective in our lives is to help us achieve our relational and vocational goals, to relieve our stress, to give us joy and peace—all at the personal level.

The result is that both the context (the Sunday setting) and the content ("God wants to meet my needs") of church as we know it in America today often serve only to reinforce the individualistic, consumer orientation of the dominant cul-ture. As long as this remains the case, our people will continue to think that they are truly going to church on Sunday morning, and our teaching on the church as a surrogate family will fall on deaf ears. We are reminded once again that what we do inevitably speaks much louder than what we say.

I have discovered in my congregation that surrogate sibling relations are bet-ter "caught" than "taught," so it is essential to provide for our people the kind of social settings in which church family relations can be experienced firsthand. We must provide environments where people can actually experience the church as a family, and we must assure our people that this relational context is what "going to church" is all about. Here is the meat and potatoes of true Christianity. Sunday is just the gravy. Such an approach will involve a significant shift in priorities for most congregations, but it is absolutely essential. Simply promoting a small-group program as a second option during the week is not enough. These relational settings must become central to the values of our church culture.

You might try what I did on a Sunday morning some time ago. I preached a sermon entitled "Why Sunday A.M. Is Not Church" in which I compared early church family values and practices with the way that we do church on Sunday morning. The application was challenging but quite straightforward. I proceeded gently but firmly to inform my people that many of them—some of whom had attended on Sunday for years—had never been to church! Then I encouraged them to begin going to church, that is, to start attending one of our home-group settings where they could cultivate the kind of surrogate sibling relationships that God intends for His children to enjoy with one another.

Some months later, I gave a presentation about Christian community at a gath-ering of our church's top-level leadership team of 20 or so people. I still recall the rather horrified look on the face of a member of our stewardship committee (these are the precious people who track Sunday attendance and Sunday giving at our church) when I informed the group that, if I had to choose, I would rather have our people attending a home group than sitting in our Sunday morning service.

Genuine spiritual formation depends upon such priorities. Consider the observations of Brad Cecil, a creative Christian leader from Arlington, Texas:

> We studied transformation. We recognized that most of the transformative things in our lives are missing from the predominant model of spiritual formation in contemporary churches. . . . Relationships are perhaps the most transformative thing in our lives, especially in areas such as values and compassion. It is very hard to teach these concepts didactically. Instead, they are shaped through a long-term process of observation, understanding, and modeling. We realized that we were not transformed by listening to sermons, even when the messages were reinforced with drama, music, and PowerPoint. As a result, we placed our priority on sharing life together. . . . we switched from a large group pattern of church to that of a network of house churches.[2]

I do not believe that it has to be an either-or, as Cecil's comments might imply. Sunday worship and teaching combined with home-group relationships is a powerful prescription for vibrant Christian living. Ideally, I want my people together both on Sunday and during the week.

But please do not miss the main point in the above quotation. We are all quite aware that Sunday attenders generally do not become spiritually formed disciples of Jesus. Here Brad Cecil is right on target. We grow most significantly as we relate closely to one another as brothers and sisters in the family of God. If we want to return to the world of New Testament Christianity, the relational environments in our churches must take precedence over our larger weekly gatherings. We will just have to leave it to God to take care of the finances and the Sunday attendance.

From Pastor to Pastors

This brings me to a final charge, directed now to those of us who are (or who are training to be) vocational Christian ministers. Many of us receive great personal satisfaction from our Sunday sermons, and so we should, for it is a tremendous honor to speak on behalf of the King of the universe. But some of us overly depend on our public teaching ministries for a weekly shot of self-esteem, and our

---

[2] Cited in E. Gibbs and R. Bolger, *Emerging Churches* (Grand Rapids: Baker, 2005), 258.

personal identities have become far too wrapped up in our role as the community's "Sunday sage."

Robust Sunday attendance and generous church offerings only compound the problem. For as a church grows, the preaching pastor will almost inevitably be affirmed in an institutional, managerial approach to ministry by a well-meaning group of elders or deacons whose ecclesiology and understanding of pastoral effectiveness are influenced more by the *Wall Street Journal* than by the letters of Paul.

It has been my observation that church leaders who spend the bulk of their week in the business world, and who have not been extensively exposed to New Testament ecclesiology, remain quite satisfied to view growth in Sunday morning attendance and the expansion of the church budget as the primary benchmarks of a healthy Christian community. As long as our key leaders remain so satisfied with so little, we will not recapture Jesus' vision for authentic Christian community.

The result of all this, ironically, is that the very leader—the preaching pastor—who can most convincingly persuade his people that Sunday morning is not church as God intended it often has the most at stake in clearly communicating that message. Our personal investment in the success of our Sunday services, and the affirmation we receive when things go well, tend to make it emotionally difficult for us as pastors to embrace the truth that our people need each other much more than they need us.

We must transcend these understandable but unhealthy feelings in order to do what is best in the long run for the people God has entrusted to us. We must preach community, and we must structure and present our church programs in such a way as to make those relational environments a first priority for the lives of our people.

Frankly, a positive step in this direction would be to engage in an extended fast from our ongoing diet of secular leadership books and principles. As one of our emerging church brothers insightfully quipped, "The business world is now quoting Scripture to help itself give leadership to its projects. Maybe it's time for the church to put down the management books and pick up the Bible to see what all the fuss is about."[3]

The responsibilities of senior church leaders go beyond encouraging church family relationships through appropriate teaching and programming. Pastors need community too—perhaps more than anyone. We pastors are not immune to the reality that spiritual formation occurs in the context of community. We

---

[3] A. Jones, quoted in Gibbs and Bolger, *Emerging Churches,* 208.

must pursue relationships with a handful of brothers in the congregation, first and foremost, for our own spiritual health. We pastors need caring brothers and sisters. And they need us.

But there is another reason that we as pastors need a group of close surrogate siblings in the church family. We ourselves need to be in community in order to model community life for our people if we truly want them to embrace church family values for their own lives. The American evangelical model of the CEO pastor who functions as a spiritual father to his congregation and as a business executive with his staff—but who relates to no one in the church as a peer brother in Christ—directly betrays the New Testament metaphor of the church as a family.

One who has no true brothers in the congregation will be unable authentically and credibly to challenge others to live together as surrogate siblings. A return to the church as God intended will begin, as is often the case, with a transformation of values and behaviors among those who lead God's people. We turn now to consider in some detail the structure and orientation of leadership in the New Testament family of God.

Chapter Nine

LEADERSHIP IN THE
FAMILY OF GOD

*"Do not call anyone on earth your father, because
you have one Father, who is in heaven."*

(Matt 23:9)

*T*he group known as The Community exhibited nearly all of the key elements of the strong-group approach to social organization that we saw evidenced in early Christianity. Like the first Christians in Jerusalem, the 40 or so members pooled their financial resources into The Community's common fund. One woman even contributed her $100,000 inheritance to the group, somewhat like Barnabas in Acts 4. Another paid cash for a 160-acre ranch in New Mexico, which served as The Community's retreat center.

The sharing of material resources was not the only evidence of collectivist behavior among members of The Community. Each member also deferred to the group for all major decisions. A sense of loyalty to The Community took absolute priority over other life commitments for those who belonged to the group.

The sharing of resources, the priority of the group over the individual, undivided group loyalty—all these ingredients were in place as we saw them functioning among the early Christians. The Community, however, was not a Christian church. It was a dangerous cult, led by a dangerous man. Former Community members portrayed the group's leader, Mark Tizer (known as Yo), as "a manipulative, alcoholic, sex-addicted despot who controls nearly every aspect of his followers' lives in a sort of spiritual slavery."[1]

In late 1997 Tizer began to capitalize on the media attention that he had attracted as a successful trainer of ultramarathoners in Colorado. This public acclamation also drove a dozen or so former members of The Community out of a self-imposed silence. The picture they painted of daily life in the cult was not a pretty one. A lawsuit filed in the state court in Boulder, Colorado, laid out a long list of Tizer's alleged practices. Among the abuses were sleep deprivation, bullying, and emotional manipulation. Specific allegations included sexual impropriety, coerced abortions, and other forms of mind control.

Tizer's marathon training regimen was also highly problematic. According to *Newsweek*,

> Children as young as 9 were required to take long, predawn runs. Coach Tizer's training regimen has adult runners training at 120 or so miles a week, half again as many as other ultramarathoners. When Celia Bertoia, 42, complained to Tizer of intense pain in her shins after a 20-mile run, he told her to take three days off, then run again. So she ran. "I was a quarter mile into my run when I heard my leg just snap," Bertoia recalls. Unabashed, Tizer blamed the fractures on Bertoia's brittleness, telling her it was a metaphor for her problems.[2]

Perhaps most indicative of Tizer's abusive and dysfunctional leadership style are the sentiments reflected in a quote by another former Community member. Chris Beh observed of the cult leader, "He takes credit for everything and responsibility for nothing."

Cults like Tizer's give us serious reservations about the strong-group approach to community life, whether Christian or otherwise. It is important to remember our description of the collectivist church model from chapter 2:

> The person perceives himself or herself to be a member of a church and responsible to the church for his or her actions, destiny, career, development, and life in general. . . . The individual person is embedded in the church and is free to do what he or she feels right and necessary only if in accord with church norms and only if the action is in the church's best interest. The church has priority over the individual member.[3]

---

[1] D. Glick and A. Murr, "The Community: Divine Madness?" *Newsweek*, August 18, 1997.
[2] Ibid.
[3] B. Malina, *Christian Origins and Cultural Anthropology* (Atlanta: John Knox, 1986), 19, paraphrased.

Substitute "The Community" for the word "church," and you have a pretty accurate description of Tizer's cult group. Cults like Tizer's understandably make many of us uncomfortable about embracing the strong-group model of the church as a family. We know that there is a tremendous danger of abuse in any community model that puts so much authority in the hands of the group and its leadership.

Nevertheless, we have seen how the strong-group church family model worked in a marvelous way among the early Christians. This tight-knit approach to social organization enabled early Christianity to turn the Roman Empire on its head. To reject God's blueprint in order to protect our churches from cultlike aberrations would be to miss out on what God has for His people. We must press ahead and recapture the social vision of Jesus. But we must do so with care.

Our culture's hermeneutic of suspicion toward power and authority makes us justly wary of heavy-handed leadership in any kind of organizational setting. Postmodern critiques of institutional forms of control, along with the regrettable church experiences a number of us have had along these lines, have produced a generation of Christians who harbor serious reservations about relinquishing control of their personal destinies to the leader of a group. In fact, the church I pastor has become somewhat of a haven for persons who have suffered various degrees of hurt and abuse at the hands of authoritarian leaders in local evangelical congregations. The problem is a real one.

Some of our younger church pioneers have reacted by disassociating themselves entirely from any formal leadership structure. Maji, an emerging Christian community in Birmingham, UK, is representative:

> The leadership is organic and open. Everyone, whether they have been around
> and in relationship with people like myself for years or they have been here
> only twice, has equal access and voice to help shape the next gathering or to
> offer assistance and participation.[4]

I must confess that in my unreflective moments I find such an approach rather appealing. I am a child of the 1960s. I have seen more than my share of the misuse of power and control, both at the local and national levels of government, and in churches and other Christian organizations. There is something attractive about a leaderless, democratic free-for-all, where the Spirit of God alone freely reigns among the people of God.

The problem, of course, is that such an extreme approach completely ignores the biblical materials on leadership. And it naively assumes that healthy, functional

---

[4] Maji facilitator Pip Piper, cited by E. Gibbs and R. Bolger, *Emerging Churches* (Grand Rapids: Baker, 2005), 202.

leaders will rise up in an organic, nondirected manner. Unfortunately, the opposite often occurs. The leadership vacuum is filled not by mature believers who qualify for the task of shepherding the people of God but by dysfunctional individuals who lead out of emptiness rather than out of a deep well of spiritual resources that only years in the Lord can provide. The leaderless church is not the answer. A special kind of leadership is required for a strong-group, surrogate family of brothers and sister in Christ.

Checks and Balances in the Family of God

We need some checks and balances that allow us to move ahead with the early Christian approach to community but that at the same time prevent the group—and especially group leaders—from exercising authority in a destructive way. This chapter explains that God has already built the necessary safeguards into the New Testament model for the church as a family. These checks and balances specifically address the way that leadership is to be structured and exercised in the church. For the abuse of authority in strong-group religious sects can almost invariably be traced to the particular orientation of the leader of the cult.

The central problem with abusive cult groups lies in the concentration of power into the hands of a single individual and the utilization of the leader's authority to manipulate rather than to serve his followers. Combine this approach to leadership with a group of dysfunctional followers who long for someone else to tell them how to live, and the result is a highly volatile situation.

In fact, authoritarian, one-man leadership is part of the very definition of the word "cult" in *The American Heritage Dictionary:* "A religion or religious sect generally considered to be extremist or false, with its followers often living in an unconventional manner under the guidance of an authoritarian, charismatic leader."[5] Marc Tizer's group, The Community, was a classic example. So were Jim Jones's People's Temple and Marshall Applewhite's Heaven's Gate. In each case authority was vested in a single individual, and in each case the cult leader used that authority to manipulate, rather than serve, the members of the group.

Thus the problem rests with both the *number* of leaders (one person) and the *nature* of leadership (manipulative and self-serving) in these cultic expressions of a strong-group social organization. A single authoritarian leader in charge of a community structured to embrace strong-group values is a recipe for spiritual and relational disaster. It is no accident that the instructions God has given for leader-

---

[5] *The American Heritage Dictionary of the English Language* (Boston: Houghton, Mifflin Company, 1992).

ship in His surrogate family include safeguards that address issues of both the number of leaders and the nature of leadership in God's group.

In Matt 23:8–12, Jesus established a pattern for community leadership that is guaranteed to ensure that the group's authority is exercised in a manner that encourages the spiritual and relational health of all involved:

> But as for you, do not be called "Rabbi," because you have one Teacher, and you are all brothers. Do not call anyone on earth your father, because you have one Father, who is in heaven. And do not be called masters either, because you have one Master, the Messiah. The greatest among you will be your servant. Whoever exalts himself will be humbled, and whoever humbles himself will be exalted.

The two principles reflected in this passage are plurality leadership and servant leadership. A biblical, strong-group church family led by a *team* of persons who exercise their authority as *servants* of their brethren will have no problem with abuse and manipulation. Plurality and servant leadership are designed to be central to God's model of the church as a strong-group family.

Plurality Leadership in the Family of God

The first biblical safeguard against the destructive authority of a misled or deranged leader is quite straightforward. The strong-group church family is not to be led by a single individual but by a group of people, variously identified in the New Testament as elders, overseers, or pastors (the terms are interchangeable). In our discussion of this important truth, the New Testament evidence and the practical benefits of team leadership are considered.

The New Testament Evidence

Hints of a plurality leadership model occur in the teachings of Jesus, and it is connected to His understanding of the fatherhood of God. Jesus' use of "Father" to refer to God constitutes some of the most obvious and extensive evidence that Jesus conceived of His group of followers in terms of a family model. For example, Jesus' use of the Semitic term "*Abba*" tells us much about the intimacy Jesus envisioned between Father and children in His surrogate family. But we must resist the temptation to explore fully the New Testament theme of the fatherhood of God. We limit our focus to a single aspect of Jesus' concept of fatherhood as it was to function in His new community.

As indicated in the quote from Matthew 23 above, Jesus intended the position of Father in the church family to be reserved for God alone: "do not call anyone on earth 'father,' for you have one Father, and he is in heaven" (NIV). The same idea subtly manifests itself in another Gospel:

> Peter began to tell Him, "Look, we have left everything and followed You." "I assure you," Jesus said, "there is no one who has left house, brothers or sisters, mother or father, children, or fields because of Me and the gospel, who will not receive 100 times more, now at this time—houses, brothers and sisters, mothers and children, and fields, with persecutions—and eternal life in the age to come." (Mark 10:28–30)

Earlier we examined this text in terms of the behavior Jesus expected His followers to demonstrate in their utilization of their material possessions. The passage also directly informs our understanding of the role of the father in Jesus' newly founded family.

The list of natural family relations that Jesus says are "left" (v. 29) should be compared with the church family relations that the faithful follower of Jesus will "receive" (v. 30). I have organized them in column format so that you can easily compare the lists:

"LEFT"	"RECEIVE"
house	houses
brothers	brothers
sisters	sisters
mother	mothers
father	*MISSING*
children	children
fields	fields

Consider what is missing among the list of relationships to be enjoyed in the church. There is going to be no "father" figure in the family Jesus is putting together—no *human* father figure, at any rate. In light of Matthew 23, the reason is quite clear: God—and God alone—is to occupy the paternal role in the family of God.

I recognize that the above understanding of these Gospel texts does not necessarily exclude one-man leadership in the local church (a single pastor or a senior pastor). One could argue that Jesus simply desired to ensure that whoever leads His church at the human level (be it a single leader or otherwise) does not usurp

God's role as the Father and final authority in the community. The single (or senior) pastor model would then be an admissible option, as long as God retains His position as sole Father of the church.

But this does not appear to be the way that Jesus' early followers understood His teaching on the topic. Evidence from at least four different New Testament writers, representing both Jewish and Gentile churches from a variety of geographical areas, arguably demonstrates that plurality leadership was the common model in the early church. Here is the biblical data with some additional comments in brackets:

Gentile Churches

When they had appointed **elders** in every church and prayed with fasting, they committed them to the Lord in whom they had believed (Acts 14:23). [Paul and Barnabas appoint leaders in the Galatian churches on their way back from the first missionary journey. Notice the emphasis upon elders (plural) in each church (singular).]

Now from Miletus, he sent to Ephesus and called for the **elders** of the church (Acts 20:17). [This refers to the leaders of the church at Ephesus, where Paul ministered for several years.]

Paul and Timothy, slaves of Christ Jesus: To all the saints in Christ Jesus who are in Philippi, including the **overseers** and **deacons** (Phil 1:1). [Paul's churches in Europe reflect the same model of plurality leadership. See also 1 Thess 5:12–13, where leaders are also referred to in the plural.]

The reason I left you in Crete was to set right what was left undone and, as I directed you, to appoint **elders** in every town (Titus 1:5). [Paul gives instructions to Titus for church organization. Again, notice the contrast between the plural (elders) and the singular (every town).]

Therefore, as a fellow elder and witness to the sufferings of the Messiah, and also a participant in the glory about to be revealed, I exhort the **elders** among you: shepherd God's flock among you, not overseeing out of compulsion but freely, according to God's will; not for the money but eagerly; not lording it over those entrusted to you, but being examples to the flock. And when the chief Shepherd appears, you will receive the unfading crown of glory (1 Pet 5:1–4). [Peter simply assumes that all the churches that will receive his letter in

"Pontus, Galatia, Cappadocia, Asia and Bithynia" (1:1) are each led by a group of elders.]

Jewish Churches

Obey your **leaders** and submit to them, for they keep watch over your souls as those who will give an account, so that they can do this with joy and not with grief, for that would be unprofitable for you (Heb 13:17). [The unknown author, writing to Jewish Christians, assumes plurality leadership.]

Is anyone among you sick? He should call for the **elders** of the church, and they should pray over him after anointing him with olive oil in the name of the Lord (Jas 5:14). [James, addressing the Jewish Christian communities in the eastern diaspora (1:1), could assume the presence of elders in every congregation in which his letter would be read.]

We also know, from the early postapostolic epistle known as 1 Clement, that the churches in Corinth and Rome (c. AD 95) were led by a plurality of elders. By contrast, there are no straightforward examples of one-man leadership until the letters of Ignatius (c. AD 110).

Some students of New Testament ecclesiology attempt to circumvent the evidence outlined above by maintaining either that plurality rule was only one option among several in the early church, or that leadership as we see it functioning in the New Testament is *descriptive* (how they did it back then) and not *prescriptive* (how we should do it today).

I am persuaded by neither line of reasoning, but this is not the place to revisit the debate over church leadership as it has been framed in the literature. I simply wish to draw attention to the continuity between Jesus and His followers regarding their conceptions of community for the early church, and to draw some implications from that continuity for the organization of church leadership.

As we saw in our analysis of his churches (chap. 4), the apostle Paul adopted the strong-group church family precisely as Jesus had envisioned and established it. All of the characteristics that we found in Jesus' teachings about God's community were replicated in the model Paul desired for his churches. The point here is that there was close continuity between Jesus and Paul with respect to the social organization of the groups they were forming. Since Paul followed so closely in Jesus' footsteps by appropriating Jesus' church family model across the board, it is reasonable to assume that Paul also patterned his ideas concerning leadership in the new family of God after the convictions of Jesus. Indeed, it would be counter-intuitive to argue otherwise.

The connection between Jesus and Paul on the issue of leadership can be observed when we compare Jesus' words (Matt 23:8–12; Mark 10:28–30) with Paul's practice of appointing a team of elders to govern each of his churches. The evidence from the Gospels is only suggestive. Jesus offered little if any explicit instruction about church polity or organization. Paul and the other New Testament writers apparently understood quite well what Jesus meant when He elevated fatherhood in the new church family to the divine realm and commanded His followers to view one another as "brothers."

Jesus intended God to be the only "solo leader" in the community. At the human level, He intended the plurality approach to serve as the inspired blueprint for church leadership. Paul and others grasped Jesus' intentions, and they established team-led churches accordingly. The continuity between Jesus and His followers in the plurality approach to leadership should caution us against summarily dismissing the team model as simply *descriptive* of a particular cultural approach to church leadership.

Some time ago I took a moment to look at all this from a different angle. I asked myself, "If one of our New Testament writers had wanted to say 'senior pastor,' how would he have done so in Greek?" The answer is quite revealing. Since "senior" in our phrase refers not to age but to the senior pastor's position of authority, a New Testament writer would likely have utilized the Greek prefix *archi*. For example, the term occurs as part of a compound word used to describe the head of a synagogue in the expression *archisunagōgos* (Acts 18:8).

This leaves us to account for the "pastor" portion of "senior pastor," an idea that would undoubtedly have been expressed by the Greek word for shepherd, *poimēn*. Interestingly enough, we do find *archi* and *poimēn* compounded together in the expression *archipoimēn* one time in the Greek New Testament. Those who wish to craft a biblical argument for a senior pastor model of church leadership will be disappointed to discover that *archipoimēn* is not used to refer to a senior pastor of a local church. It is used to refer to Jesus in the passage from 1 Peter cited earlier: "And when the *chief Shepherd* appears, you will receive the unfading crown of glory" (5:4). Peter assumed that the churches to which he wrote are led by pastors (5:1). He reserved the position of "senior pastor" for Jesus. Whether the metaphor is family (God is Father) or flock (Jesus is Chief Shepherd), the New Testament pattern of plurality leadership at the human level appears to be preserved in every case.

The Pragmatic Arguments

The biblical evidence should be reason enough to consider the team approach to local church leadership. But there are also some very practical benefits of following God's blueprint. Plurality leadership is in the best interests of both followers and leaders in the family of God. I offer six pragmatic arguments for the team approach. The first four address primarily the needs of the flock, and the last two demonstrate the value of the plurality model for the pastors involved.

(1) A Safeguard against abuse. I have already illustrated the most important pragmatic argument for plurality leadership in the local church. The team approach is an absolutely indispensable safeguard against the potential abuse of authority inherent in the strong-group approach to community.

As long as we continue with a low-group, individualist approach to church life in evangelical America, one-man leadership presents no serious problems in the area of abuse and manipulation. Authority resides in the individual church member, and each person can simply leave and find another church should pastoral authority be exercised in an unhealthy way. But if we desire to adopt the strong-group family approach to ecclesiology and make the kind of commitments the early Christians made to their local churches, this will no longer be the case. Combining the strong-group church with one-man leadership opens the door to the possibility of cultlike aberrations like those documented above. Strong-group churches must be led by a team of pastor-elders in order to prevent group authority from falling into the hands of a single individual.

This is not to say that a collectivist church led by a single pastor will inevitably become an abusive cult. The early church soon left behind the New Testament model of plurality leadership, so that by the early second century one-man rule was the norm throughout the Roman Empire. But the strong-group mentality remained intact. Interestingly, although the church departed from Jesus' model in form, church leaders for the most part remained faithful to Jesus' model in principle.

Cyprian of Carthage (see chap. 5) is a good illustration of this. As Bishop of Carthage, Cyprian wielded a great deal of authority. He was the single Christian leader presiding over a large geographical area in North Africa. But Cyprian never usurped God's role as Father of the community or challenged his flock to obey him as such (like a modern-day pastor functioning as a CEO). Cyprian reserved the father metaphor for God. Instead, the word he used again and again in his letters to refer to himself is "brother." This explicitly places Cyprian on the same level as the lowliest church member and helps to prevent the kind of abuse associated with strong-group authority in cultlike communities.

Perhaps most single (or senior) pastor figures in America would lead their strong-group churches like Cyprian if our communities adopted the New Testament family model. But some certainly would not, and here is where the danger lies. The parade of cult aberrations in contemporary American society strongly cautions us against placing strong-group authority into the hands of a single individual.

The clear biblical pattern for plurality leadership, combined with the potential for the abuse of authority in a strong-group community setting, persuasively argues for team leadership at the local church level. And there are several other practical benefits of plurality leadership in American evangelical churches today.

(2) A safeguard against "celebrity-ism." Plurality leadership provides God's people with a visible reminder that Christ is the head of the church—a truth perhaps more important in our society than ever before in the history of the church. At a conference I attended recently, a speaker offered a striking observation. He noted that Americans used to have heroes. Now we have celebrities.

The difference is profound. Heroes are persons we try to emulate. We admire their character qualities, and we want to have those qualities in our own lives. Abraham Lincoln is a great example of a hero. Every pastor I know has told the story of Lincoln's string of almost incessant failures—until, that is, he became president and proved to be one of the greatest leaders America has ever had. Reflecting upon a hero like Lincoln makes us want to persevere through failure after failure. We want to be like our heroes.

Celebrities are another story. We do not emulate the character qualities of celebrities. We cannot hope to be *like* them. Instead, we try to live *through* them. Americans vicariously live out their lives through the experiences of their media celebrities.

My wife has her hair cut by a woman in her forties named Gladys who comes to our home. On one occasion several years ago, Gladys arrived at the door for a 10:00 a.m. appointment quite dismayed that she had scheduled Joann's haircut at the very time she usually watches her favorite television show. Much to her relief, Gladys noticed that our television set was visible from the kitchen where she cuts Joann's hair. Joann reluctantly agreed to let Gladys watch the Jerry Springer Show.

I have never watched Jerry Springer. Nor had Joann until that morning. All it took was a few minutes of viewing for Joann to conclude that the show is pure trash—classic TV talk-show sensationalism and titillation. Joann asked Gladys why she enjoyed the show so much. Her reply was highly revealing. Gladys claimed that her own life was so boring that she enjoyed seeing more interesting lives on television. And, according to Gladys, "the trashier the better." Gladys basically lives out her life vicariously through the lives of "celebrities" on the tube.

Unfortunately, the same dynamic has found its way into the church. People like Gladys, who lack a strong sense of personal identity and who therefore need to live their lives vicariously through the experiences of others, occupy our pews every Sunday. In Christian circles there is always the temptation to transfer this celebrity attachment to the pastor figure in the local church, and the temptation is only fueled further by having the same gifted individual in the pulpit week after week. Christians caught up in this unhealthy dynamic proceed to live out their lives through a spiritual celebrity—the pastor of a church (or perhaps a noted radio preacher). Jesus, the head of the church, quietly recedes into the background.[6]

Take Bob, for example. Bob's own spiritual life is rather boring. He just kind of plugs along day by day. Bob's pastor, on the other hand, seems bigger than life. From Bob's seat in the twenty-fifth row of that huge auditorium on Sundays, Pastor Smith's experience of God appears vibrant and exciting. Bob puts his pastor on a distant pedestal, and Pastor Smith becomes Bob's spiritual celebrity. Week after week, Bob gets pumped up hearing Pastor Smith talk about his relationship with Jesus. But Bob never seems to get going himself. Pastor Smith is Bob's celebrity, while Christ, the head of the church, somehow gets left out of the picture.

Bob would probably be devastated to discover that Pastor Smith likely wrestles with the same ups and downs as Bob does in his daily walk with Christ. High times and low times. Dry times and times of refreshment. Pastor Smith's experience is not a whole lot different than Bob's. There really are no spiritual celebrities when the truth is told.

You can spot the Christians who view their pastors as celebrities. For one thing, they ditch church when the senior pastor is out of town. After all, they don't go to their local Christian community to hear from the head of the church, Jesus. They go to church to listen to their celebrity pastor. And how do such people respond when the truth is told, that is, when they discover that their larger-than-life spiritual icon is just a real, hurting, normal human being like them? They tend to run for cover. Or, worse yet, they go into denial.

---

[6] I am indebted to J. P. Moreland for a number of the above insights. See especially pp. 88–94 of *Love Your God with All Your Mind* (Colorado Springs: NavPress, 1997), where Moreland discussed the "empty self."

One Sunday one of my co-pastors at Oceanside Christian Fellowship shared with our congregation that he was going through a real tough time in his life. He said that he needed their support and encouragement both emotionally and ministerially to deal with a severe bout of depression. The response was revealing. To their credit, most of our people rallied to the man's side, some perhaps almost relieved to discover that their pastor was a genuine, fallible human being just like them. But a small group of key church members just could not handle my partner's transparency. They told him in no uncertain terms, "We need you to have it all together. We can't stay in a church with a pastor who has these kinds of problems." Then they left.

Sometimes, when a spiritual celebrity is dethroned, the truth hurts so much that denial is the only available response. A friend of mine was a real podcast junkie. John had a favorite radio preacher whose every sermon he downloaded and played repeatedly. Pastor Bill's theology was John's theology. Pastor Bill's interpretation of the Scriptures was John's interpretation. I knew John was in trouble when he would quote Pastor Bill to me instead of the Bible.

Then Pastor Bill fell into immorality—more than once. But because Pastor Bill was John's celebrity, because he was bigger than life, John just could not accept it. Despite the fact that Pastor Bill lost his radio show and was removed from his church ministry, John refused to believe what had really happened. John insisted that Pastor Bill was "set up." Pretty scary to think just how far some Christians will go in order to maintain their allegiance to their spiritual celebrities.

Christians in America do not need pastors who are celebrities. They need pastors who are mature brothers—pastors who walk alongside them hand-in-hand, overcoming the same spiritual obstacles that their sheep face, in the context of the interpersonal accountability and relational integrity that God has provided in His church family.

The church is a family, not a show. And the biblical blueprint for plurality leadership—in which the Sunday teaching ministry of the church is shared by several pastors—would go a long way to prevent the unhealthy dynamic of "celebrity-ism" discussed and illustrated in the above paragraphs. One of the most tangible ways to communicate to our people that Jesus is the head of the church is to lead and feed our churches in a team format at the human level.

(3) A balanced spiritual diet. Plurality leadership also provides God's people with a balanced perspective in the area of Bible teaching. All pastors have their passions and their "hobby horses"—even those who teach chapter by chapter through the Bible. For example, in the church I serve, I repeatedly emphasize

to our people the themes found in this book because I have been consumed with them for the past decade. I am convinced that our people need to hear over and over about the counter-cultural New Testament strong-group model for Christian community.

But collectivist Christianity is not all the people of Oceanside Christian Fellowship need to hear. Our worship leader, Margy, constantly exhorts our people through word and song to pursue a passionate individual relationship with God—and rightly so. Such emphasis needs equal time in the teaching of our church. A balanced diet of spiritual food is one of the greatest benefits of being taught and discipled by a team of Christian leaders.

Even in the apostle Paul's home church, the members received a balanced spiritual diet. Paul was not the only teacher of the community: "In the local church at Antioch there were prophets and teachers: Barnabas, Simeon who was called Niger, Lucius the Cyrenian, Manaen, a close friend of Herod the tetrarch, and Saul" (Acts 13:1). Imagine this: "Sorry, Paul, this Sunday we want to hear from Lucius or Manaen." Wait a minute. If Paul was in one of our churches, we would want to hear from *him*—every Sunday!

The early Christians knew better. They knew that they needed a balanced diet. Even Paul did not have the whole truth. (That is probably why God did not let him write the whole New Testament!) Upon further reflection, I suspect that the team-teaching approach at Antioch explains why the church was able to send Paul and Barnabas off to the mission field and remain a healthy and vibrant congregation. The church did not depend upon the great attraction of either Paul, the commissioned apostle, or Barnabas, the great orator, to draw a crowd on Sunday. They had plenty of teachers to instruct their people.

I share a preaching rotation with two other pastors. One Sunday after the service was over, a member met me as I was walking up the aisle, and he was full of affirmation for my sermon that morning. "Great sermon, Joe!" he exclaimed. Well, just as I was beginning to feel pretty good about myself, I went through the auditorium doors out into the lobby and overhead another person say to one of our elders, "When is that other pastor, Brandon, going to be preaching again? I really like *his* sermons."

Ouch! We pastors are most vulnerable emotionally right after we pour our hearts out in the pulpit on Sunday mornings. My initial emotional reaction to the above comment was not one that I am proud of, so I'll save the details. Once I got over myself, though, I could not help but smile inwardly and think, "That's it! That's exactly why we share the preaching!" Different pastors on our team connect with different personality types in our church. As a result, both our teaching and our church membership rolls remain much more well-rounded than would be the case if the same person fed the flock week after week.

(4) A model for church family life. The fourth benefit of the plurality approach to leadership is the help it provides in modeling Christian maturity to others. We cannot read our Bibles without concluding that the number one evidence of Christian maturity is our ability to engage in intimate, authentic relationships with our fellow human beings.

There is no other consistently reliable benchmark of our growth in Christ—certainly not Bible knowledge or effectiveness in ministry—by which to evaluate our Christian walk. A person who cannot get along with people is simply immature in his spiritual walk. And the beauty of plurality leadership is that it models relational integrity and teamwork at the top level of church life.

As you can gather from what you have read so far in this book, I have some rather strong opinions about how we should do church. The other six elders at my church are also men of deep conviction. It is challenging for us to work together interpersonally, to appreciate our differences without becoming defensive, and then to come to consensus on important and potentially divisive issues.

The people in our church are well aware of our differences in temperament and orientation. And from what I gather they are tremendously encouraged to watch from a distance as we make the plurality approach to ministry work by deferring to one another and (together) to our Lord Jesus as the head of the church. Our pastoral team's determination to experience Christian community together, as flawed as it sometimes is, gives our people a tangible model for interpersonal relationships in their own lives.

In our day of dysfunctional families and increasing relational chaos, the local church needs more than a solitary preacher who talks eloquently about getting along with others but who answers to no one in his everyday ministry. A church needs a team of pastors who model people skills in their relationships with one another. Plurality leadership provides the context for just such modeling.

(5) Moral accountability. The final two practical reasons for the biblical blueprint of plurality leadership more directly benefit the leaders involved. First of all, a plurality approach provides interpersonal accountability at the leadership level. I find it troubling that numerous pastors exhort their people to join Bible study and accountability groups, while they themselves answer to no one for their own moral and spiritual lives. This recipe for disaster has cooked up some pretty sad stories in American evangelicalism in recent decades, as leader after leader has

fallen to some form of immorality. The lone-ranger approach to pastoral ministry is not only unbiblical; it is also dangerous. Team leadership done correctly
results in both moral and ministerial accountability for the pastor-elders of God's
church.

I am on a short leash at Oceanside Christian Fellowship. All of our pastor-
elders are. Every Tuesday morning at 6:30 a.m. I can count on my fellow-elders to
ask me the tough questions about the important relationships in my life. "How's
your relationship with Joann, Joe? How's your walk with the Lord?" I welcome
this kind of accountability because I know the level to which I am capable of sinking if left on my own.

I might add that the close bonds we build with one another on Tuesday mornings greatly facilitate the decision-making process when we meet together on Sat-
urdays to discuss church business. Because we have shared, prayed, and wept
together nearly every Tuesday morning for more than ten years now, we enjoy
the kind of relationships with one another that allow us to drop our defenses and
receive challenges to our opinions, as we wrestle through important church ministry decisions in those Saturday meetings.

(6) Prevention of pride and discouragement. Being a pastor is often like being
strapped to an emotional roller coaster. When things go well in the ministry, when
people get saved and grow, when Sunday attendance increases, the pastor feels
great. When the numbers decline, when complaints multiply, when the church
refuses to budge in important areas of change, the pastor is in the pits.

Pride and depression unfortunately occupy the extreme ends of this emotional
spectrum. The successful pastor struggles to remind himself that God and not the
pastor is responsible for all the good things that have happened in the church. But
the pastor whose ministry limps along tends to get depressed and blame himself
for church failures.

From what we learned about the New Testament model for church leadership,
it appears that God never intended the burdens and blessings of pastoral ministry
to fall on the shoulders of a single individual. The team approach ensures that no
one person will take the credit or the blame for the often unpredictable twists and
turns of local church ministry.

I spent most of my early years of ministry in a large, multistaffed church.
Although we had a senior-pastor model, Pastor John was a real team player. I
do not believe that the church would be as healthy as it is today if that had not
been the case. During John's five-year tenure as senior pastor, we led the church
through a painful transition in style of ministry. It was crystal clear to us on staff

that a Baptist church with a traditional approach to music ministry—hymns, choir, and organ—was not going to connect with persons in the southern California beach city where we were located. We needed to complement our traditional Sunday service with a more contemporary worship experience, one led by a live band with guitars, bass, keyboards, and drums.

Many of our key leaders were convinced otherwise. After all, this was a Baptist church that had done things pretty much the same way every Sunday for 75 years. Actually, the "worship war" that resulted was a rather mild one compared to some stories I have heard. But the pastoral staff took a lot of shots during this time of change, some of them right in the back—like the time our music minister was accused in an anonymous note of being "a tool of the devil."

Pastor John's response to all this was gracious and levelheaded. Most importantly, he made sure we spent considerable time together weekly as a staff, praying for strength for one another and wrestling together through the sticky interpersonal issues that major change inevitably brought our way.

The result was that the church—and the staff—survived the transition with little fallout. No one on staff had to face the flak we received alone. The burden was shared. Pastor John soon left the church on great terms to take a teaching job in a local seminary, and the stage was set to bring in a new pastor whose contemporary approach to ministry and great communication skills have resulted in tremendous growth for the congregation. I had always heard it said that a strong leader is needed to direct a church through a difficult period of change. I would rather have a strong team of leaders any day.

I trust that you have begun to see the way that plurality leadership both protects the leadership team and safeguards the church against the kind of abuse and manipulation characteristic of the cult groups that so often appear in the headlines. Had Jim Jones and Marshall Applewhite found themselves networked into the kind of accountability outlined above, they would have had little or no room to move in their misguided and ultimately tragic attempts to direct the lives of their followers. We need to return to Jesus' blueprint in Matthew 23 now to consider yet another safeguard against the abuse of authority in the strong-group church family.

Servant Leadership

God not only intends the *number* of leaders to provide a check against abuse; he is also concerned with the *nature* of leadership—probably even more so. Jesus challenged His listeners with an approach to leadership that flew in the face of the whole social fabric of ancient society: "The greatest among you will be your servant. Whoever exalts himself will be humbled, and whoever humbles himself will be exalted" (Matt 23:11–12).

Again and again Jesus taught and modeled for His disciples a single nonnegotiable truth about the orientation of leaders in His new community: humility and sacrifice constitute the quintessential qualities for leadership in the kingdom of God. God's leaders are, in short, servant leaders. Among the various reasons for a servant approach to leadership is an eminently practical one. Servant leadership provides yet another safeguard against the abuse of authority in the strong-group church family. Leaders who serve will not abuse or manipulate.

Our Great Example

Jesus, of course, is our model of servant leadership, and there is no better description of what being a servant entailed for Jesus—and should entail for us— than this from Paul:

> Do nothing out of rivalry or conceit, but in humility consider others as more important than yourselves. Everyone should look out not only for his own interests, but also for the interests of others.
> Make your own attitude that of Christ Jesus,
>> who, existing in the form of God, did not consider equality with God
>> as something to be used for His own advantage.
>> Instead He emptied Himself by assuming the form of a slave,
>> taking on the likeness of men.
>> And when He had come as a man in His external form,
>> He humbled Himself by becoming obedient
>> to the point of death—even to death on a cross. (Phil 2:3–8)

Much ink has been spilled over the centuries in efforts to mine from this wonderful passage all of its spiritual jewels. I find the key to the whole picture of the humiliation of Jesus in a single short phrase at the end of v. 6: Paul said that Jesus "did not consider equality with God as something to be used for His own advantage."

Now that is a profound statement. Not the part about Jesus being equal with God. That was becoming pretty standard fare for people who had been exposed to Paul's teaching for a while. What would have stopped Paul's ancient readers right in their tracks is his assertion that *Jesus did not use His deity to serve Himself.* In antiquity, people who possessed power almost invariably used their power in their own interests. That was the way of the world. It still is. But it is not the way of the kingdom.

The meaning of the phrase "something to be used for His own advantage" (v. 6)—a single term *(harpagmos)* in the original Greek—has received much needed clarification through several extensive studies of the usage of this word in ancient writings. The HCSB translation cited above reflects recent scholarship on the word. Our most recent commentators and translators of Philippians now understand the term *harpagmos* to mean not "something to be grasped" (NIV) but "something to be used for His own advantage" (HCSB; similarly, NRSV: "something to be exploited").

Thus the meaning of v. 6 is not that Jesus somehow lacked equality with God and resisted the temptation to "grasp" it. Rather, equality with God was something Jesus already possessed and which He chose not to selfishly exploit. Gordon Fee elaborates,

> Thus, Christ did not consider "equality with God" to consist of "grasping" or being "selfish"; rather he rejected this popular view of kingly power by "pouring himself out" for the sake of others. . . . equality with God means not "grasping" but "giving away."[7]

Notice Fee's comparison of Jesus' view of the utilization of power with the "popular view of kingly power." As taxes flowed from the hinterlands of the empire into Rome and into the various capitals of the provinces, the rulers of Jesus' day lived in extreme luxury compared with those whom they oppressed. They served themselves by "grasping" and "seizing" (two good translations of *harpagmos*) anyone's possessions that they could get their hands on.

Jesus, in contrast, did not regard His power as an opportunity for grasping. It is all quite amazing when you think about it. Jesus had it all, needed nothing, and yet "made himself nothing" (Phil 2:7, NIV) for the sake of the subjects of His kingdom. This is what servant leadership is really all about. And this is the kind of leadership Jesus desires for His group, the Christian church.

A Servant Leader in a Most Unlikely Place

My most memorable introduction to servant leadership did not occur in a church. It happened in a sweatshop of sorts. Among my various vocational adventures was a stint in the garment industry back in the early 1970s. We manufactured women's sportswear. Our administrative team consisted of two managers, an industrial engineer, and a production control clerk (me).

---

[7] G. D. Fee, *Paul's Letter to the Philippians*, in *New International Commentary on the New Testament*, ed. G. D. Fee (Grand Rapids: Eerdmans, 1995), 206.

My job was to track the various orders of clothing through the sewing process and to make sure we had enough thread on hand to sew the stuff together. All four of us in the office were American citizens, but the great majority of the 120 men and women who ran the sewing machines and steam presses were not. They had entered the United States illegally from Mexico, Central America, and Thailand.

Please do not be offended by the issue of illegal immigration that surfaces in the story that follows. I am about to describe the behavior of our plant manager at Joshua Tree Manufacturing, a man named Al Barlovitz, who risked his own status—indeed, his very job—to protect a group of marginalized immigrants from treatment that Al thought was unjust. It is not my intention to make a value judgment one way or another on the issue of illegal immigration. I simply want us to appreciate the profound sacrifice that Al was willing to make for persons whom he perceived to be at the mercy of those in power. It is Al's attitude towards the weak and the vulnerable—not illegal immigration—that is at the heart of this remarkable story.

Our factory was one of many in the garment district that employed illegal immigrants in those days, and the Immigration and Naturalization Service (INS) regularly paid surprise visits to shops like ours in order to apprehend and deport such workers. The surprise nature of the visits meant that the INS had no legal access to a factory's premises. The agents could only line up their large passenger vans (paddy wagons) outside, knock on the door, and announce their presence.

An unspoken rule prevailed that guaranteed the INS a degree of success even without a search warrant, while allowing factory production to continue relatively unimpeded. The arrangement also meant that an INS raid typically worked itself out in a predictable way.

The understanding ran something like this. If a plant manager allowed the INS to apprehend a token number of illegals—say 5 to 10 percent of the factory's employees—the INS would disappear and leave the business unmolested for a period of time. But if the shop manager refused the INS access to his facility on their surprise visit, the agents would soon return with a search warrant and take all the illegals they could get their hands on. But before this would happen, word would get out and most of the employees would stay away from work until the heat died down.

A full-blown raid with a search warrant was bad news for the economic health of the business. Work would stop for days at a time, and in an industry dominated by fleeting fashion trends and delivery schedules this was simply unacceptable. So most plant managers caved in to the unannounced INS visitors, gave them access to their premises, and sacrificed a few of their workers in spite of the lack of a search warrant.

Except for Al Barlovitz. Al, our plant manager, was passionately faithful to the Latino and Asian men and women who worked so hard for him on the floor of the steamy converted bowling alley that served as our production area. Al was not about to stand around and allow any of them to be apprehended. Why? Al was a Jewish man who had experienced his own kind of discrimination and marginalization when he was forced out of business in Salt Lake City because he had failed to conform to the social and religious norms of the community in which his factory was located. So now Al was not about to subject even a few of his faithful but vulnerable workers to what he perceived to be similar mistreatment at the hands of the INS.

I will never forget the day the INS showed up at Joshua Tree. It was an amazing sight. In a matter of seconds, the whole block was surrounded by white Ford paddy wagons. What was more amazing—almost surreal as I recall it so vividly today—was the scene on the inside. Twenty men and nearly 100 women began to hide themselves throughout the facility as soon as they realized what was going down. They obviously knew the rules. The first 10 or 20 poor souls found by INS agents would serve as the token apprehensions. The ones who hid themselves better would escape.

Many of our workers managed to climb up into a false ceiling. At one point, I was trying hard to keep focused on my work, and I was sitting at my desk running some figures on the calculator. Suddenly, two feet came crashing through the ceiling tiles directly above my chair as one immigrant frantically grabbed for the supporting rafters so she would not fall to the ground. Soon ceiling tiles were falling everywhere, and by this time the whole place was filled with chaos. All eyes were on Al Barlovitz. The INS wanted in. What would Al do?

Al was not about to play the game. He refused to open the door to the INS. He would not give up a single employee. Al chided the agents to go ahead and get their search warrant. "By the time you suckers get back," Al said, "my people will all be gone. Then you can do what you want with that search warrant of yours!" (Al's language was actually a bit more colorful.)

Soon the INS left. Then all our workers left. Our management team spent the rest of the afternoon alone in the office considering the ramifications of Al's decision for the economic health of Joshua Tree Manufacturing. After all, we did not expect a large number of seamstresses to show up for work for the next week or so. And I was a whole lot more proficient at a calculator than a sewing machine. It looked like Joshua Tree was not going to meet shipping deadlines for the foreseeable future. Al's response: "Heck with Joshua Tree, I'd do it all over again if I had the chance!"

I was just a young man in the working world for the first time, and Al Barlovitz had become my hero. Al remains one of my heroes to this day. After walking with Jesus and studying the Bible for nearly three decades, I think I have a pretty clear picture of what servant leadership is all about. Now I just have to learn to *do* it. And in retrospect I see the model reflected perfectly in Al Barlovitz.

Like Jesus, Al resisted the temptation to view his position of authority as Joshua Tree's plant manager as "something to be used for his own advantage" (Phil 2:6). Instead, Al Barlovitz served those lowly illegal immigrants who had sought economic refuge on American soil, and he risked his own job in the process.

Al's attitude toward his employees had a profound effect on the relational atmosphere of Joshua Tree Manufacturing. This non-Christian man united 125 people from nearly every conceivable racial background into the most harmonious work community I have ever seen. Many of the illegal immigrants at Joshua Tree were alone in America. Al and their co-workers at Joshua Tree became their family away from home. And the loyalty Al expressed to his workers did not travel on a one-way street. It was reciprocated. The employees of Joshua Tree Manufacturing loved Al like a father. Yes, we lost a few days of production. But because of the immigrants' commitment to Al, when they finally did return after the INS dust settled, they worked hard enough to put the schedule all back in place in a matter of just a few weeks.

Conclusion

The two aspects of leadership we have observed in this chapter form an indispensable part of the strong-group church family model. We need not fear that the collectivist church will turn into a cultlike aberration. We need only to ensure that leadership is structured and exercised in the way that Jesus intended.

The first precaution Jesus took had to do with the number of leaders He designated for the group He was establishing. Jesus reserved the role of Father in His surrogate family of followers for God alone. Further, several Gospel passages appear to suggest that Jesus designed His church to be led by a plurality of leaders. This interpretation of Jesus' intentions finds confirmation in the activities of Paul and other missionaries of the New Testament era, who established local Christian communities that were each governed by a team of pastor-elders.

A second key value relates to the nature of leadership as it is to function in the surrogate family of God. God's leaders must exercise their authority not "from the top down" but "from the bottom up." Leaders in God's church must be servant leaders.

The combination of these two safeguards will go a long way to ensure the relational health of the strong-group church family model. A team of leaders who hold one another accountable to serve those entrusted to their charge—and who are held accountable to do so by the broader church family—will not turn a local Christian church into a destructive self-serving cult.

But these two key leadership characteristics exercise more than merely a precautionary function in God's strong-group surrogate family. There are significant positive benefits to God's design also. A group of pastor-elders, who equally share the ministry as servants to their brothers and sisters in the broader church family, provides a living example of relational integrity at the top level of church leadership. Such an example cannot help but overflow into the life of the congregation to produce a healthy and vibrant family of believers.

CONCLUSION

Look at how great a love the Father has given us, that we
should be called God's children. And we are!

(1 John 3:1)

I conclude our exploration of the church as a family with a glance backward and a gaze ahead. In view of the amount (and newness) of the material covered, it should prove useful to retrace our steps by summarizing the main ideas of the book. I then offer some steps we might take as leaders to implement the church family model in local congregational life.

A Glance Backward

We began our adventure by looking in some detail at the social values and family priorities of people in the world of the early Christians (chaps. 1 and 2). We then proceeded to explore the ways that Jesus and His followers appropriated and contextualized the family model in local church settings throughout the Roman Empire (chaps. 3, 4, and 5). Let us briefly revisit the social world of Mediterranean antiquity and then reconsider Jesus' vision for authentic Christian community.

Mediterranean Culture and Ancient Family Systems

Three fundamental characteristics of Mediterranean society and ancient family systems served as the conceptual and relational building blocks for Jesus' plan for His church to function as a surrogate kinship group:

1. *The group comes first.* In the social world of the early Christians the survival and health of the group took priority over the needs and desires of the individual.

2. *It's all about family:* The extended (patrilineal) family system was the group to which persons in Mediterranean antiquity expressed primary relational allegiance.

3. *I am my brother's keeper:* The closest same generation family bond in the New Testament world was the bond between consanguine siblings.

The group comes first. The most salient difference between our social outlook and the cultural orientation of ancient persons is to be found in the degree of loyalty that people express toward the various groups in their lives. People in the New Testament world put the group first. We give the individual pride of place.

Social anthropologists refer to modern America as a weak-group society where the needs, goals, and desires of the individual come first. Personal allegiance to the group—whether that group is my family, my church, my co-workers, or a civic organization of some sort—is a secondary consideration. We tend to view the groups in our lives in a rather utilitarian way. These broader social entities serve as resources that we as individuals draw on in order to realize our own goals and to navigate our personal pathways through life.

The decision-making opportunities we possess as modern Americans reflect our cultural priorities. I as an individual choose my own career, mate, and place of residence. And I give little thought to how these choices might impact the broader social networks to which I belong. All of this illustrates a fundamental cultural axiom in contemporary Western society: the individual comes first.

Among strong-group peoples a radically different ethos determines behavior in nearly every area of life. Collectivist societies value the group over the individual. And ancient Mediterranean society exhibits a decidedly strong-group social outlook. For people in the world of the early Christians the survival and health of the group took precedence over the desires or preferences of individual group members. Personal decisions were made with a view to group honor and social solidarity.

It's all about family. The social unit to which strong-group Mediterranean persons expressed primary relational allegiance was the family. People in the world of Jesus and Paul readily embraced the idea that the good of the family was to take priority over one's personal desires and aspirations. An individual therefore deferred to the wishes of the extended family—generally represented in the preferences of the family patriarch—whenever he or she faced a major life decision. Family served as the primary locus of relational loyalty and solidarity for persons in Mediterranean antiquity.

Family solidarity manifests itself most transparently when people marry in traditional societies. In our social world individuals pair up for personal relational satisfaction. The bride and groom generally give little thought to the effect of the union upon their extended families. But people in strong-group cultures marry with a view to the way in which the couple's relationship will affect the broader social collective.

Marriages in traditional societies (like the New Testament world) are almost exclusively contracted to enhance the social standing of the respective families involved. Very little (if any) consideration is given to the relational satisfaction of the couple. The family has the first and final word in any discussion about "who marries who" in collectivist societies.

And marriage strategies are not the only expression of family loyalty among strong-group peoples. We recounted the sacrifice of Juan Espiritu, the young man from Tijuana, Mexico, who readily surrendered his individual vocational aspirations so that his younger siblings could get an education. "Perhaps," Juan said of his brothers and sisters, "one of them will become a doctor. That is my desire." [1] For Juan, the group is more important than the individual. And the most important group in this regard is Juan's family.

I am my brother's keeper. Strong-group people conceive of family quite differently than modern Americans. For people in the world of Jesus and Paul, family consisted of those who were related by blood—the father's blood. The bloodline, which marked family membership, traveled from generation to generation solely through male offspring. This is why anthropologists call these family systems patrilineal kinship groups.

This way of structuring family necessarily generated a rather curious (to us) set of relational priorities for people in the New Testament world. Consider first the connection between marriage and family and, by implication, the connection between husband and wife. For Westerners the connection is self-evident. Marriage *is* family, or it is the fundamental building block of family, at any rate. And we expect marriage to function as our closest same-generational relationship.

Not so for the ancients. Because a husband and wife came from two different patrilines, they were not considered family in the same way as those who shared a father's bloodline. In Mediterranean antiquity a man's family consisted of the members of the patrilineal kinship group into which he was born. A woman's family consisted of the members of the patrilineal kinship group into which she was born. Marriage did little to change this. As odd as it seems to us, husbands

---

[1] *Los Angeles Times*, January 26, 1998.

and wives never actually belonged to the same family system in the strong-group world of early Christianity because they did not share the same patriline.

The practical result of all this for people in ancient society strikes us as rather counterintuitive, but it is perhaps the most important bit of data gleaned from our study of the Mediterranean family. The closest relational bond in a given generation of people in the New Testament world was not the bond between a husband and a wife. It was the bond between siblings.

The emotional intimacy and support that we typically expect to characterize a good marriage relationship are experienced by strong-group persons in their relationships with their brothers and sisters—even after they marry. The sibling bond takes priority. For the ancient readers of Genesis 4, the answer to Cain's question "Am I my brother's keeper?" could only be a resounding "Yes!"

We are not surprised to encounter numerous stories of sibling relations both in the Old Testament and in secular literature from the ancient world. Narratives portraying sibling solidarity or sibling betrayal captivated the minds of the first readers of the Bible precisely because collectivist peoples are more deeply committed to their siblings than to anyone else in their circle of family relations, including their husbands and wives.

Sibling solidarity is of great significance for appreciating the community orientation of the New Testament church. Jesus established His followers as a faith family, and practical expressions of brotherhood soon came to epitomize what it meant for the early Christians to relate to one another as Jesus had intended. Whatever else they might have been, the first followers of Jesus were preeminently a society of surrogate siblings.

When the Church Was a Family

The heart of our study focused on the way that Jesus and His followers appropriated the patrilineal family as the central social model for relational life in the early Christian church. We considered the process as it unfolded in three stages:

1. *Jesus and family:* Jesus viewed His followers as a surrogate family, challenged them to reconsider their loyalty to their families of origin, and modeled surrogate family values in His own life by publicly distancing Himself from His own natural family.

2. *Paul and the family of God:* The apostle Paul expected the communities of Christians he established throughout the eastern Roman Empire to function as surrogate families, and he utilized the family metaphor to

encourage his converts to act like siblings in their relationships with one another.

3. *The ancient church as family:* The ancient church retained the family model and exhibited sibling social solidarity throughout the pre-Constantine era of early church history.

What follows is a brief review of these developments in the order in which they occurred.

Jesus and family. Among the cultural givens that Jesus encountered in first-century Palestine was the strong-group orientation of ancient society. Now Jesus was hardly shy about challenging social norms that conflicted with His vision for a renewed people of God. For example, He adamantly rejected the Pharisees' purity laws, and He forcefully addressed abuses in the Jerusalem temple.

But Jesus did not appear to have had a problem with the strong-group outlook of His social world, an outlook that prioritized the good of the group over that of the individual. This is not to say that Jesus was insensitive to individual needs. It simply means that Jesus directly affirmed His world's relational priorities when He adopted the Mediterranean family—the primary locus of relational solidarity in collectivist antiquity—as the social model for the group He established. Apparently, Jesus assumed that the individual needs of His followers would best be met in the context of this strong-group surrogate family, and this is certainly what we encounter in Acts and the Epistles.

Jesus spoke about family in three rather distinct ways, and some of these teachings appear to be mutually contradictory. At times Jesus unequivocally affirmed natural family relationships. He reiterated the fifth of the Ten Commandments to honor father and mother. He upheld marriage and disallowed divorce. And He welcomed little children into His arms. In these texts Jesus was unreservedly family-friendly.

Other passages portray Jesus in precisely the opposite light. At more than one point in His ministry Jesus promised that the gospel would bring not solidarity but division to the natural family (Matt 10:34–35; Mark 13:12), and He asserted, "If anyone comes to Me and does not hate his own father and mother, wife and children, brothers and sisters—yes, and even his own life—he cannot be My disciple" (Luke 14:26). To a man who wished to bury his father—the honorable thing to do—Jesus enjoined, "Follow Me, and let the dead bury their own dead" (Matt 8:22).

In addition to these apparently mixed messages about the natural family, Jesus instructed His disciples about another kind of family entirely, one based not on blood but on a common relationship with God. "You are all brothers," Jesus informed His disciples (Matt 23:8). And Jesus modeled such an outlook in His own family relations:

> Then His mother and His brothers came, and standing outside, they sent word to Him and called Him. A crowd was sitting around Him and told Him, "Look, Your mother, Your brothers, and Your sisters are outside asking for You."
>
> He replied to them, "Who are My mother and My brothers?" And looking about at those who were sitting in a circle around Him, He said, "Here are My mother and My brothers! Whoever does the will of God is My brother and sister and mother." (Mark 3:31–35)

Jesus here exhibited a loyalty to His new surrogate family that exceeds any ongoing loyalty toward His natural family, and He encouraged His followers to do the same.

Several considerations allow us satisfactorily to harmonize Jesus' variegated teachings about family. It is important to recognize at the outset that following Jesus in the strong-group world of Mediterranean antiquity meant joining Jesus' group. In a social setting where each and every person found his identity in the group to which he belonged, a call to leave one's primary group—the family—in order to follow an individual would make sense only if following that individual meant joining his group.

Of course, this would be particularly true if the new group itself was viewed as a family of sorts. This is precisely the case with Jesus and His followers. When Jesus utilized phrases such as "come to Me" and "be My disciple," Jesus is not calling us to relate to Him solely at the personal level. Jesus assumes that a relationship with Him will find tangible expression in commitment to His newly formed society of surrogate siblings.

Additionally, Jesus expected loyalty to His new family to take priority over His followers' natural family commitments. This is certainly the most reasonable way to read the anti-family sayings in the Gospels and still preserve their prophetic force. And I suspect that this is one of the reasons that Jesus initially chose to adopt the family model. Jesus intentionally framed His movement in terms of family to emphasize the kind of uncompromising relational loyalty Jesus desired among His followers.

Therefore, the challenge in Jesus' radical call to discipleship is not simply a challenge to prioritize loyalty to Jesus as an individual over loyalty to one's family. Rather, a disciple must choose between two families: the disciple's natural family and Jesus' newly formed surrogate family of believers. For example, N. T. Wright came to this conclusion about Jesus' uncompromising charge to the would-be follower who wanted first to bury his father ("let the dead bury their own dead," Matt 8:22): "[the] only explanation for Jesus' astonishing command is that he envisaged loyalty to himself and his kingdom-movement as creating *an alternative family*."[2] Jesus' "alternative family" is to take priority over the natural family, and this accounts for the apparently anti-family sayings in the Gospels.

Finally, wherever possible within this new set of family priorities, Jesus clearly encouraged ongoing loyalty to natural family relations. Commitment to Jesus' new family did not necessarily preclude natural family loyalty, particularly in situations where whole households converted to the Jesus movement. But the focus remained on the faith family, not on the disciple's family of origin. And where conflict between the natural family and God's family did arise, Jesus' new family was to become the primary sphere of group loyalty and relational solidarity.

Paul and the family of God. It has become rather trendy in some scholarly circles to drive a wedge between Jesus of Nazareth and Paul of Tarsus. Jesus promised the kingdom, but Paul gave us the church. Paul had little or no interest in the historical Jesus. Paul was influenced solely in his theology by his interactions with the risen Christ, the Christ of faith. And Paul's program for the inclusion of Gentiles among the people of God had little in common with Jesus' agenda for the renewal of ethnic Israel. Or so we are told.

To be sure, Jesus and Paul ministered in different social contexts, and the two figures played markedly different roles in the unfolding drama of salvation history. But there are some striking similarities that should caution against assuming that Paul was disinterested in Jesus' earthly ministry. For example, the postulation of radical discontinuity between Jesus and Paul struggles significantly to account for the commonalities in the respective communal visions of the two men.

Paul picked up Jesus' vision for a society of surrogate siblings, and he ran with it. From the earliest days of Paul's ministry, the family idea was absolutely central to Paul's ecclesiology. Sibling terminology ("brothers," "sisters") and other kinship expressions ("Father," "inheritance," "children of God") occur in nearly every chapter of Paul's letters.

For Paul, as for Jesus, the church was a family, and the most reasonable way to account for this is to assume that Paul had received—likely through the Jerusalem apostles—instructions from Jesus about surrogate family relations. For as his letters so clearly reveal, Paul passionately sought the realization of Jesus' social vision.

---

[2] N. T. Wright, *Jesus and the Victory of God* (Minneapolis: Fortress, 1996), 401 (italics added).

Paul expected sibling solidarity to function in some very specific behaviors in the Jesus communities he established in the eastern Roman Empire. For example, he assumed that the members of his churches would experience a deep affective connection with one another, like that enjoyed by blood siblings in the natural families of their social world. Patrilineal kinship ideals, such as family unity and the absence of discord, were also among the characteristics Paul cultivated in his congregations.

In harmony with ancient family values Paul also challenged his converts to exhibit sibling solidarity by sharing their material resources with a brother or sister—or another church family—in need. And Paul rebuked people in his congregations who betrayed sibling values by engaging in litigation when wronged by a brother in the community. Finally, Paul, like Jesus, appears to have prioritized the faith family over the natural family. For example, in 1 Corinthians he encouraged both singles and married persons to view their respective life-situations under the overarching rubric of Jesus' broader kingdom agenda.

Paul was not always successful in getting his converts to treat one another like surrogate siblings. But Paul's grief has become our gain since his preoccupation in his letters with the relational problems in his churches speaks volumes about the apostle's understanding of Christian community. Again and again Paul drew on the family model to encourage his churches to live like siblings in the faith. For Paul, as for Jesus, the church was to function as a family.

The ancient church as family. At the dawn of the second century AD, Christianity had little in its favor from the perspective of the dominant culture. The movement had begun with a group of lower-class Jewish peasants and fishermen worshiping a crucified carpenter in a backwater province of the empire. The initial expansion of Christianity among nonelite Gentiles in the Greek cities of the Roman East did little to enhance the movement's credibility.

In the eyes of one Roman senator, Christianity was just another one of those "degraded and shameful" practices that somehow made their way to Rome from the extreme ends of the Empire (Tacitus, *Annals,* 15.47). Christians had no temples, no sacrifices, no priesthoods, no liturgy—just an informal weekly meeting in a local home where they broke bread and sang a hymn "in honor of Christ as if to a god" (Pliny, *Epistles,* 10.96). This is hardly the stuff of a major world religion.

Monotheism did exert some appeal to people paralyzed with fear in the face of a multitude of gods and goddesses, spirits and demons. For the most part, however, it was not Christian theology that encouraged thousands to endure social ostracization and to risk state persecution by joining the Jesus movement as the church proceeded to spread like a holy fire throughout the Roman world. It was Christian behavior that did this.

At least that is how pagan intellectuals explained the rise of Christianity. It was patently clear to Julian the Apostate—the emperor who wanted to revive pagan religion—that the expansion of the Jesus movement had a whole lot to do with Christian social solidarity. And Julian could hardly suppress his exasperation over the connection:

> Why do we not observe that it is their [the Christians'] benevolence to strang-
> ers, their care for the graves of the dead and the pretended holiness of their
> lives that have done the most to increase atheism? . . . When . . . the impious
> Galileans support not only their own poor, but ours as well, all men see that our
> people lack aid from us.[3]

Lucian of Samosata, another elite opponent of the Jesus movement, readily acknowledged that the Christians' "first lawgiver [Jesus] persuaded them that they are all brothers of one another." And it was self-evident to Lucian that this family orientation accounted for the movement's social solidarity: "Therefore they despise all things indiscriminately and consider them common property" (Lucian, *The Passing of Peregrinus*, 13).

Affective solidarity, the sharing of material resources, primary loyalty to Jesus' group—all of these now-familiar traits of the Mediterranean family continued to mark community life among Jesus' followers during the second and third centuries of Christian history. The ancient church lived out Jesus' vision for authentic Christian community, and they attracted converts in droves.

We considered in an earlier chapter the pilgrimage of the teenaged mother Perpetua, whose commitment to her surrogate family of faith cost the young woman not only her relationship with her father but her very life also. During her time in prison, Perpetua noted in her diary,

> my father was so angered by the word "Christian" that he moved towards me
> as though he would pluck my eyes out. But he left it at that and departed, van-
> quished along with his diabolical arguments. For a few days afterward I gave
> thanks to the Lord that I was separated from my father, and I was comforted by
> his absence. (*Passion of Perpetua*, 3.3)

As the time of Perpetua's martyrdom drew near, her father refused even to address Perpetua as "daughter." Here is a poignant picture of what it meant for the early

---

[3] *The Works of the Emperor Julian*, vol. 3, trans. W. Wright, in Loeb Classical Library (London: W. Heinemann, 1923) 17, 69.

Christians to prioritize loyalty to God and His family over and above loyalty to their natural families. And we can reasonably assume that this scenario played itself out again and again, particularly during times of state persecution.

One of the more tangible expressions of family solidarity in the ancient church was the sharing of material resources. In addition to the pagan sources cited above, we encounter evidence of such behavior in the writings of Christian leaders throughout the empire. As Tertullian remarked, "We who are united in mind and soul have no hesitation about sharing what we have" (*Apologeticus* 39.10–11).

The church ransomed kidnapped brothers and sisters, fed imprisoned confessors, and met the basic needs of people whose conversion to Christianity had cost them their jobs. And the world around stood up and took notice: "The practice of such a special love brands us in the eyes of some. 'See,' they say, 'how they love one another'" (Tertullian, *Apol.* 39.5–7).

Against all odds the early Christians won thousands to the Savior and ultimately triumphed completely over competing religious options in the Roman Empire. And we can trace much of the vitality of the Christian movement to the surrogate family values and behaviors that characterized local church life. It was just as Jesus had promised: "By this all people will know that you are My disciples, if you have love for one another" (John 13:35).

Summary

Our cultural, biblical, and historical tour through the world of early Christianity is now complete. The first three bullets below underscore what we have learned about the social world of Mediterranean antiquity. The last three bullets trace the development of the family metaphor through the first three centuries of church history:

- *The group comes first:* In the social world of the early Christians, the survival and health of the group took priority over the needs and desires of the individual.
- *It's all about family:* The extended (patrilineal) family system was the group to which people in Mediterranean antiquity expressed primary relational allegiance.
- *I am my brother's keeper:* The closest same-generation family bond in the New Testament world was the bond between consanguine siblings.
- *Jesus and family:* Jesus viewed His followers as a surrogate family, challenged them to reconsider their loyalty to their families of origin, and

modeled surrogate family values in His own life by publicly distancing Himself from His own natural family.

- *Paul and the family of God:* The apostle Paul expected the communities of Christians he established throughout the eastern Roman Empire to function as surrogate families, and he utilized the family metaphor to encourage his converts to act like siblings in their relationships with one another.
- *The ancient church as family:* The ancient church retained the family model and exhibited sibling social solidarity throughout the pre-Constantine era of early church history.

We turn now to consider some ways in which we might recapture Jesus' vision for the church as a family in our own cultural settings.

A Gaze Ahead

As a springboard for our discussion we will revisit the spiritual and social pilgrimage of our North African actor friend Marcus (chap. 5). The Roman theater was an unambiguously pagan environment. Local magistrates dedicated theatrical productions to pagan deities, and immorality was rampant on the stage.

The church's response was unequivocal. Christian leaders such as Tertullian discouraged their congregants from attending the shows, and they insisted that actors who wanted to follow Jesus disassociate themselves from the theater entirely. Marcus's conversion to Christ cost him his very livelihood.

In an attempt to make ends meet, this enterprising actor opened an acting school. This did not sit well with Marcus's pastor, nor with Pastor Eucratius's mentor, Cyprian, the Bishop of Carthage. Cyprian charged Eucratius in no uncertain terms to excommunicate Marcus from the rural congregation in Thena where Marcus had found Jesus, if Marcus continued to teach acting.

But what if Marcus was willing to align himself with the church's moral standards and shut down his acting school? In that case, Cyprian instructed Eucratius to see to it that Marcus lacked none of life's basic necessities—food, clothing, and shelter—in order to assist the former actor in his newfound faith. And if the little congregation in rural Thena lacked the resources to foot the bill, Eucratius was to send Marcus to Carthage, where Cyprian promised to meet Marcus's material needs.

Robust Boundaries and Relational Solidarity

We have much to learn from Marcus's pilgrimage. I find here two essential values that gave the ancient church much of its social capital and relational integrity, values that ought to characterize any community that seeks to identify itself as Christian.

I call the first value "robust boundaries"—boundaries that served to distinguish those who belonged to the local Christian community from those who did not.

The particular boundary Marcus had to wrestle with related to church convictions about the Roman theater. As we read through early Christian literature, we find robust boundaries reflected in other areas, both behavioral and theological. In the Roman world a follower of Jesus was someone who both behaved a certain way and believed a certain way. These boundaries were well enough established—and widely enough known—that both believers and unbelievers knew where the pagan world ended and the Christian community began.

"Relational solidarity" is what I call the second social value we glean from Marcus's experience. I have in mind here the way in which the early Christians took care of one another—like family. We have engaged this theme throughout the book and can summarize our findings as follows: Christianity in the Roman world was a community endeavor organized around a surrogate family model in which (1) individual Christians placed the good of the church family above their own personal goals, desires, and aspirations, and in which (2) church members could count on support from the community to meet the material and emotional challenges that often came with commitment to Jesus. Marcus is a prime example on both counts. Marcus deferred to the church family's moral demands, and his brothers and sisters, in turn, made sure that his basic needs were met.

So, here are two fundamental ancient church community values: robust boundaries and relational solidarity. They are wonderfully illustrated in the pilgrimage of Marcus and the North African church at Thena, and I suggest that a people that wishes to be identified as a Christian community today should seek to have both of these values realized in their local congregation.

How are we doing along these lines? We begin by comparing the early church's relational solidarity with community in the evangelical church in America today. Initially, the picture is not particularly encouraging. American evangelicals of the baby-boomer generation have increasingly moved away from maintaining long-term commitments to our local churches. As a result fewer and fewer of us enjoy deep and meaningful relationships with others in the churches we attend.

Sadly, for many believers Christianity is no longer a community endeavor. Instead, many choose to focus on experiencing God at the individual level. And the way we do church only reinforces and perpetuates this lone-ranger spirituality.

That which we call "church"—our Sunday service—occurs in a social environment that does little to encourage the kind of mutually interactive community that we find among the early Christians. The person sitting next to me in the large

Sunday gathering could be painfully undergoing any number of physical or relational hardships in his life, and I might never know it. And it would not take us long to identify other structural and institutional obstacles to family-like relationships in the typical American evangelical church.

I remain hopeful, however, about relational solidarity. God often works among us in spite of ourselves, and we see His determination break through on occasion as He knits us together as family, right in the midst of a Christian culture that has been taken captive by American individualism. Many of us have enjoyed family-like relationships at various times and places in our churches, notwithstanding institutional structures and programming that tend to inhibit rather than encourage such virtues. God will have His way whatever our cultural orientation.

We would do better, however, to join our Lord Jesus in His community-building kingdom project. And the future looks quite bright for relational solidarity. There is a fresh wind blowing among a new generation of believers who are intentionally seeking to recapture the relational integrity of the early church in ways that baby-boomer Christians have not. Leaders of a movement that some have labeled the "emerging church" are looking for more where Christian community is concerned.

Emerging Christians desire a church that is not an institution but the kind of supportive, encouraging surrogate family that people in our broken world intuitively long for, but which many have never experienced, even in their own natural families. Our new generation of Christians wants church leaders to be genuine brothers and sisters, and gentle shepherds, not just polished rhetoricians and efficient managers. And our emerging brothers and sisters prefer worship services that are not programmatic and impersonal in nature, but organic and relational.

Finally, emerging Christians increasingly insist upon a community that not only loves and cares for its own, but also extends its arms beyond the boundaries of the church to offer compassionate help to a broken world. Sounds a bit like what Julian the Apostate reluctantly acknowledged about the social practices of the early Christians: "[They] support not only their own poor, but ours as well."

All of this bodes well for the relational life of the next generation of the faithful, and I find such sentiments quite encouraging. So I am relatively optimistic about the future of the Western church where relational solidarity is concerned.

But it does not appear that robust boundaries get equal time in the current buzz about Christian community. And it is not hard to see why, given the association of certain segments of Christianity with philosophical and theological perspectives that have exchanged a robust degree of epistemological optimism for skeptical forms of postmodern relativism. Such approaches to truth and knowledge inevitably render it nearly impossible to make the kind of categorical pronouncements about community boundaries—be they moral or theological—that leaders in the early Christian movement could make.

Philosophical and theological considerations aside, from a purely pragmatic perspective, those of us who are leaders in the local church minister to a culture that increasingly resists embracing categorical truth-claims of any kind. As a result, we find it easy to get on the bandwagon of relational solidarity—to preach love, authenticity, and mutual support and encouragement. And so we should.

But the idea that we might also need to have robust boundaries in place to define the contours of an authentic Christian community does not particularly resonate with our culture. And I get the impression that this key social value of the ancient church does not particularly resonate with some of our emerging church leaders either.

So I find it necessary to remind us that categorical truth-claims—about both beliefs and behaviors—were simply an indispensable part of the biblical worldview of early Christianity. And these convictions, in turn, generated the kind of robust boundaries that are illustrated in the story of our actor friend Marcus and that defined Christian community throughout the pre-Constantine era of church history.

Issues that served to delineate the robust boundaries of the New Testament church included sexual immorality (1 Cor 5:1–8), lack of repentance when sinning against a brother (Matt 18:15–18), unwillingness to forgive a repentant brother (Matt 18:21–35), the propagation of false doctrine (2 Tim 3:1–8), divisiveness (Titus 3:10–11), and even sloth (2 Thess 3:6–15). People who lived their lives according to community standards remained part of the family of God, but those who did not were excluded.

Those of us who somehow, in the name of tolerance and inclusion, think the church needs to redefine the time-tested, biblically-based boundaries that characterized community in early Christianity have something to learn from the ongoing debate in the Episcopal church over the issue of homosexuality. I quote at length from M. Pearse's marvelous little book, *Why the Rest Hates the West*. This quote describes the 1998 Lambeth Conference, which gathered together the bishops of the worldwide Anglican church. Pearse wrote:

> The Conference surprised a number of commentators by its decision to uphold
> traditional biblical teaching in condemning homosexual practices, since it had
> been calculated by many that the liberal, permissive wing of the church would

predominate. However, evangelicals and other traditionalists were strengthened at the conference by the augmented battalion of bishops from the growing community of the African church. As representatives of traditional cultures, these bishops had no problem with biblical injunctions on the subject of homosexuality and expressed considerable bewilderment when confronted by Westerners who did. As one of them commented, "You came over to our country 150 years ago and gave us the Bible. . . . Now you are telling us the Bible is not true."

The most telling moment was when, after the motion upholding traditional teaching was passed, Jack Spong, the stridently liberal bishop of Newark, New Jersey, denounced the African bishops as "superstitious" and "uneducated." It must have been a moment of madness; the politically correct, antiracist, multiculturalist Jack Spong would never have uttered such words, even in defense of a cause so dear to the heart of the antihomophobic Jack Spong, except under the influence of some extreme emotion. Of course, if the Africans really had been superstitious and uneducated, then only the politically correct *illuminati* would have denied the fact. For them, problems should never be addressed as problems; instead they should be sublimated into the realm of politics, thereby rendering even a frank description of the issues—let alone any possibility of resolution—impossible. In this case, however, Spong was plainly wrong on matters of fact; the African bishops were, on the whole, as educated as he. And concerning superstition, their real offense consisted of the fact that they had dared to touch one of Spong's sacred cows. For they had failed to come to the kind of moral judgment about homosexuality that a liberal-minded, tolerant, open Westerner—as exemplified by Spong himself—would and should have come to. In other words, the trouble with the Africans was that they were not Western enough![4]

Here, finally, is the rub, is it not? When we define Christian community in such a way as to embrace the biblical teaching about relational solidarity, while at the same time rejecting the robust boundaries we see reflected in early Christian literature, we are left with nothing but an emasculated, localized, postmodern, Western version of "community" that bears little resemblance to the surrogate family model of the ancient Christian church, and which is actually no longer worthy of the name Christian at all.

This is hardly rocket science. The concept of the church as a family finds its origins in the relational values and practices of the natural family. And as any family therapist would tell us, a healthy family needs both love (relational solidarity)

---

[4] M. Pearse, *Why the Rest Hates the West* (Downers Grove: InterVarsity, 2004), 21–22.

and discipline (robust boundaries). Experience demonstrates again and again that
to place a high priority on relationships, while ignoring the need for boundaries in
the name of love or tolerance, inevitably results in a highly dysfunctional family
unit—one that ultimately undermines those very relationships themselves.

A woman with whom I am acquainted often requests prayer for her 35-year-
old, unemployed, drug-addicted son. The problem is patently obvious to all who
know the family's situation: the derelict son lives rent-free in the parents' home.
What we have here is a family that gets high marks in the area of relational solidarity. The son receives all the financial support and encouragement he wants. What
has been totally lacking, of course, probably for years and years, are the kind of
robust boundaries that characterize any healthy family and that keep its younger
members from remaining—like our 35-year-old junkie—dependent, unproduc-
tive infants well into their adult lives.

As it goes with our natural families, so it goes with the family of God. Any
church that calls itself Christian, emerging or otherwise, and which longs to blaze
a trail back to community as it was experienced in early Christianity, will firmly
establish along that path two indispensable sociological trail-markers: relational
solidarity and robust boundaries. Only with both of these values solidly in place
can we hope to recapture in our congregations the social capital and prophetic
power that characterized the ancient Christian church.

Restoring a Holistic Gospel

We wrestled in chapter 6 with the thorny issue of the relationship between
soteriology and ecclesiology. I suggested that God's primary objective throughout salvation history has been the creation of a people for His own possession, a
community inhabited by the Holy Spirit and characterized by justice and mercy
exercised in the context of relational accountability. At both Sinai and Pentecost
the salvation of God's people was a community-creating event.

My intention is not to downplay God's concern for us as individuals. Nor do I
wish to deemphasize the necessity of individual regeneration. But it must be recognized that in the New Testament era, a person was saved not solely to enjoy a
personal relationship with Jesus. A person was saved to community. Our truncated
evangelical conception of Jesus as personal Savior turns out to be an unfortunate
distortion of radical American individualism, not a holistic reflection of biblical
soteriology.

It is not by accident that the phrase "personal relationship with God" is conspicuously absent from the pages of Scripture. According to the New Testament,

we are saved to community. Salvation involves adoption into the family of God. Indeed, salvation *is* becoming a member of God's family—a family that includes both a new Father and a new set of brothers and sisters. Biblical salvation is a community-creating event.

To be sure, a convert to Christianity needs to do business with God as an individual. Each of us must trust Jesus' blood atonement for the forgiveness of his sins. That is a given, and it is foundational for all that follows. But a new believer's pilgrimage with Jesus does not end at the foot of the cross. Indeed, the cross of Christ—and all that it implies—becomes the doorway to membership in God's group and the pattern for our life together. We are saved not simply to enjoy a personal relationship with God; we are saved to community. There is no room in biblical Christianity for an unchurched Christian.

What then is the message of the gospel? And how do we know whether a person has truly converted to Christ? These have always been thorny theological questions. The issue becomes even more complex when we add to the mix our strong-group understanding of church life and soteriology. Let us begin with the latter of the two questions and return afterward to the former.

When is a person truly saved? My intention here is not to split theological hairs by attempting to define the point at which the "line of salvation" is crossed and an individual is truly regenerated. I will leave it to our theologians to tackle the daunting task of harmonizing what we have learned about salvation-to-community with the doctrine of individual justification by faith. The observations that follow are designed simply to help God's shepherds exercise some discernment in our evangelistic strategies and in the spiritual oversight of our people.

My key point is a straightforward one. If salvation is a community-creating event, if conversion to Christianity means being saved to community, then it would seem that for a conversion to be genuine, this relational aspect of salvation must somehow find expression in the everyday life of a professing Christian. *Amen!*

After all, we would wonder about the faith of someone who showed no ongoing evidence or concern for his relationship with God the Father. And as we saw earlier, the positional reality of our "familification" is just as real in God's eyes as our justification. We gain both a new Father and a new set of surrogate siblings when we become followers of Jesus. So it makes sense to expect a genuine salvation experience to cash out in some degree of concern for those horizontal relationships with one's brothers and sisters in Christ, as well.

This is certainly the pattern in the New Testament. In the early church, a person who became a Christian quickly found himself deeply embedded in God's group, in the sphere of relational accountability and mutuality. All of the references to "one another" and "each other" in the epistles assume as much.

In a single chapter in the book of Acts, for example, we see people both converting to Christ *and* sharing their material resources with one another (Acts 2). A saving relationship with God and a commitment to God's group were apparently inseparable in the early church. One became a follower of Jesus, and the family of God took first priority in his life.

But there is an important difference between then and now. People in the ancient world were collectivists in their worldview before they ever heard the gospel. They were already up-to-speed on group-oriented social values simply because of the culture in which they lived. The people Peter and Paul evangelized knew quite well what it meant to make a commitment to a strong-group family. This must be taken into account in our efforts to reproduce the New Testament model in our own cultural matrix.

Evangelism today is a whole lot different. We share Jesus with people steeped in the radical individualism of American society. So we need to educate and socialize our newcomers into strong-group thinking and behavior, if we wish to reproduce the biblical blueprint of the church as a family. This will inevitably be a process, and we must refrain from questioning an individual's salvation ✳ just because he has yet to make a strong-group commitment to a local family of believers.

We will derail the whole project at the outset, however, if we continue to share an individualistic gospel about Jesus as "personal Savior" that tacks on church involvement as some kind of utilitarian afterthought. The family of God is not an institution that I as an individual Christian utilize to help me grow in my personal relationship with Jesus. The family of God is the place where I join together in community with my siblings in the faith, in order to engage in God's great missional adventure of world evangelization. The family of God is the place where I lose my life in order to gain it.   ↳ *Kingdom advancement.*

What is the message of the gospel? This leads us to consider the content of our gospel presentations. What *is* this good news that we should be sharing with our friends and neighbors? Here I would challenge us to think outside the traditional box a bit. I suggest that we inform our potential converts in no uncertain terms that commitment to Jesus also involves commitment to God's group.

We need to explain to our unsaved friends that they will gain a new Father *and* a new set of siblings when they give their lives to Jesus. And we must help them to see that the two relationships are inseparable. As Cyprian of Carthage boldly asserted,

"You cannot have God for your Father unless you have the church for your Mother" (*On the Unity of the Church*, 3.1.214). Accordingly, I am no longer satisfied with a summary of the gospel that assures the hearer of individual salvation apart from any emphasis on the importance of commitment to the family of God.

The idea of encouraging people to pray a prayer of personal repentance—to "accept Jesus as personal Savior" and thereby become a child of God—must therefore be complemented with a challenge to become part of God's family. Otherwise, we simply perpetuate the radical individualism that has rendered American evangelicalism culturally and morally impotent, and we blatantly ignore the New Testament picture of regeneration as a community-creating event.

We would do well to do neither. To reject God's blueprint for salvation to community is essentially to remain satisfied with the present state of affairs. This just guarantees that our so-called converts will continue to take their "personal Saviors" from relationship to relationship, from marriage to marriage, and from church to church, much to their own social and spiritual demise.

Most of them may not even do that well. Many who embrace the truncated "bar-code gospel" of American Christendom leave the community of the faithful altogether.[5] A 1997 study found that more than one-half of the people who made first-time "decisions for Christ" were no longer connected to a Christian church within just eight weeks of having made such a decision.[6]

An illustration from the natural world will drive the point home. Under normal circumstances, babies are born into families. The social chaos characterizing America in recent decades has generated, among its various casualties, unwanted newborn babies who are left in dumpsters to die. These babies are obviously not born into families. It has become tragically clear to anyone who follows news stories like these that babies who are not born into families do not have a chance for survival.

So it is with Christians who are not born into the local family of God. Receiving Christ as Savior without church involvement is a sure recipe for stillbirth. And when I say "church involvement," I trust you understand by now that I am not talking about showing up at the Sunday morning service or serving on the stewardship committee on Tuesday nights.

Church involvement in the New Testament sense means the development of intimate, healthy, long-lasting relationships with one's brothers and sisters in Christ. This kind of commitment to a local church might not begin to manifest

---

[5] The phrase "bar-code gospel" is from D. Willard, *The Divine Conspiracy: Rediscovering Our Hidden Life in God* (San Francisco: HarperSanFrancisco, 1998), 38. See chap. 6.

[6] G. Barna, *The Second Coming of the Church* (Waco, Texas: Word, 1998), 2.

itself immediately after the person trusts Christ, like it did for the early Christians in Acts 2. But it needs to happen, and it needs to happen sooner rather than later. For, to become a Christian is to become *both* a child of God *and* a sibling in God's strong-group family. We should clearly communicate this holistic gospel to people who express an interest in giving their lives to Jesus.

Thus it may be just as important to begin to familiarize our non-Christian friends with the horizontal aspect of salvation, as it is to talk to them about reconciliation with God the Father through the work of God the Son. People with whom we share Jesus need to be informed concerning expectations and opportunities for relationships in God's family, so that they can make professions of faith that embrace both halves of the biblical teaching about salvation—both the individual and the corporate. We must tell the world that following Jesus involves both commitment to God *and* commitment to God's group.

They Like Jesus but Not the Church

Encouraging our friends and co-workers to make a commitment to Jesus *and* His church generates another set of challenges. Unfortunately, most non-Christians have a profoundly distorted view of what church is really all about. The title of D. Kimball's recent book pretty much sums it up: *They Like Jesus but Not the Church*.[7] Dan is right. My unchurched friends who hang around the local fishing tackle shop are rather intrigued by Jesus, but they are turned off by the church.

This puts the ball right back in our court as leaders. Our friends and neighbors often have good reason not to like church. Most of them have never experienced church as we see it functioning in early Christianity. They only know church as an American cultural institution. They only know church as we have designed it.

The solution to this dilemma is readily apparent. We need to cultivate in our churches the kind of social environments where our non-Christian friends can come and experience firsthand Jesus' vision for authentic Christian community. Then our friends and neighbors will not only be intrigued by Jesus; they will also begin to see how following Jesus works out in the context of real-life human relationships. They will make informed decisions for Christ—decisions that embrace both the vertical and the horizontal dimensions of New Testament soteriology.

I will leave it to you as a reader to determine what those environments might look like in your particular church setting. Except for some occasional asides about our Sunday services, I have attempted to keep the discussion centered around general family values and behaviors, rather than specific church programs or minis-

---

[7] D. Kimball, *They Like Jesus but Not the Church: Insights from Emerging Generations* (Grand Rapids: Zondervan, 2007).

tries—and intentionally so. The best church programs for cultivating community are inevitably contextually rooted and contextually circumscribed. By this I mean that they grow naturally out of the unique relational soil of a given congregation, and they are not easily transferable to another church setting.

But the family values and behaviors we encountered in the early church transcend culture. We can contextualize these values and behaviors in any local church setting, provided that we are willing to exercise a degree of determination, stumble a bit through trial and error, and make ample room for the community-creating power of the Holy Spirit of God.

There remains a final ingredient that will prove absolutely essential for recapturing Jesus' vision for authentic Christian community. We need church leaders who have the courage both to teach *and* to model a radically counter-cultural approach to doing church in their local congregations. And, frankly, it will take more courage to do the latter than the former.

"Who Are My Brothers?"

"Who are my brothers?" asked Jesus. We as the shepherds of God's flock had better wrestle with this question ourselves before we challenge our people with it. Who can you point to in your congregation who knows your weaknesses as well as your strengths? Who in your church rejoices with you in your vocational successes and family milestones? Who is aware of the challenges you face in keeping your thoughts pure? Who upholds you in prayer when you experience times of deep discouragement in your ministry? Who among your people knows the ups and downs of your marriage and how you struggle to keep your children on track? In summary: *Who in your congregation knows you as a brother and not simply as a pastor?*

Pastors need brothers for many reasons, not the least of which are moral accountability and mutual encouragement along the path of life. But we could find this kind of brotherhood outside of our congregations, perhaps with other Christian leaders in the denomination or in the broader civic community. Do we really need to engage in sibling-like relations with people in our own congregations? Some would say no. They think it is actually unwise to open ourselves up to people in the churches we pastor.

I spent the first 20 years of my Christian life in a conservative Baptist church. My first pastor was a senior saint named Barney Andrews, who faithfully served Christ's church for nearly 40 years before retiring from the ministry in 1985. Pastor Andrews left a remarkable legacy. But even this man of God had his blind spots, areas where Christian culture clouded and ultimately obscured the message of the Bible on this issue or that. We all do. In Pastor Andrews's case the problem area had to do with how a pastor should relate to his flock.

Back in the 1970s Pastor Andrews was mentoring a friend of mine who was in seminary training for the ministry. Carefully consider the following bit of advice that this well-intentioned old-school shepherd gave to a future minister: "Do not make any close friends in your church! You will make yourself vulnerable, and you will likely get hurt."

To get grammatical for a moment, we have here in Pastor Andrews's advice an imperative and an indicative, an exhortation and an observation. The observation can hardly be disputed. Open yourself up to others, and you *will* make yourself vulnerable. And yes, you will likely get hurt. To one degree or another, pain and vulnerability play a part in all of our intimate relationships, and many of us have experienced this firsthand in the church.

What about the imperative about not making any close friends? Should pastors truly avoid developing deep relationships with people in their congregations? Is Pastor Andrews's exhortation biblical? No, it is not. Jesus made Himself vulnerable, and He got hurt. F. Buechner, writing of the incarnation, put it like this:

> For those who believe in God, it means, this birth, that God himself is never
> safe from us, and maybe that is the dark side of Christmas. He comes in such a
> way that we can always turn him down, as we could crack the baby's skull like
> an eggshell, or nail him up when he gets too big for that.[8]

It began in Bethlehem. It ended on a Roman cross. Along the way, God the Son was rejected by His fellow-countrymen, dismissed as mentally troubled by his family, and abandoned or betrayed by the 12 men He had loved the most. Finally, for you and for me, Jesus experienced what must have been an eternal moment of utter alienation from God the Father Himself: "My God, My God," He exclaimed, "why have You forsaken Me?" (Matt 27:46). Jesus made Himself vulnerable, and He got hurt. We are to follow in His footsteps.

What about Paul? Listen to what he wrote to the Thessalonians: "We cared so much for you that we were pleased to share with you not only the gospel of God but also our own lives, because you had become dear to us" (1 Thess 2:8). Did Paul make close friends at church? Did Paul make himself vulnerable to the members of his congregations? Apparently so.

Did Paul get hurt? Perhaps not by the Thessalonians, but consider his relationship with the Corinthians—the rejection of Paul's authority, the painful visit. In 2 Corinthians 6 is the climax of Paul's entire defense of his ministry to the church

---

[8] F. Buechner, *The Hungering Dark* (San Francisco: HarperOne, 1985), 13–14.

family at Corinth, a defense that began some four chapters earlier in the letter. Paul's relational pain just permeates the passage:

> We have spoken openly to you, Corinthians; our heart has been opened wide. You are not limited by us, but you are limited by your own affections. Now in like response—I speak as to children—you also should be open to us. (2 Cor 6:11–13)

P. Barnett cuts to the very heart of the issue: "Here in 2 Corinthians 6 we hear Paul in his most *human* self-disclosure. The apostolic office, which is to a significant degree a model for subsequent pastoral and missionary ministry, is a *human* ministry; it can never be a mere institution."[9] *Don't make friends in the church. You'll make yourself vulnerable, and you might get hurt.* Like Jesus. Like Paul. So much for Pastor Andrews' well-intended advice.

The inclination of pastors to remain relationally removed from their people can often be traced to an unfortunate experience in a previous church or ministry. Many of us have seen close relationships with church members explode in our faces, when our "friends" turned on us and used privileged information shared in confidence to undermine our ministries. Numbers of pastors have become determined to protect themselves from further incidents like these by discussing intimate life details only with friends from outside the church.

Strategies designed to protect ourselves from hurt and betrayal are understandable, but they ultimately serve only to undermine the community-building work God desires to do in our midst. Such an approach to pastor-member relations renders a pastor powerless prophetically to challenge his people to experience the kind of strong-group sibling relationships that characterized the early Christian church. This reality simply cannot be overemphasized. One who has no true brothers in the congregation will be unable to authentically and credibly challenge others in his church family to live together as surrogate siblings.

This is why we must answer the question *Who are my brothers and sisters?* in terms of the people in our own congregations. It will not do for us to share our lives only with other leaders in the broader Christian community, as helpful as that might be on occasion. If a pastor is unwilling to risk openness with a handful of brothers *in his church*—for whatever reason—then the members will surely do likewise. We simply cannot take our people where we are unwilling to go. We must be willing to go there whatever the cost.

---

[9] P. Barnett, *The Second Epistle to the Corinthians,* in *New International Commentary on the New Testament,* ed. G. D. Fee (Grand Rapids: Eerdmans, 1997), 335 (italics added).

Pastors must cultivate sibling-like relationships with a handful of people in their own congregations so they can model "church as a family" to the rest of the flock. Perhaps the best place for that to happen is at the top, where leadership is shared according to the New Testament model of plurality leadership in the family of God (see chap. 9). Only when pastors set aside our misled need to *father* our flocks, and instead share the oversight and instruction of our congregations with other mature *brothers*, will we tangibly and persuasively communicate to others the absolute centrality of the biblical model of the church as a society of surrogate siblings. *As well as fathers* 1 JN 2:13

I have now met with the same five men in my church every week for the past ten years. We lead Oceanside Christian Fellowship as a team of elders. We share the preaching. We share the leadership. We share the joys and heartaches of ministry.

Most importantly—for both the relational health of my natural family and the relational health of my church family—the men that I meet with on Tuesday mornings no longer relate to me according to the title (pastor) that precedes my name. Nor are they particularly impressed with the academic abbreviations (M.A., M.Div., Th.M., Ph.D.) that follow my name. This is because Denny, Dan, Ed, Stan, and Brandon have become, first and foremost, my brothers in this adventure called the family of God. I have become their brother also. I only wish the same for you, as you seek to recapture Jesus' vision for authentic Christian community in your own pilgrimage as a leader in the family of God.

Summary

Somehow, against all odds, Christianity prevailed. A small Jewish sectarian movement, which arose on the eastern fringes of the great Roman Empire, steadily added Gentiles to the mix and continued to expand right in the face of the most vehement opposition. First Jerusalem, then Antioch, then Asia, then Rome, then Egypt, then more of Africa—finally the whole Roman Empire bowed its knees to Jesus Christ as Lord.

How did they do it? According to Luke it happened like this: "with great power the apostles were giving testimony to the resurrection of the Lord Jesus, and great grace was on all of them" (Acts 4:33). Substitute "early Christians" for "apostles" and you have a pretty accurate picture of the evangelistic vitality of the Jesus movement from its inception in first-century Judea all the way down to the end of the Christian persecutions, at the dawn of the fourth century AD.

How I long for that to be an accurate description of my congregation! *With great power the people of Oceanside Christian Fellowship were giving testimony to the resurrection of the Lord Jesus, and great grace was on all of them.* Where do we get this "great power" and "great grace"? From God, of course. But I think we can be a bit more specific.

Let us place Luke's glowing description of the evangelistic power of the Jerusalem church back into its biblical context:

> Now the multitude of those who believed were of one heart and soul, and no one said that any of his possessions was his own, but instead they held everything in common. *And with great power the apostles were giving testimony to the resurrection of the Lord Jesus, and great grace was on all of them.* For there was not a needy person among them, because all those who owned lands or houses sold them, brought the proceeds of the things that were sold, and laid them at the apostles' feet. This was then distributed to each person as anyone had a need. (Acts 4:32–35, italics added)

Notice what precedes and follows Luke's comments about the "power" and "grace" that marked the Jerusalem church: social solidarity, the sharing of material resources—in a word, the church as a family. That little word "For" at the beginning of v. 34 is not there by accident. Apparently, the proclamation of the resurrected Lord Jesus in the Jerusalem church gained much of its credibility from the family values and behaviors that characterized that first Christian congregation.

And so it was for the early Christians throughout the empire. "See how they love one another!" the world exclaimed (Tertullian, *Apol.* 39.7). "Their first lawgiver persuaded them that they are all brothers of one another" (Lucian, *The Passing of Peregrinus*, 13). "The impious Galileans support not only their own poor, but ours as well" (*Works of Julian*, 69).

Jesus and His followers took their culture's strong-group approach to family life, appropriated it as the preeminent social model for their local Christian communities, and lived with one another like Mediterranean brothers and sisters. And the early Christians turned the world upside down. When the church was a family, the church was on fire. May God help us recapture Jesus' vision for authentic Christian community in our churches today.

NAME INDEX

SUBJECT INDEX

Scripture Index